A GUIDE TO MYSQL®

FINAL 2678

A GUIDE TO MYSQL®

Philip J. Pratt
Grand Valley State University

Mary Z. Last
University of Mary Hardin-Baylor

THOMSON
COURSE TECHNOLOGY

Australia • Canada • Mexico • Singapore • Spain • United Kingdom • United States

THOMSON
COURSE TECHNOLOGY

A Guide to MySQL®

by Philip J. Pratt and Mary Z. Last

Senior Acquisitions Editor:
Maureen Martin

Editorial Assistant:
Allison Murphy

Copyeditor:
Mark Goodin

Product Manager:
Beth Paquin

Marketing Manager:
Karen Seitz

Proofreader:
Nancy Lamm

Developmental Editor:
Jessica Evans

Cover Designer:
Laura Rickenbach

Indexer:
Rich Carlson

Production Editor:
Brooke Booth

Text Designer:
Books by Design

Associate Product Manager:
Jennifer Smith

Manufacturing Coordinator:
Justin Palmeiro

TABLE OF CONTENTS

PREFACE

Structured Query Language (or SQL, which is pronounced *se-quel*, or *ess-cue-ell*) is a popular computer language that is used by diverse groups such as home computer owners, owners of small businesses, end users in large organizations, and programmers. Although this text uses the SQL implementation in MySQL and the Windows XP operating system as a vehicle for teaching SQL, its chapter material, examples, and exercises can be completed using MySQL 4.1 or higher and with other operating systems, such as Linux.

A Guide to MySQL is written for a wide range of teaching levels, from students taking introductory computer science classes to those students in advanced information systems classes. This text can be used for a standalone course on SQL or in conjunction with a database concepts text where students are required to learn SQL.

MySQL is freely available as open source software. The most recent version of MySQL can be downloaded from the Internet at *http://dev.mysql.com/downloads/*. The MySQL Query Browser and MySQL Administrator are separate MySQL programs that use a graphical user interface. These tools, which are covered in Chapter 8, also can be downloaded from the Internet. With the exception of Chapter 2, the chapters in this text should be covered in order. If this text is being used in conjunction with a database concepts text, Chapter 2 can be omitted. Chapter 2 also can be taught later in the course.

Relationship to *Concepts of Database Management, Fifth Edition*

For database courses featuring SQL, this MySQL text can be bundled with *Concepts of Database Management, Fifth Edition* by Pratt and Adamski (Course Technology). The data and pedagogy between the two texts is consistent.

DISTINGUISHING FEATURES

Use of Examples

Each chapter contains multiple examples that use SQL to solve a problem. Following each example, students will read about the commands that are used to solve the stated problem, and then they will see the SQL commands used to arrive at the solution. For most students, learning through examples is the most effective way to master material. For this reason, instructors should encourage students to read the chapters at the computer and input the commands shown in the figures.

Case Studies

A running case study—Premiere Products—is presented in all of the examples within the chapters, and also in the first set of exercises at the end of each chapter. Although the database is small in order to be manageable, the examples and exercises for the Premiere Products database simulate what a real business can accomplish using SQL commands. Using the same case study as examples within the chapter and in the end-of-chapter exercises ensures a high level of continuity to reinforce learning.

A second case study—the Henry Books database—is used in a second set of exercises at the end of each chapter. A third case study—the Alexamara Marina Group database—is used in a third set of exercises at the end of each chapter. The second and third case studies give students a chance to venture out "on their own" without the direct guidance of examples from the text.

Question and Answer Sections

A special type of exercise, called a Q&A, is used throughout the book. These exercises force students to consider special issues and understand important questions before continuing with their study. The answer to each Q&A appears after the question. Students are encouraged to formulate their own answers before reading the ones provided in the text to ensure that they understand new material before proceeding.

Review Material

A Summary and Key Terms list appear at the end of each chapter, followed by Review Questions that test students' recall of the important points in the chapter and occasionally test their ability to apply what they have learned. The answers to the odd-numbered Review Questions are provided in Appendix C. Each chapter also contains exercises related to the Premiere Products, Henry Books, and Alexamara Marina Group databases.

Appendices

Three appendices appear at the end of this text. Appendix A is a reference that describes the purpose and syntax for the major SQL commands featured in the text. Students can use Appendix A to identify how and when to use commands quickly. Appendix B includes a "How Do I" reference, which lets students cross-reference the appropriate section in Appendix A by searching for the answer to a question. Appendix C includes answers to the odd-numbered Review Questions.

Instructor Support

The Instructor's Resources include a package of proven supplements for instructors and students. The Instructor's Resources offer a detailed electronic Instructor's Manual, figure files, Microsoft PowerPoint presentations, and the ExamView® Test Bank. The Instructor's Manual includes suggestions and strategies for using this text, as well as answers to Review Questions and solutions to the end-of-chapter exercises. Figure files allow instructors to create their own presentations using figures appearing in the text. Instructors can also take advantage of lecture presentations provided on PowerPoint slides; these presentations follow each chapter's coverage precisely, include chapter figures, and can be customized. ExamView® is a powerful objective-based test generator that enables instructors to create paper, LAN, or Web-based tests from test banks designed specifically for this Course Technology text. Users can utilize the ultra-efficient QuickTest Wizard to create tests in less than five minutes by taking advantage of Course Technology's question banks, or can customize their own exams from scratch.

Distance Learning (I) is also offered. Course Technology is proud to present online test banks in WebCT and Blackboard to provide the most complete and dynamic learning experience possible. For more information on how to access the online test bank, contact your local Course Technology sales representative.

The Instructor's Resources also include text files corresponding to the commands shown in most figures in the text. After opening the text files in Notepad or in a word processor, commands can be copied and pasted in MySQL rather than being typed directly.

ORGANIZATION OF THE TEXT

The text contains eight chapters and three appendices, which are described in the following sections.

Chapter 1: Introduction to Premiere Products, Henry Books, and Alexamara Marina Group

Chapter 1 introduces the three database cases that are used throughout the text: Premiere Products, Henry Books, and Alexamara Marina Group. Many Q&A exercises are provided throughout the chapter to ensure that students understand how to manipulate the database on paper before they begin working in SQL.

Chapter 2: Database Design Fundamentals

Chapter 2 covers important concepts and terminology associated with relational databases, functional dependence, and primary keys, followed by a method for designing a database to satisfy a given set of requirements. It also illustrates the normalization process for finding and correcting a variety of potential problems in database designs. Finally, it shows how to represent database designs graphically using Entity-Relationship diagrams.

Chapter 3: An Introduction to SQL

In Chapter 3, students begin using MySQL by creating and running SQL commands to create tables, use data types, and add rows to tables. Chapter 3 also discusses the role of and use of nulls.

Chapter 4: Single-Table Queries

Chapter 4 is the first of two chapters about using SQL commands to query a database. The queries in Chapter 4 all involve single tables. Students use simple and compound conditions; computed columns; the SQL BETWEEN, LIKE, and IN operators; SQL functions; and nested queries. Students also group data and retrieve columns with null values.

Chapter 5: Multiple-Table Queries

Chapter 5 completes the discussion of querying a database by demonstrating queries that join more than one table. Included in this chapter are discussions of the SQL IN and EXISTS operators, nested subqueries, using aliases, joining a table to itself, SQL set operations, and the use of the ALL and ANY operators. The chapter also includes coverage of various types of joins.

Chapter 6: Updating Data

In Chapter 6, students learn how to use the SQL COMMIT, ROLLBACK, UPDATE, INSERT, and DELETE commands to update table data. Students also learn how to create a new table from an existing table and how to change the structure of an existing table. The chapter also includes coverage of transactions, including both their purpose and implementation.

Chapter 7: Database Administration

Chapter 7 covers the database administration features of SQL, including the use of views; granting and revoking database privileges to users; creating, dropping, and using an index; using and obtaining information from the system catalog; and using integrity constraints.

Chapter 8: MySQL Special Topics

In Chapter 8, students learn how to use MySQL to import and export data. Students also learn how to use SQL commands to fine-tune a database so it processes data quickly and efficiently. The ANALYZE TABLE, CHECK TABLE, and OPTIMIZE TABLE commands are discussed as ways to assess table performance. Two techniques for assessing query performance—the EXPLAIN command and the PROCEDURE ANALYSE() function—are also illustrated. Finally, students learn how to use two of the graphical user interface (GUI) tools that MySQL provides: the MySQL Query Browser and the MySQL Administrator. Because these tools are separate programs, they must be downloaded from the Internet at *http://dev.mysql.com/downloads/*.

Appendix A: SQL Reference

Appendix A includes a command reference for all the major SQL clauses and operators that are featured in the chapters. Students can use Appendix A as a quick resource when constructing commands. Each command includes a short description, a table that shows the required and optional clauses and operators, and an example and its results. It also contains a reference to the pages in the text where the command is covered.

Appendix B: How Do I Reference

Appendix B provides students with an opportunity to ask a question, such as "How do I delete rows?," and to identify the appropriate section in Appendix A to use to find the answer. Appendix B is extremely valuable when students know what task they want to accomplish, but can't remember the exact SQL command they need.

Appendix C: Answers to Odd-Numbered Review Questions

Answers to the odd-numbered Review Questions in each chapter appear in this appendix so students can make sure that they are completing the Review Questions correctly.

GENERAL NOTES TO THE STUDENT

You can download the script files that you can use to create or drop the Alexamara Marina Group, Henry Books, and Premiere Products databases used in this book. The script files have the following functions:

- **MySQL-Alexamara**: Creates and activates the Alexamara database, creates all the tables in the Alexamara database, and loads all the data into the tables. Run this script file to create the Alexamara Marina Group database. (*Note:* This script file assumes you have not previously created the database or any of the tables in the database. If you have created any of the tables, you should run the MySQL-DropAlexamara script prior to running the MySQL-Alexamara script.)

- **MySQL-Henry**: Creates and activates the Henry database, creates all the tables in the Henry database, and loads all the data into the tables. Run this script file to create the Henry Books database. (*Note:* This script file assumes you have not previously created the database or any of the tables in the database. If you have created any of the tables, you should run the MySQL-DropHenry script prior to running the MySQL-Henry script.)

- **MySQL-Premiere**: Creates and activates the Premiere database, creates all the tables in the Premiere database, and loads all the data into these tables. Run this script file to create the Premiere Products database. (*Note:* This script file assumes you have not previously created the database or any of the tables in the database. If you have created any of the tables, you should run the MySQL-DropPremiere script prior to running the MySQL-Premiere script.)

- **MySQL-DropAlexamara**: Drops (deletes) all the tables and data in the Alexamara database. (To delete the Alexamara database from the MySQL Server, execute the DROP DATABASE ALEXAMARA; command.)

- **MySQL-DropHenry**: Drops (deletes) all the tables and data in the Henry database. (To delete the Henry database from the MySQL Server, execute the DROP DATABASE HENRY; command.)

- **MySQL-DropPremiere**: Drops (deletes) all the tables and data in the Premiere database. (To delete the Premiere database from the MySQL Server, execute the DROP DATABASE PREMIERE; command.)

For details on running script files in MySQL, check with your instructor. You can also refer to Chapter 3 in the text for information about creating and using scripts.

Embedded Questions

In many places, you'll find Q&A sections to ensure that you understand some crucial material before you proceed. In some cases, the questions are designed to give you the chance to consider some special concept in advance of its actual presentation. In all cases, the answer to each question appears immediately after the question. You can simply read the question and its answer, but you will benefit from taking time to determine the answer to the question before checking your answer against the one given in the text.

End-of-Chapter Material

The end-of-chapter material consists of a Summary, a Key Terms list, Review Questions, and exercises for the Premiere Products, Henry Books, and Alexamara Marina Group cases. The Summary briefly describes the material covered in the chapter. The Key Terms list gives you a chance to review the terms defined in the chapter. The Review Questions require you to recall and apply the important material in the chapter. The answers to the odd-numbered Review Questions appear in Appendix C so you can check your progress. The Premiere Products, Henry Books, and Alexamara Marina Group exercises test your knowledge of the chapter material; your instructor will assign one or more of these exercises for you to complete.

ACKNOWLEDGMENTS

We would like to acknowledge several individuals for their contributions in the preparation of this text. We appreciate the efforts of the following individuals who reviewed the manuscript and made many helpful suggestions: Sarah Jones, Santa Fe Community College; Georgia Brown, Northern Illinois University; Gary Savard, Champlain College; and Vickee Stedham, St. Petersburg College.

The efforts of the following members of the staff at Course Technology, Inc. have been invaluable and have made this text possible: Maureen Martin, Senior Acquisitions Editor; Beth Paquin, Product Manager; Brooke Booth, Production Editor; and Quality Assurance testers Chris Scriver, Danielle Shaw, and Serge Palladino.

We have had the great pleasure to work with an absolutely amazing Developmental Editor, Jessica Evans, on several books. Thanks for all your efforts, Jess. You're the best!

CHAPTER 1

INTRODUCTION TO PREMIERE PRODUCTS, HENRY BOOKS, AND ALEXAMARA MARINA GROUP

LEARNING OBJECTIVES

Objectives

- Introduce Premiere Products, a company whose database is used as the basis for many of the examples throughout the text
- Introduce Henry Books, a company whose database is used as a case that runs throughout the text
- Introduce Alexamara Marina Group, a company whose database is used as an additional case that runs throughout the text
- Introduce MySQL, a database management system

INTRODUCTION

In this chapter, you will examine the database requirements of Premiere Products, a company that will be used in the examples throughout the text. Then you will examine the database requirements for Henry Books and Alexamara Marina Group, whose databases are featured in the exercises that appear at the end of each chapter. Finally, you will learn about MySQL, a database management system.

WHAT IS A DATABASE?

Throughout this text, you will work with databases for three organizations: Premiere Products, Henry Books, and Alexamara Marina Group. A **database** is a structure that contains different categories of information and the relationships between these categories. The Premiere Products database, for example, contains information about categories such as sales representatives (sales reps), customers, orders, and parts. The Henry Books database contains information about categories such as books, publishers, authors, and branches. The Alexamara Marina Group database contains information about categories such as marinas, slips and the boats in them, service categories, and service requests.

Each database also contains relationships between categories. For example, the Premiere Products database contains information that relates sales reps to the customers they represent and customers to the orders they have placed. The Henry Books database contains information that relates publishers to the books they publish and authors to the books they have written. The Alexamara Marina Group database contains information that relates the boats in the slips at the marina to the owners of the boats.

As you work through the chapters in this text, you will learn more about these databases and how to view and update the information they contain. As you read each chapter, you will see examples from the Premiere Products database. At the end of each chapter, your instructor might assign the exercises for the Premiere Products, Henry Books, or Alexamara Marina Group databases.

THE PREMIERE PRODUCTS DATABASE

The management of Premiere Products, a distributor of appliances, housewares, and sporting goods, has determined that the company's recent growth no longer makes it feasible to maintain customer, order, and inventory data using its manual systems. With the data stored in a database, management will be able to ensure that the data is current and more accurate than in the present manual systems. In addition, managers will be able to obtain answers to their questions concerning the data in the database easily and quickly, with the option of producing a variety of useful reports.

Management has determined that Premiere Products must maintain the following information about its sales reps, customers, and parts inventory in the new database:

- The number, last name, first name, address, total commission, and commission rate for each sales rep
- The customer number, name, address, current balance, and credit limit for each customer, as well as the number of the sales rep who represents the customer
- The part number, description, number of units on hand, item class, number of the warehouse where the item is stored, and unit price for each part in inventory

Premiere Products also must store information about orders. Figure 1-1 shows a sample order.

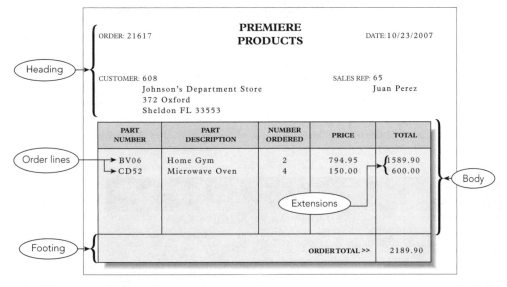

FIGURE 1-1 Sample order

The sample order shown in Figure 1-1 has three sections:

- The heading (top) of the order contains the company name; the order number and date; the customer's number, name, and address; and the sales rep's number and name.
- The body of the order contains one or more order lines, sometimes called line items. Each order line contains a part number, a part description, the number of units of the part ordered, and the quoted price for the part. Each order line also contains a total, usually called an extension, which is the result of multiplying the number ordered by the quoted price.
- Finally, the footing (bottom) of the order contains the order total.

Premiere Products also must store the following items in the database for each customer's order:

- For each order, the database must store the order number, the date the order was placed, and the number of the customer that placed the order. The customer's name and address and the number of the sales rep who represents the customer are stored with customer information. The name of the sales rep is stored with the sales rep information.

- For each order, the database must store the order number, the part number, the number of units ordered, and the quoted price for each order line. The part description is stored with the information about parts. The result of multiplying the number of units ordered by the quoted price is not stored because the computer can calculate it when needed.
- The overall order total is not stored. Instead, the database calculates the total whenever an order is printed or displayed on the screen.

Figure 1-2 shows sample data for Premiere Products.

REP

REP_NUM	LAST_NAME	FIRST_NAME	STREET	CITY	STATE	ZIP	COMMISSION	RATE
20	Kaiser	Valerie	624 Randall	Grove	FL	33321	$20,542.50	0.05
35	Hull	Richard	532 Jackson	Sheldon	FL	33553	$39,216.00	0.07
65	Perez	Juan	1626 Taylor	Fillmore	FL	33336	$23,487.00	0.05

CUSTOMER

CUSTOMER_NUM	CUSTOMER_NAME	STREET	CITY	STATE	ZIP	BALANCE	CREDIT_LIMIT	REP_NUM
148	Al's Appliance and Sport	2837 Greenway	Fillmore	FL	33336	$6,550.00	$7,500.00	20
282	Brookings Direct	3827 Devon	Grove	FL	33321	$431.50	$10,000.00	35
356	Ferguson's	382 Wildwood	Northfield	FL	33146	$5,785.00	$7,500.00	65
408	The Everything Shop	1828 Raven	Crystal	FL	33503	$5,285.25	$5,000.00	35
462	Bargains Galore	3829 Central	Grove	FL	33321	$3,412.00	$10,000.00	65
524	Kline's	838 Ridgeland	Fillmore	FL	33336	$12,762.00	$15,000.00	20
608	Johnson's Department Store	372 Oxford	Sheldon	FL	33553	$2,106.00	$10,000.00	65
687	Lee's Sport and Appliance	282 Evergreen	Altonville	FL	32543	$2,851.00	$5,000.00	35
725	Deerfield's Four Seasons	282 Columbia	Sheldon	FL	33553	$248.00	$7,500.00	35
842	All Season	28 Lakeview	Grove	FL	33321	$8,221.00	$7,500.00	20

FIGURE 1-2 Sample data for Premiere Products

ORDERS

ORDER_NUM	ORDER_DATE	CUSTOMER_NUM
21608	10/20/2007	148
21610	10/20/2007	356
21613	10/21/2007	408
21614	10/21/2007	282
21617	10/23/2007	608
21619	10/23/2007	148
21623	10/23/2007	608

ORDER_LINE

ORDER_NUM	PART_NUM	NUM_ORDERED	QUOTED_PRICE
21608	AT94	11	$21.95
21610	DR93	1	$495.00
21610	DW11	1	$399.99
21613	KL62	4	$329.95
21614	KT03	2	$595.00
21617	BV06	2	$794.95
21617	CD52	4	$150.00
21619	DR93	1	$495.00
21623	KV29	2	$1,290.00

PART

PART_NUM	DESCRIPTION	ON_HAND	CLASS	WAREHOUSE	PRICE
AT94	Iron	50	HW	3	$24.95
BV06	Home Gym	45	SG	2	$794.95
CD52	Microwave Oven	32	AP	1	$165.00
DL71	Cordless Drill	21	HW	3	$129.95
DR93	Gas Range	8	AP	2	$495.00
DW11	Washer	12	AP	3	$399.99
FD21	Stand Mixer	22	HW	3	$159.95
KL62	Dryer	12	AP	1	$349.95
KT03	Dishwasher	8	AP	3	$595.00
KV29	Treadmill	9	SG	2	$1,390.00

FIGURE 1-2   Sample data for Premiere Products (continued)

In the REP table, you see that there are three sales reps, whose numbers are 20, 35, and 65. The name of sales rep 20 is Valerie Kaiser. Her street address is 624 Randall. She lives in Grove, Florida, and her zip code is 33321. Her total commission is $20,542.50, and her commission rate is 5% (0.05).

In the CUSTOMER table, 10 Premiere Products customers are identified with the numbers 148, 282, 356, 408, 462, 524, 608, 687, 725, and 842. The name of customer number 148 is Al's Appliance and Sport. This customer's address is 2837 Greenway in Fillmore, Florida, with a zip code of 33336. The customer's current balance is $6,550.00, and its credit limit is $7,500.00. The number 20 in the REP_NUM column indicates that Al's Appliance and Sport is represented by sales rep 20 (Valerie Kaiser).

Skipping to the table named PART, you see that there are 10 parts, whose part numbers are AT94, BV06, CD52, DL71, DR93, DW11, FD21, KL62, KT03, and KV29. Part AT94 is an iron, and the company has 50 units of this part on hand. Irons are in item class HW (housewares) and are stored in warehouse 3. The price of an iron is $24.95. Other item classes are AP (appliances) and SG (sporting goods).

Moving back to the table named ORDERS, you see that there are seven orders, which are identified with the numbers 21608, 21610, 21613, 21614, 21617, 21619, and 21623. Order number 21608 was placed on October 20, 2007, by customer 148 (Al's Appliance and Sport).

NOTE

In some database systems, the word *order* has a special purpose. Having a table named ORDER could cause problems in such systems. For this reason, Premiere Products uses the table name ORDERS instead of ORDER.

The table named ORDER_LINE might seem strange at first glance. Why do you need a separate table for the order lines? Could they be included in the ORDERS table? The answer is technically yes. The table named ORDERS could be structured as shown in Figure 1-3. Notice that this table contains the same orders as shown in Figure 1-2, with the same dates and customer numbers. In addition, each table row in Figure 1-3 contains all the order lines for a given order. Examining the fifth row, for example, you see that order 21617 has two order lines. One of these order lines is for two BV06 parts at $794.95 each, and the other order line is for four CD52 parts at $150.00 each.

ORDERS

ORDER_NUM	ORDER_D ATE	CUSTOMER_NUM	PART_NUM	NUM_ORDERED	QUOTED_PRICE
21608	10/20/2007	148	AT94	11	$21.95
21610	10/20/2007	356	DR93	1	$495.00
			DW11	1	$399.99
21613	10/21/2007	408	KL62	4	$329.95
21614	10/21/2007	282	KT03	2	$595.00
21617	10/23/2007	608	BV06	2	$794.95
			CD52	4	$150.00
21619	10/23/2007	148	DR93	1	$495.00
21623	10/23/2007	608	KV29	2	$1,290.00

FIGURE 1-3 Alternative ORDERS table structure

Q & A

Question: How is the information from Figure 1-2 represented in Figure 1-3?
Answer: Examine the ORDER_LINE table shown in Figure 1-2 and note the sixth and seventh rows. The sixth row indicates that there is an order line on order 21617 for two BV06 parts at $794.95 each. The seventh row indicates that there is an order line on order 21617 for four CD52 parts at $150.00 each. Thus, the information that you find in Figure 1-3 is represented in Figure 1-2 in two separate rows rather than in one row.

It might seem inefficient to use two rows to store information that could be represented in one row. There is a problem, however, with the arrangement shown in Figure 1-3—the table is more complicated. In Figure 1-2, there is a single entry at each location in the table. In Figure 1-3, some of the individual positions within the table contain multiple entries, making it difficult to track the information between columns. In the row for order number 21617, for example, it is crucial to know that the BV06 corresponds to the 2 in the NUM_ORDERED column (not the 4) and that it corresponds to the $794.95 in the QUOTED_PRICE column (not the $150.00). In addition, a more complex table raises practical issues, such as:

- How much room do you allow for these multiple entries?
- What if an order has more order lines than you have allowed room for?
- For a given part, how do you determine which orders contain order lines for that part?

Although none of these problems is unsolvable, they do add a level of complexity that is not present in the arrangement shown in Figure 1-2. In Figure 1-2, there are no multiple entries to worry about, it does not matter how many order lines exist for any order, and finding every order that contains an order line for a given part is easy (just look for all order lines with the given part number in the PART_NUM column). In general, this simpler structure is preferable, and that is why order lines appear in a separate table.

To test your understanding of the Premiere Products data, use Figure 1-2 to answer the following questions.

Q & A

Question: What are the numbers of the customers represented by Valerie Kaiser?
Answer: 148, 524, and 842. (Look up the REP_NUM value of Valerie Kaiser in the REP table and obtain the number 20. Then find all customers in the CUSTOMER table that have the number 20 in the REP_NUM column.)

Q & A

Question: What is the name of the customer that placed order 21610, and what is the name of the rep who represents this customer?
Answer: Ferguson's is the customer; Juan Perez is the sales rep. (Look up the CUSTOMER_NUM value in the ORDERS table for order number 21610 and obtain the number 356. Then find the customer in the CUSTOMER table with the CUSTOMER_NUM value of 356. Using the REP_NUM value, which is 65, find the name of the rep in the REP table.)

Q & A

Question: List all parts that appear in order 21610. For each part, give the description, number ordered, and quoted price.
Answer: Part number: DR93; part description: Gas Range; number ordered: 1; and quoted price: $495.00. Also, part number: DW11; part description: Washer; number ordered: 1; and quoted price: $399.99. (Look up each ORDER_LINE table row in which the order number is 21610. Each of these rows contains a part number, the number ordered, and the quoted price. Use the part number to look up the corresponding part description in the PART table.)

Q & A

Question: Why is the QUOTED_PRICE column part of the ORDER_LINE table? Can you not just use the part number and look up the price in the PART table?
Answer: If the QUOTED_PRICE column did not appear in the ORDER_LINE table, you would need to obtain the price for a part on an order line by looking up the price in the PART table. Although this might not be a bad practice, it prevents Premiere Products from charging different prices to different customers for the same part. Because Premiere Products wants the flexibility to quote and charge different prices to different customers, the QUOTED_PRICE column is included in the ORDER_LINE table. If you examine the ORDER_LINE table, you will see cases in which the quoted price matches the actual price in the PART table and cases in which it differs. For example, in order number 21608, Al's Appliance and Sport bought 11 irons, and Premiere Products charged only $21.95 per iron, rather than the regular price of $24.95.

THE HENRY BOOKS DATABASE

Ray Henry is the owner of a bookstore chain named Henry Books. Like the management of Premiere Products, Ray has decided to store his data in a database. He wants to achieve the same benefits; that is, he wants to ensure that his data is current and accurate. He also needs to create forms to interact with the data and to produce reports from that data. In addition, he wants to be able to ask questions concerning the data and to obtain answers to these questions easily and quickly.

In running his chain of bookstores, Ray gathers and organizes information about branches, publishers, authors, and books. Figure 1-4 shows sample branch and publisher data for Henry Books. Each branch has a number that uniquely identifies the branch. In addition, Ray tracks the branch's name, location, and number of employees. Each publisher has a code that uniquely identifies the publisher. In addition, Ray tracks the publisher's name and city.

BRANCH

BRANCH_NUM	BRANCH_NAME	BRANCH_LOCATION	NUM_EMPLOYEES
1	Henry Downtown	16 Riverview	10
2	Henry On The Hill	1289 Bedford	6
3	Henry Brentwood	Brentwood Mall	15
4	Henry Eastshore	Eastshore Mall	9

PUBLISHER

PUBLISHER_CODE	PUBLISHER_NAME	CITY
AH	Arkham House	Sauk City WI
AP	Arcade Publishing	New York
BA	Basic Books	Boulder CO
BP	Berkley Publishing	Boston
BY	Back Bay Books	New York
CT	Course Technology	Boston
FA	Fawcett Books	New York
FS	Farrar Straus and Giroux	New York
HC	HarperCollins Publishers	New York
JP	Jove Publications	New York
JT	Jeremy P. Tarcher	Los Angeles
LB	Lb Books	New York
MP	McPherson and Co.	Kingston
PE	Penguin USA	New York
PL	Plume	New York
PU	Putnam Publishing Group	New York
RH	Random House	New York
SB	Schoken Books	New York
SC	Scribner	New York
SS	Simon and Schuster	New York
ST	Scholastic Trade	New York
TA	Taunton Press	Newtown CT
TB	Tor Books	New York
TH	Thames and Hudson	New York
TO	Touchstone Books	Westport CT
VB	Vintage Books	New York
WN	W.W. Norton	New York
WP	Westview Press	Boulder CO

FIGURE 1-4   Sample branch and publisher data for Henry Books

Figure 1-5 shows sample author data for Henry Books. Each author has a number that uniquely identifies the author. In addition, Ray records each author's last and first names.

AUTHOR

AUTHOR_NUM	AUTHOR_LAST	AUTHOR_FIRST
1	Morrison	Toni
2	Solotaroff	Paul
3	Vintage	Vernor
4	Francis	Dick
5	Straub	Peter
6	King	Stephen
7	Pratt	Philip
8	Chase	Truddi
9	Collins	Bradley
10	Heller	Joseph
11	Wills	Gary
12	Hofstadter	Douglas R.
13	Lee	Harper
14	Ambrose	Stephen E.
15	Rowling	J.K.
16	Salinger	J.D.
17	Heaney	Seamus
18	Camus	Albert
19	Collins, Jr.	Bradley
20	Steinbeck	John
21	Castelman	Riva
22	Owen	Barbara
23	O'Rourke	Randy
24	Kidder	Tracy
25	Schleining	Lon

FIGURE 1-5 Sample author data for Henry Books

Figure 1-6 shows sample book data for Henry Books. Each book has a code that uniquely identifies the book. For each book, Ray also tracks the title, publisher, book type, price, and whether the book is a paperback.

BOOK

BOOK_CODE	TITLE	PUBLISHER_CODE	TYPE	PRICE	PAPERBACK
0180	A Deepness in the Sky	TB	SFI	$7.19	Yes
0189	Magic Terror	FA	HOR	$7.99	Yes
0200	The Stranger	VB	FIC	$8.00	Yes
0378	Venice	SS	ART	$24.50	No
079X	Second Wind	PU	MYS	$24.95	No
0808	The Edge	JP	MYS	$6.99	Yes
1351	Dreamcatcher: A Novel	SC	HOR	$19.60	No
1382	Treasure Chests	TA	ART	$24.46	No
138X	Beloved	PL	FIC	$12.95	Yes
2226	Harry Potter and the Prisoner of Azkaban	ST	SFI	$13.96	No
2281	Van Gogh and Gauguin	WP	ART	$21.00	No
2766	Of Mice and Men	PE	FIC	$6.95	Yes
2908	Electric Light	FS	POE	$14.00	No
3350	Group: Six People in Search of a Life	BP	PSY	$10.40	Yes
3743	Nine Stories	LB	FIC	$5.99	Yes
3906	The Soul of a New Machine	BY	SCI	$11.16	Yes
5163	Travels with Charley	PE	TRA	$7.95	Yes
5790	Catch-22	SC	FIC	$12.00	Yes
6128	Jazz	PL	FIC	$12.95	Yes
6328	Band of Brothers	TO	HIS	$9.60	Yes
669X	A Guide to SQL	CT	CMP	$37.95	Yes
6908	Franny and Zooey	LB	FIC	$5.99	Yes
7405	East of Eden	PE	FIC	$12.95	Yes
7443	Harry Potter and the Goblet of Fire	ST	SFI	$18.16	No
7559	The Fall	VB	FIC	$8.00	Yes
8092	Godel, Escher, Bach	BA	PHI	$14.00	Yes
8720	When Rabbit Howls	JP	PSY	$6.29	Yes
9611	Black House	RH	HOR	$18.81	No
9627	Song of Solomon	PL	FIC	$14.00	Yes
9701	The Grapes of Wrath	PE	FIC	$13.00	Yes
9882	Slay Ride	JP	MYS	$6.99	Yes
9883	The Catcher in the Rye	LB	FIC	$5.99	Yes
9931	To Kill a Mockingbird	HC	FIC	$18.00	No

FIGURE 1-6 Sample book data for Henry Books

To check your understanding of the relationship between publishers and books, answer the following questions.

Q & A

Question: Who published *Jazz*? Which books did Jove Publications publish?
Answer: Plume published *Jazz*. In the row in the BOOK table for *Jazz* (see Figure 1-6), find the publisher code PL. Examining the PUBLISHER table (see Figure 1-4), you see that PL is the code assigned to Plume. Jove Publications published *The Edge*, *When Rabbit Howls*, and *Slay Ride*. To find the books published by Jove Publications, find its code (JP) in the PUBLISHER table. Next, find all records in the BOOK table for which the publisher code is JP.

The table named WROTE, as shown in Figure 1-7, is used to relate books and authors. The SEQUENCE field indicates the order in which the authors of a particular book are listed on the cover. The table named INVENTORY in the same figure is used to indicate the number of copies of a particular book that are currently on hand at a particular branch of Henry Books. The first row, for example, indicates that there are two copies of the book with the code 0180 at branch 1.

WROTE

BOOK_CODE	AUTHOR_NUM	SEQUENCE
0180	3	1
0189	5	1
0200	18	1
0378	11	1
079X	4	1
0808	4	1
1351	6	1
1382	23	2
1382	25	1
138X	1	1
2226	15	1
2281	9	2
2281	19	1
2766	20	1
2908	17	1
3350	2	1
3743	16	1

INVENTORY

BOOK_CODE	BRANCH_NUM	ON_HAND
0180	1	2
0189	2	2
0200	1	1
0200	2	3
0378	3	2
079X	2	1
079X	3	2
079X	4	3
0808	2	1
1351	2	4
1351	3	2
1382	2	1
138X	2	3
2226	1	3
2226	3	2
2226	4	1
2281	4	3

FIGURE 1-7 Sample data that relates books to authors and books to branches for Henry Books

WROTE

BOOK_CODE	AUTHOR_NUM	SEQUENCE
3906	24	1
5163	20	1
5790	10	1
6128	1	1
6328	14	1
669X	7	1
6908	16	1
7405	20	1
7443	15	1
7559	18	1
8092	12	1
8720	8	1
9611	5	2
9611	6	1
9627	1	1
9701	20	1
9882	4	1
9883	16	1
9931	13	1

INVENTORY

BOOK_CODE	BRANCH_NUM	ON_HAND
2766	3	2
2908	1	3
2908	4	1
3350	1	2
3743	2	1
3906	2	1
3906	3	2
5163	1	1
5790	4	2
6128	2	4
6128	3	3
6328	2	2
669X	1	1
6908	2	2
7405	3	2
7443	4	1
7559	2	2
8092	3	1
8720	1	3
9611	1	2
9627	3	5
9627	4	2
9701	1	2
9701	2	1
9701	3	3
9701	4	2
9882	3	3
9883	2	3
9883	4	2
9931	1	2

FIGURE 1-7 Sample data that relates books to authors and books to branches for Henry Books (continued)

To check your understanding of the relationship between authors and books, answer the following questions.

Q & A

Question: Who wrote *Black House*? (Make sure to list the authors in the correct order.) Which books did Toni Morrison write?

Answer: Stephen King and Peter Straub wrote *Black House*. First examine the BOOK table (see Figure 1-6) to find the book code for *Black House* (9611). Next, look for all rows in the WROTE table in which the book code is 9611. There are two such rows. In one row, the author number is 5, and in the other, it is 6. Then, look in the AUTHOR table to find the authors who have been assigned the numbers 5 and 6. The answers are Peter Straub (5) and Stephen King (6). The sequence number for author number 5 is 2 and the sequence number for author number 6 is 1. Thus, listing the authors in the proper order results in Stephen King and Peter Straub.

Toni Morrison wrote *Beloved*, *Jazz*, and *Song of Solomon*. To find the books written by Toni Morrison, look up her author number in the AUTHOR table (it is 1). Then look for all rows in the WROTE table for which the author number is 1. There are three such rows. The corresponding book codes are 138X, 6128, and 9627. Looking up these codes in the BOOK table, you find that Toni Morrison wrote *Beloved*, *Jazz*, and *Song of Solomon*.

Q & A

Question: A customer in branch 1 wants to purchase *The Soul of a New Machine*. Is this book currently in stock at branch 1?

Answer: No. Looking up the code for *The Soul of a New Machine* in the BOOK table, you find it is 3906. To find out how many copies are in stock at branch 1, look for a row in the INVENTORY table with 3906 in the BOOK_CODE column and 1 in the BRANCH_NUM column. Because there is no such row, branch 1 doesn't have any copies of *The Soul of a New Machine*.

Q & A

Question: You would like to obtain a copy of *The Soul of a New Machine* for this customer. Which other branches currently have this book in stock, and how many copies does each branch have?

Answer: Branch 2 has one copy, and branch 3 has two copies. You already know that the code for *The Soul of a New Machine* is 3906. (If you did not know the book code, you would look it up in the BOOK table.) To find out which branches currently have copies, look for rows in the INVENTORY table with 3906 in the BOOK_CODE column. There are two such rows. The first row indicates that branch 2 currently has one copy. The second row indicates that branch 3 currently has two copies.

THE ALEXAMARA MARINA GROUP DATABASE

Alexamara Marina Group offers in-water storage to boat owners by providing boat slips that boat owners can rent on an annual basis. Alexamara owns two marinas: Alexamara East and Alexamara Central. Each marina has several boat slips available. Alexamara also provides a variety of boat repair and maintenance services to the boat owners who rent the slips. Alexamara stores the data it needs to manage its operations in a relational database containing the tables described in the following section.

Alexamara stores information about its two marinas in the MARINA table shown in Figure 1-8. A marina number uniquely identifies each marina. The table also includes the marina name, street address, city, state, and zip code.

MARINA

MARINA_NUM	NAME	ADDRESS	CITY	STATE	ZIP
1	Alexamara East	108 2nd Ave.	Brinman	FL	32273
2	Alexamara Central	283 Branston	W. Brinman	FL	32274

FIGURE 1-8 Sample marina data for Alexamara Marina Group

Alexamara stores information about the boat owners to whom it rents slips in the OWNER table shown in Figure 1-9. An owner number that consists of two uppercase letters followed by a two-digit number uniquely identifies each owner. For each owner, the table also includes the last name, first name, address, city, state, and zip code.

OWNER

OWNER_NUM	LAST_NAME	FIRST_NAME	ADDRESS	CITY	STATE	ZIP
AD57	Adney	Bruce and Jean	208 Citrus	Bowton	FL	31313
AN75	Anderson	Bill	18 Wilcox	Glander Bay	FL	31044
BL72	Blake	Mary	2672 Commodore	Bowton	FL	31313
EL25	Elend	Sandy and Bill	462 Riverside	Rivard	FL	31062
FE82	Feenstra	Daniel	7822 Coventry	Kaleva	FL	32521
JU92	Juarez	Maria	8922 Oak	Rivard	FL	31062
KE22	Kelly	Alyssa	5271 Waters	Bowton	FL	31313
NO27	Norton	Peter	2811 Lakewood	Lewiston	FL	32765
SM72	Smeltz	Becky and Dave	922 Garland	Glander Bay	FL	31044
TR72	Trent	Ashton	922 Crest	Bay Shores	FL	30992

FIGURE 1-9 Sample owner data for Alexamara Marina Group

Each marina contains slips that are identified by slip numbers. Marina 1 (Alexamara East) has two sections (A and B) and slips are numbered within each section. Thus, slip numbers at marina 1 consist of the letter A or B followed by a number (for example, A3 or B2). At marina 2 (Alexamara Central), a number (1, 2, 3) identifies each slip.

Information about the slips in the marinas is contained in the MARINA_SLIP table shown in Figure 1-10. Each row in the table contains a slip ID that identifies the particular slip. The table also contains the marina number and slip number, the length of the slip (in feet), the annual rental fee, the name of the boat currently occupying the slip, the type of boat, and the boat owner's number.

MARINA_SLIP

SLIP_ID	MARINA_NUM	SLIP_NUM	LENGTH	RENTAL_FEE	BOAT_NAME	BOAT_TYPE	OWNER_NUM
1	1	A1	40	$3,800.00	Anderson II	Sprite 4000	AN75
2	1	A2	40	$3,800.00	Our Toy	Ray 4025	EL25
3	1	A3	40	$3,600.00	Escape	Sprite 4000	KE22
4	1	B1	30	$2,400.00	Gypsy	Dolphin 28	JU92
5	1	B2	30	$2,600.00	Anderson III	Sprite 3000	AN75
6	2	1	25	$1,800.00	Bravo	Dolphin 25	AD57
7	2	2	25	$1,800.00	Chinook	Dolphin 22	FE82
8	2	3	25	$2,000.00	Listy	Dolphin 25	SM72
9	2	4	30	$2,500.00	Mermaid	Dolphin 28	BL72
10	2	5	40	$4,200.00	Axxon II	Dolphin 40	NO27
11	2	6	40	$4,200.00	Karvel	Ray 4025	TR72

FIGURE 1-10   Sample data about slips at Alexamara Marina Group

Alexamara provides boat maintenance service for owners at its two marinas. The types of service provided are stored in the SERVICE_CATEGORY table shown in Figure 1-11. A category number uniquely identifies each service that Alexamara performs. The table also contains a description of the category.

SERVICE_CATEGORY

CATEGORY_NUM	CATEGORY_DESCRIPTION
1	Routine engine maintenance
2	Engine repair
3	Air conditioning
4	Electrical systems
5	Fiberglass repair
6	Canvas installation
7	Canvas repair
8	Electronic systems (radar, GPS, autopilots, etc.)

FIGURE 1-11   SERVICE_CATEGORY table

Information about the services requested by owners is stored in the SERVICE_REQUEST table shown in Figure 1-12. Each row in the table contains a service ID that identifies each service request. The slip ID identifies the location (marina number and slip number) of the boat to be serviced. For example, the slip ID on the second row is 5. As indicated in the MARINA_SLIP table in Figure 1-10, the slip ID 5 identifies the boat in marina 1 and slip number B2.

The SERVICE_REQUEST table shown in Figure 1-12 also contains the category number of the service to be performed, plus a description of the specific service to be performed, and a description of the current status of the service. It also contains the estimated number of hours required to complete the service. For completed jobs, the table contains the actual number of hours it took to complete the service. If another appointment is required to complete additional service, the appointment date appears in the NEXT_SERVICE_DATE column.

SERVICE_REQUEST

SERVICE_ID	SLIP_ID	CATEGORY_NUM	DESCRIPTION	STATUS	EST_HOURS	SPENT_HOURS	NEXT_SERVICE_DATE
1	1	3	Air conditioner periodically stops with code indicating low coolant level. Diagnose and repair.	Technician has verified the problem. Air conditioning specialist has been called.	4	2	7/12/2007
2	5	4	Fuse on port motor blown on two occasions. Diagnose and repair.	Open	2	0	7/12/2007

FIGURE 1-12   Sample data about service requests at Alexamara Marina Group

SERVICE_REQUEST

SERVICE_ ID	SLIP_ ID	CATEGORY_ NUM	DESCRIPTION	STATUS	EST_ HOURS	SPENT_ HOURS	NEXT_ SERVICE DATE
3	4	1	Oil change and general routine maintenance (check fliud levels, clean sea strainers, etc.).	Service call has been scheduled.	1	0	7/16/2007
4	1	2	Engine oil level has been dropping drastically. Diagnose and repair.	Open	2	0	7/13/2007
5	3	5	Open pockets at base of two stantions.	Technician has completed the initial filling of the open pockets. Will complete the job after the initial fill has had sufficient time to dry.	4	2	7/13/2007
6	11	4	Electric-flush system periodically stops functioning. Diagnose and repair.	Open	3	0	
7	6	2	Engine overheating. Loss of coolant. Diagnose and repair.	Open	2	0	7/13/2007
8	6	2	Heat exchanger not operating correctly.	Technician has determined that the exchanger is faulty. New exchanger has been ordered.	4	1	7/17/2007
9	7	6	Canvas severely damaged in windstorm. Order and install new canvas.	Open	8	0	7/16/2007
10	2	8	Install new GPS and chart plotter.	Scheduled	7	0	7/17/2007

FIGURE 1-12 Sample data about service requests at Alexamara Marina Group (continued)

SERVICE_REQUEST

SERVICE_ ID	SLIP_ ID	CATEGORY_ NUM	DESCRIPTION	STATUS	EST_ HOURS	SPENT_ HOURS	NEXT_ SERVICE DATE
11	2	3	Air conditioning unit shuts down with HHH showing on the control panel.	Technician not able to replicate the problem. Air conditioning unit ran fine through multiple tests. Owners to notify technician if the problem recurs.	1	1	
12	4	8	Both speed and depth readings on data unit are significantly less than the owner thinks they should be.	Technician has scheduled appointment with owner to attempt to verify the problem.	2	0	7/16/2007
13	8	2	Customer describes engine as making a clattering sound.	Technician suspects problem with either propeller or shaft and has scheduled the boat to be pulled from the water for further investigation.	5	2	7/12/2007
14	7	5	Owner accident caused damage to forward portion of port side.	Technician has scheduled repair.	6	0	7/13/2007
15	11	7	Canvas leaks around zippers in heavy rain. Install overlap around zippers to prevent leaks.	Overlap has been created. Installation has been scheduled.	8	3	7/17/2007

FIGURE 1-12   Sample data about service requests at Alexamara Marina Group (continued)

The Alexamara Marina Group exercises at the end of this chapter will give you a chance to check your understanding of the data in this database.

To work with a database on a computer, you must use a database management system. A **database management system (DBMS)** is a software program that lets you create a database and then use it to add, change, delete, sort, and view the data in a database. In this text, you will learn how to use the database management system called MySQL.

MySQL is freely available as open source software. **Open source software** is software for which the source code is freely and publicly available. Open source promotes software reliability and quality by supporting independent peer review and rapid evolution of source code. Users are encouraged to contribute corrections, enhancements, and suggestions for new features to the software's developer. The Linux operating system is an example of a popular open source program.

MySQL was created in the 1990s by Michael Widenius of TeX DataKonsult AB in Sweden. Users in the Internet community quickly realized the potential of MySQL for developing databases for Web applications. MySQL continues to evolve as new functionality is added to the program. The version of MySQL used in this text is MySQL 4.1; however, this text can be used with earlier and later versions of MySQL as the focus of this text is on the SQL command language, which is not version specific. **SQL**, which stands for **Structured Query Language**, is one of the most popular and widely used languages for retrieving and manipulating database data. You will learn more about SQL as you complete the chapters in this text.

MySQL, which has been installed over six million times, is currently the world's most popular open source database. MySQL is particularly suited for client server applications running on the Internet. Organizations that use MySQL for their database needs range from small not-for-profit organizations to global manufacturing companies, government agencies, multinational news organizations, and major Internet service providers. For more information on MySQL, you can explore its Web site at *www.mysql.com*.

MySQL is available for many different operating environments, including Windows, Linux, UNIX, and Mac OS. In this text, you will learn to use MySQL version 4.1 for the Windows XP environment. You can download the most recent version of the MySQL program for your operating system from the Internet at *http://dev.mysql.com/downloads/*. Click the MySQL 4.1 (or the most recent generally available release) link, and then download the version for your operating system. The version used in this text is MySQL 4.1 for Windows. You can use this text with any version of MySQL, however, as the commands used in this text are not affected by different operating systems.

Chapter Summary

Premiere Products is an organization whose information requirements include sales reps, customers, parts, orders, and order lines.

Henry Books is an organization whose information requirements include branches, publishers, authors, books, inventory, and author sequences.

Alexamara Marina Group is an organization whose information requirements include marinas, owners, slips, service categories, and service requests.

MySQL is an open source database management system that is freely available and can be downloaded from the Internet. Currently, MySQL is the most popular open source database. It is particularly suited for Web-based applications. The software runs on many different operating systems.

Key Terms

database

database management system (DBMS)

MySQL

open source software

Structured Query Language (SQL)

Exercises

Premiere Products

Answer each of the following questions using the Premiere Products data shown in Figure 1-2. No computer work is required.

1. List the names of all customers that have a credit limit of $7,500.00 or less.
2. List the order numbers for orders placed by customer number 608 on 10/23/2007.
3. List the part number, part description, and on-hand value for each part in item class SG. (*Hint*: On-hand value is the result of multiplying the number of units on hand by the price.)
4. List the part number and part description of all parts that are in item class HW.
5. How many customers have a balance that exceeds their credit limit?
6. What is the part number, description, and price for the least expensive part in the database?
7. For each order, list the order number, order date, customer number, and customer name.
8. For each order placed on October 21, 2007, list the order number, customer number, and customer name.
9. List the sales rep number and name for every sales rep who represents at least one customer with a credit limit of $10,000.00.
10. For each order placed on October 21, 2007, list the order number, part number, part description, and item class for each part ordered.

Henry Books

Answer each of the following questions using the Henry Books data shown in Figures 1-4 through 1-7. No computer work is required.

1. List the name of each publisher that is located in New York.
2. List the name of each branch that has at least nine employees.
3. List the book code and title of each book that has the type FIC.
4. List the book code and title of each book that has the type FIC and that is in paperback.
5. List the book code and title of each book that has the type FIC or whose publisher code is SC.
6. List the book code and title of each book that has the type MYS and a price of less than $20.00.
7. Customers who are part of a special program get a 10 percent discount off regular book prices. For the first five books in the BOOK table, list the book code, title, and discounted price. (Use the PRICE column to calculate the discounted price.)
8. Find the name of each publisher containing the word *and*.
9. List the book code and title of each book that has the type FIC, MYS, or ART.
10. How many books have the type SFI?
11. Calculate the average price for books that have the type ART.
12. For each book published by Penguin USA, list the book code and title.
13. List the book code, book title, and units on hand for each book in branch number 3.

Alexamara Marina Group

Answer each of the following questions using the Alexamara Marina Group data shown in Figures 1-8 through 1-12. No computer work is required.

1. List the owner number, last name, and first name of every boat owner.
2. List the last name and first name of every owner located in Bowton.
3. List the marina number and slip number for every slip whose length is equal to or less than 30 feet.
4. List the marina number and slip number for every boat with the type Dolphin 28.
5. List the slip number for every boat with the type Dolphin 28 that is located in marina 1.
6. List the boat name for each boat located in a slip whose length is between 25 and 30 feet.
7. List the slip number for every slip in marina 1 whose annual rental fee is less than $3,000.00.
8. Labor is billed at the rate of $60.00 per hour. List the slip ID, category number, estimated hours, and estimated labor cost for every service request. To obtain the estimated labor cost, multiply the estimated hours by 60. Use the column name ESTIMATED_COST for the estimated labor cost.
9. List the marina number and slip number for all slips containing a boat with the type Sprite 4000, Sprite 3000, or Ray 4025.
10. How many Dolphin 25 boats are stored at both marinas?

11. For every boat, list the marina number, slip number, boat name, owner number, owner's first name, and owner's last name.

12. For every service request for routine engine maintenance, list the slip ID, the description, and the status.

13. For every service request for routine engine maintenance, list the slip ID, marina number, slip number, estimated hours, spent hours, owner number, and owner's last name.

CHAPTER 2

DATABASE DESIGN FUNDAMENTALS

LEARNING OBJECTIVES

Objectives

- Understand the terms *entity*, *attribute*, and *relationship*
- Understand the terms *relation* and *relational database*
- Understand functional dependence and be able to identify when one column is functionally dependent on another
- Understand the term *primary key* and identify primary keys in tables
- Design a database to satisfy a set of requirements
- Convert an unnormalized relation to first normal form
- Convert tables from first normal form to second normal form
- Convert tables from second normal form to third normal form
- Create an entity-relationship diagram to represent the design of a database

INTRODUCTION

In Chapter 1, you reviewed the tables and columns in the Premiere Products, Henry Books, and Alexamara Marina Group databases that you will use to complete the rest of this text. The process of determining the particular tables and columns that will comprise a database is known as **database design**. In this chapter, you will learn a method for designing a database to satisfy a set of requirements. In the process, you will learn how to identify the tables and columns in the database. You also will learn how to identify the relationships between the tables.

This chapter begins by examining some important concepts related to databases. It also presents the design method using the set of requirements that Premiere Products identified to produce the appropriate database design. The chapter then examines the process of normalization, in which you identify and fix potential problems in database designs. Finally, the chapter shows a way of visually representing the design of a database.

DATABASE CONCEPTS

Before learning how to design a database, you need to be familiar with some important database concepts related to relational databases, which are the types of databases you examined in Chapter 1 and that you will use throughout the rest of this text. The terms entity, attribute, and relationship are important to understand when designing a database; the concepts of functional dependence and primary keys are critical when learning about the database design process.

Relational Databases

A **relational database** is a collection of tables like the ones you examined for Premiere Products in Chapter 1 and that also appear in Figure 2-1. Formally, these tables are called relations, and this is how this type of database gets its name.

REP

REP_NUM	LAST_NAME	FIRST_NAME	STREET	CITY	STATE	ZIP	COMMISSION	RATE
20	Kaiser	Valerie	624 Randall	Grove	FL	33321	$20,542.50	0.05
35	Hull	Richard	532 Jackson	Sheldon	FL	33553	$39,216.00	0.07
65	Perez	Juan	1626 Taylor	Fillmore	FL	33336	$23,487.00	0.05

FIGURE 2-1 Sample data for Premiere Products

CUSTOMER

CUSTOMER_NUM	CUSTOMER_NAME	STREET	CITY	STATE	ZIP	BALANCE	CREDIT_LIMIT	REP_NUM
148	Al's Appliance and Sport	2837 Greenway	Fillmore	FL	33336	$6,550.00	$7,500.00	20
282	Brookings Direct	3827 Devon	Grove	FL	33321	$431.50	$10,000.00	35
356	Ferguson's	382 Wildwood	Northfield	FL	33146	$5,785.00	$7,500.00	65
408	The Everything Shop	1828 Raven	Crystal	FL	33503	$5,285.25	$5,000.00	35
462	Bargains Galore	3829 Central	Grove	FL	33321	$3,412.00	$10,000.00	65
524	Kline's	838 Ridgeland	Fillmore	FL	33336	$12,762.00	$15,000.00	20
608	Johnson's Department Store	372 Oxford	Sheldon	FL	33553	$2,106.00	$10,000.00	65
687	Lee's Sport and Appliance	282 Evergreen	Altonville	FL	32543	$2,851.00	$5,000.00	35
725	Deerfield's Four Seasons	282 Columbia	Sheldon	FL	33553	$248.00	$7,500.00	35
842	All Season	28 Lakeview	Grove	FL	33321	$8,221.00	$7,500.00	20

ORDERS

ORDER_NUM	ORDER_DATE	CUSTOMER_NUM
21608	10/20/2007	148
21610	10/20/2007	356
21613	10/21/2007	408
21614	10/21/2007	282
21617	10/23/2007	608
21619	10/23/2007	148
21623	10/23/2007	608

ORDER_LINE

ORDER_NUM	PART_NUM	NUM_ORDERED	QUOTED_PRICE
21608	AT94	11	$21.95
21610	DR93	1	$495.00
21610	DW11	1	$399.99
21613	KL62	4	$329.95
21614	KT03	2	$595.00
21617	BV06	2	$794.95
21617	CD52	4	$150.00
21619	DR93	1	$495.00
21623	KV29	2	$1,290.00

FIGURE 2-1 Sample data for Premiere Products (continued)

PART

PART_NUM	DESCRIPTION	ON_HAND	CLASS	WAREHOUSE	PRICE
AT94	Iron	50	HW	3	$24.95
BV06	Home Gym	45	SG	2	$794.95
CD52	Microwave Oven	32	AP	1	$165.00
DL71	Cordless Drill	21	HW	3	$129.95
DR93	Gas Range	8	AP	2	$495.00
DW11	Washer	12	AP	3	$399.99
FD21	Stand Mixer	22	HW	3	$159.95
KL62	Dryer	12	AP	1	$349.95
KT03	Dishwasher	8	AP	3	$595.00
KV29	Treadmill	9	SG	2	$1,390.00

FIGURE 2-1 Sample data for Premiere Products (continued)

NOTE

The names of columns and tables in this text follow a common naming convention in which column names use uppercase letters and replace spaces between words with underscores (_). For example, Premiere Products uses the column named LAST_NAME to store last names and the column named CREDIT_LIMIT to store credit limits.

Entities, Attributes, and Relationships

There are some terms and concepts that are very important for you to know when working in the database environment. The terms entity, attribute, and relationship are fundamental when discussing databases. An **entity** is like a noun; it is a person, place, thing, or event. The entities of interest to Premiere Products, for example, are such things as customers, orders, and sales reps. The entities that are of interest to a school include students, faculty, and classes; a real estate agency is interested in clients, houses, and agents; and a used car dealer is interested in vehicles, customers, and manufacturers.

An **attribute** is a property of an entity. The term is used here exactly as it is used in everyday English. For the entity *person*, for example, the list of attributes might include such things as eye color and height. For Premiere Products, the attributes of interest for the entity *customer* are such things as name, address, city, and so on. For the entity *faculty* at a school, the attributes would be such things as faculty number, name, office number, phone, and so on. For the entity *vehicle* at a car dealership, the attributes are such things as the vehicle identification number, model, color, year, and so on.

A **relationship** is the association between entities. There is an association between customers and sales reps, for example, at Premiere Products. A sales rep is associated with all of his or her customers, and a customer is associated with his or her sales rep. Technically, you say that a sales rep is *related* to all of his or her customers, and a customer is *related* to his or her sales rep.

The relationship between sales reps and customers is an example of a **one-to-many relationship** because one sales rep is associated with many customers, but each customer is associated with only one sales rep. (In this type of relationship, the word *many* is used in a way that is different from everyday English; it might not always mean a large number. In this context, for example, the term *many* means that a sales rep might be associated with *any* number of customers. That is, one sales rep can be associated with zero, one, or more customers.)

How does a relational database handle entities, attributes of entities, and relationships between entities? Entities and attributes are fairly simple. Each entity has its own table. In the Premiere Products database, there is one table for sales reps, one table for customers, and so on. The attributes of an entity become the columns in the table. In the table for sales reps, for example, there is a column for the sales rep number, a column for the sales reps' names, and so on.

What about relationships? At Premiere Products, there is a one-to-many relationship between sales reps and customers (each sales rep is related to the *many* customers that he or she represents, and each customer is related to the *one* sales rep who represents the customer). How is this relationship implemented in a relational database?

Consider Figure 2-1 again. If you want to determine the name of the sales rep who represents Brookings Direct (customer number 282), you would locate the row for Brookings Direct in the CUSTOMER table and determine that the value for REP_NUM is 35. Then you would look for the row in the REP table on which the REP_NUM is 35. The *one* rep with REP_NUM 35 is Richard Hull, who represents Brookings Direct.

On the other hand, if you want to determine the names of all the customers of the rep named Valerie Kaiser, you would locate the row for Valerie Kaiser in the REP table and determine that the value in the REP_NUM column is 20. Then you would look for all the rows in the CUSTOMER table on which the REP_NUM is 20. After identifying Valerie Kaiser's rep number, you find that the *many* customers she represents are numbered 148 (Al's Appliance and Sport), 524 (Kline's), and 842 (All Season).

These relationships are implemented by having common columns in two or more tables. The REP_NUM column in the REP table and the REP_NUM column in the CUSTOMER table are used to implement the relationship between sales reps and customers. Given a sales rep, you can use these columns to determine all the customers that he or she represents; given a customer, you can use these columns to find the sales rep who represents the customer.

In this context, a relation is essentially a two-dimensional table. If you consider the tables shown in Figure 2-1, however, you can see that certain restrictions are placed on relations. Each column should have a unique name, and entries within each column should "match" this column name. For example, if the column name is CREDIT_LIMIT, all entries in that column must be credit limits. Also, each row should be unique—if two rows are identical, the second row does not provide any new information. For maximum flexibility, the order of the columns and rows should be immaterial. Finally, the table's design should be as simple as possible by restricting each position to a single entry and by preventing multiple entries (also called **repeating groups**) in an individual location in the table. Figure 2-2 shows a table design that includes repeating groups.

ORDERS

ORDER_ NUM	ORDER_ DATE	CUSTOMER_ NUM	PART_ NUM	NUM_ ORDERED	QUOTED_ PRICE
21608	10/20/2007	148	AT94	11	$21.95
21610	10/20/2007	356	DR93	1	$495.00
			DW11	1	$399.99
21613	10/21/2007	408	KL62	4	$329.95
21614	10/21/2007	282	KT03	2	$595.00
21617	10/23/2007	608	BV06	2	$12.95
			CD52	4	$150.00
21619	10/23/2007	148	DR93	1	$495.00
21623	10/23/2007	608	KV29	2	$325.99

FIGURE 2-2 Table with repeating groups

Figure 2-3 shows a better way to represent the same information shown in Figure 2-2, as you learned in Chapter 1. In Figure 2-3, every position in the table contains a single value.

ORDERS

ORDER_ NUM	ORDER_ DATE	CUSTOMER_ NUM	PART_ NUM	NUM_ ORDERED	QUOTED_ PRICE
21608	10/20/2007	148	AT94	11	$21.95
21610	10/20/2007	356	DR93	1	$495.00
21610	10/20/2007	356	DW11	1	$399.99
21613	10/21/2007	408	KL62	4	$329.95
21614	10/21/2007	282	KT03	2	$595.00
21617	10/23/2007	608	BV06	2	$12.95
21617	10/23/2007	608	CD52	4	$150.00
21619	10/23/2007	148	DR93	1	$495.00
21623	10/23/2007	608	KV29	2	$325.99

FIGURE 2-3 ORDERS data without repeating groups

When you remove the repeating groups from Figure 2-2, all of the rows in Figure 2-3 are single-valued. This structure is formally called a relation. A **relation** is a two-dimensional table in which the entries in the table are single-valued (each location in the table contains a single entry), each column has a distinct name, all values in the column match this name, the order of the rows and columns is immaterial, and each row contains unique values. A relational database is a collection of relations.

NOTE

Rows in a table (relation) are also called **records** or **tuples**. Columns in a table (relation) are also called **fields** or attributes. This text uses the terms *tables*, *columns*, and *rows* unless the more formal terms of *relation*, *attributes*, and *tuples* are necessary for clarity.

31

There is a commonly accepted shorthand representation to show the tables and columns in a relational database: For each table, you write the name of the table and then within parentheses list all of the columns in the table. In this representation, each table appears on its own line. Using this method, you represent the Premiere Products database as follows:

```
REP (REP_NUM, LAST_NAME, FIRST_NAME, STREET,
     CITY, STATE, ZIP, COMMISSION, RATE)
CUSTOMER (CUSTOMER_NUM, CUSTOMER_NAME, STREET,
     CITY, STATE, ZIP, BALANCE, CREDIT_LIMIT,
     REP_NUM)
ORDERS (ORDER_NUM, ORDER_DATE, CUSTOMER_NUM)
ORDER_LINE (ORDER_NUM, PART_NUM, NUM_ORDERED,
     QUOTED_PRICE)
PART (PART_NUM, DESCRIPTION, ON_HAND, CLASS,
     WAREHOUSE, PRICE)
```

Notice that some tables contain columns with duplicate names. For example, the REP_NUM column appears in both the REP table *and* the CUSTOMER table. Suppose a situation existed wherein someone (or the DBMS) might confuse the two columns. For example, if you write REP_NUM, it is not clear which REP_NUM column you want to use. You need a mechanism for indicating the REP_NUM column to which you are referring. One common approach to solving this problem is to write both the table name and the column name, separated by a period. Thus, the REP_NUM column in the CUSTOMER table is written as CUSTOMER.REP_NUM, whereas the REP_NUM column in the REP table is written as REP.REP_NUM. Technically, when you write columns in this format, you say that you **qualify** the names. It is *always* acceptable to qualify column names, even if there is no potential for confusion. If confusion might arise, however, it is *essential* to qualify column names.

FUNCTIONAL DEPENDENCE

The concept of functional dependence is crucial to understanding the rest of the material in this chapter. Functional dependence is a formal name for what is basically a simple idea. To illustrate functional dependence, suppose that the REP table for Premiere Products is structured as shown in Figure 2-4. The only difference between the REP table shown in Figure 2-4 and the one shown in Figure 2-1 is the addition of an extra column named PAY_CLASS.

REP

REP_NUM	LAST_NAME	FIRST_NAME	STREET	CITY	STATE	ZIP	COMMISSION	PAY_CLASS	RATE
20	Kaiser	Valerie	624 Randall	Grove	FL	33321	$20,542.50	1	0.05
35	Hull	Richard	532 Jackson	Sheldon	FL	33553	$39,216.00	2	0.07
65	Perez	Juan	1626 Taylor	Fillmore	FL	33336	$23,487.00	1	0.05

FIGURE 2-4 REP table with a PAY_CLASS column

Suppose that one of the policies at Premiere Products is that all sales reps in any given pay class earn their commissions at the same rate. If you were asked to describe this situation, you might say that a sales rep's pay class *determines* his or her commission rate. Alternatively, you might say that a sales rep's commission rate *depends on* his or her pay class. This phrasing uses the words *determines* and *depends on* in the same way that you describe functional dependency. If you wanted to be formal, you would precede either expression with the word *functionally*. Thus you might say, "A sales rep's pay class *functionally determines* his or her commission rate," and "A sales rep's commission rate *functionally depends on* his or her pay class." You can also define functional dependency by saying that if you know a sales rep's pay class, you can determine his or her commission rate.

In a relational database, column B is **functionally dependent** on another column (or a collection of columns), A, if at any point in time a value for A determines a single value for B. You can think of this as follows: If you are given a value for A, do you know that you can find a single value for B? If so, B is functionally dependent on A (often written as A → B). If B is functionally dependent on A, you also can say that A **functionally determines** B.

At Premiere Products, is the LAST_NAME column in the REP table functionally dependent on the REP_NUM column? Yes, it is. If you are given a value for REP_NUM, such as 20, there is a *single* LAST_NAME, Kaiser, associated with it. This is represented as:

REP_NUM → LAST_NAME

Q & A

Question: In the CUSTOMER table, is CUSTOMER_NAME functionally dependent on REP_NUM?

Answer: No. Given the REP_NUM 20, for example, you would not be able to find a single customer name, because 20 appears on more than one row in the table.

Q & A

Question: In the ORDER_LINE table, is NUM_ORDERED functionally dependent on ORDER_NUM?

Answer: No. An ORDER_NUM might be associated with several items in an order, so having just an ORDER_NUM does not provide enough information.

Q & A

Question: Is NUM_ORDERED functionally dependent on PART_NUM?

Answer: No. Again, just as with ORDER_NUM, a PART_NUM might be associated with several items in an order, so PART_NUM does not provide enough information.

Q & A

Question: On which columns in the ORDER_LINE table is NUM_ORDERED functionally dependent?

Answer: To determine a value for NUM_ORDERED, you need both an order number and a part number. In other words, NUM_ORDERED is functionally dependent on the combination (formally called the **concatenation**) of ORDER_NUM and PART_NUM. That is, given an order number *and* a part number, you can find a single value for NUM_ORDERED.

At this point, a question naturally arises: How do you determine functional dependencies? Can you determine them by looking at sample data, for example? The answer is no.

Consider the REP table in Figure 2-5, in which last names happen to be unique. It is very tempting to say that LAST_NAME functionally determines STREET, CITY, STATE, and ZIP (or equivalently that STREET, CITY, STATE, and ZIP are all functionally dependent on LAST_NAME). After all, given the last name of a rep, you can find the single address.

REP

REP_NUM	LAST_NAME	FIRST_NAME	STREET	CITY	STATE	ZIP	COMMISSION	RATE
20	Kaiser	Valerie	624 Randall	Grove	FL	33321	$20,542.50	0.05
35	Hull	Richard	532 Jackson	Sheldon	FL	33553	$39,216.00	0.07
65	Perez	Juan	1626 Taylor	Fillmore	FL	33336	$23,487.00	0.05

FIGURE 2-5 REP table

What happens when rep 85, whose last name is also Kaiser, is added to the database? You then have the situation illustrated in Figure 2-6. Because there are now two reps with the last name of Kaiser, you can no longer find a single address using a rep's last name. Thus you were misled by the original sample data. The only way to determine functional dependencies is to examine the user's policies. This process can involve discussions with users, examination of user documentation, and so on. If, for example, you discover that Premiere Products has a rule never to hire two reps with the same last name (a very strange rule, to say the least), then LAST_NAME would indeed determine the other columns. Without such a rule, however, LAST_NAME would not.

REP

REP_NUM	LAST_NAME	FIRST_NAME	STREET	CITY	STATE	ZIP	COMMISSION	RATE
20	Kaiser	Valerie	624 Randall	Grove	FL	33321	$20,542.50	0.05
35	Hull	Richard	532 Jackson	Sheldon	FL	33553	$39,216.00	0.07
65	Perez	Juan	1626 Taylor	Fillmore	FL	33336	$23,487.00	0.05
85	Kaiser	William	172 Bahia	Norton	FL	39281	$0.00	0.05

FIGURE 2-6   REP table with two reps named Kaiser

PRIMARY KEYS

Another important concept of database design is that of the primary key. In the simplest terms, the **primary key** is the unique identifier for a table. For example, the REP_NUM column is the unique identifier for the REP table. Given a rep num in the table, such as 20, there will only be one row on which that rep number occurs. Thus, the rep number 20 uniquely identifies a row (in this case, the first row, and the rep named Valerie Kaiser).

In this text, the definition of primary key needs to be more precise than a unique identifier for a table. Specifically, column A (or a collection of columns) is the primary key for a table if:

Property 1. *All* columns in the table are functionally dependent on A.
Property 2. No subcollection of the columns in A (assuming A is a collection of columns and not just a single column) also has property 1.

Q & A

Question: Is the CLASS column the primary key for the PART table?
Answer: No, because the other columns are not functionally dependent on CLASS. Given the class HW, for example, you cannot determine a part number, description, or anything else, because there are several rows on which the class is HW.

Q & A

Question: Is the CUSTOMER_NUM column the primary key for the CUSTOMER table?
Answer: Yes, because customer numbers are unique. A specific customer number cannot appear on more than one row. Thus, all columns in the CUSTOMER table are functionally dependent on CUSTOMER_NUM.

Q & A

Question: Is the ORDER_NUM column the primary key for the ORDER_LINE table?
Answer: No, because it does not functionally determine either NUM_ORDERED or QUOTED_PRICE.

Q & A

Question: Is the combination of the ORDER_NUM and PART_NUM columns the primary key for the ORDER_LINE table?
Answer: Yes, because you can determine all columns by this combination of columns, and, further, neither the ORDER_NUM nor the PART_NUM alone has this property.

Q & A

Question: Is the combination of the PART_NUM and DESCRIPTION columns the primary key for the PART table?
Answer: No. Although it is true that you can determine all columns in the PART table by this combination, PART_NUM alone also has this property.

Primary keys are usually indicated in a shorthand representation of a database by underlining the column or collection of columns that comprise the primary key. Thus, the complete shorthand representation for the Premiere Products database is:

```
REP (REP_NUM, LAST_NAME, FIRST_NAME, STREET,
     CITY, STATE, ZIP, COMMISSION, RATE)
CUSTOMER (CUSTOMER_NUM, CUSTOMER_NAME, STREET,
     CITY, STATE, ZIP, BALANCE, CREDIT_LIMIT,
     REP_NUM)
ORDERS (ORDER_NUM, ORDER_DATE, CUSTOMER_NUM)
ORDER_LINE (ORDER_NUM, PART_NUM, NUM_ORDERED,
     QUOTED_PRICE)
PART (PART_NUM, DESCRIPTION, ON_HAND, CLASS,
     WAREHOUSE, PRICE)
```

NOTE

Sometimes you might identify one or more columns that you can use as a table's primary key. For example, if the Premiere Products database included an EMPLOYEE table that contains employee numbers and Social Security numbers, either the employee number or the Social Security number could serve as the table's primary key. In this case, both columns are referred to as candidate keys. Like a primary key, a **candidate key** is a column or collection of columns on which all columns in the table are functionally dependent—the definition for primary key really defines candidate key as well. From all the candidate keys, you would choose one to be the primary key.

NOTE

According to the definition of a candidate key, a Social Security number is a legitimate primary key. Many databases, such as those that store data about students at a college or university or those that store data about employees at a company, use a person's Social Security number as a primary key. However, many institutions and organizations are moving away from using Social Security numbers as primary keys because of privacy issues. Instead of using Social Security numbers, many institutions and organizations use unique student numbers or employee numbers as primary keys.

NOTE

Some institutions prefer to assign values to use as primary keys for such items as customer numbers, part numbers, and student numbers. Others simply let the computer generate the values. In this case, the DBMS simply assigns the next available number. For example, if customer numbers 1000–1436 have already been assigned, the next customer added to the database will be assigned customer number 1437.

DATABASE DESIGN

This section presents a specific method you can follow to design a database, given a set of requirements that the database must support. The determination of the requirements is part of the process known as systems analysis. A systems analyst interviews users, examines existing and proposed documents, and examines organizational policies to determine exactly the type of data needs the database must support. This text does not cover this analysis. Rather, it focuses on how to take the set of requirements that this process produces and determine the appropriate database design.

After presenting the database design method, this section presents a sample set of requirements and illustrates the design method by designing a database to satisfy these requirements.

Design Method

To design a database for a set of requirements, complete the following steps:

1. Read the requirements, identify the entities (objects) involved, and name the entities. For example, if the design involves departments and employees, you might use the entity names DEPARTMENT and EMPLOYEE. If the design involves customers and sales reps, you might use the entity names CUSTOMER and REP.

2. Identify the unique identifiers for the entities you identified in Step 1. For example, if one of the entities is PART, determine what information is required to uniquely identify each individual part. In other words, what information does the organization use to distinguish one part from another? For a PART entity, the unique identifier for each part might be a PART_NUM; for a CUSTOMER entity, the unique identifier might be a CUSTOMER_NUM. If no unique identifier is available from the data you know about the entity, you need to create one. For example, you might use a unique number to identify parts when no part numbers exist.

3. Identify the attributes for all the entities. These attributes become the columns in the tables. It is possible for two or more entities to contain the same attributes. At Premiere Products, for example, reps and customers both have addresses, cities, states, and zip codes. To clarify this duplication of attributes, follow the name of the attribute with the corresponding entity in parentheses. Thus, ADDRESS (CUSTOMER) is a customer address and ADDRESS (REP) is a sales rep address.

4. Identify the functional dependencies that exist among the attributes. Ask yourself the following question: If you know a unique value for an attribute, do you also know the unique values for other attributes? For example, if you have the three attributes REP_NUM, LAST_NAME, and FIRST_NAME, and if you know a unique value for REP_NUM, do you also know a unique value for LAST_NAME and FIRST_NAME? If so, then LAST_NAME and FIRST_NAME are functionally dependent on REP_NUM (REP_NUM → LAST_NAME, FIRST_NAME).

5. Use the functional dependencies to identify the tables by placing each attribute with the attribute or minimum combination of attributes on which it is functionally dependent. The attribute or attributes for an entity on which all other attributes are dependent will be the primary key of the table. The remaining attributes will be the other columns in the table. Once you have determined all the columns in the table, you can give the table an appropriate name. Usually the name will be the same as the name you identified for the entity in Step 1.

6. Identify any relationships between tables. In some cases, you might be able to determine the relationships directly from the requirements. It might be clear, for example, that one rep is related to many customers and that each customer is related to exactly one rep. If it is not, look for matching columns in the tables you created. For example, if both the REP table and the CUSTOMER table contain a REP_NUM column and the values in these columns must match, you know that reps and customers are related. The fact that the REP_NUM column is the primary key in the REP table tells you that the REP table is the "one" part of the relationship and the CUSTOMER table is the "many" part of the relationship.

In the next section, you will apply this process to produce the design for the Premiere Products database using the collection of requirements that this database must support.

Database Design Requirements

The analyst has interviewed users and examined documents at Premiere Products and has determined that the database must support the following requirements:

1. For a sales rep, store the sales rep's number, last name, first name, street address, city, state, zip code, total commission, and commission rate.

2. For a customer, store the customer's number, name, street address, city, state, zip code, balance, and credit limit. In addition, store the number, last name, and first name of the sales rep who represents this customer. The analyst has also determined that a sales rep can represent many customers, but a customer must have exactly one sales rep (in other words, a sales rep must represent a customer; a customer cannot be represented by zero or more than one sales reps).

3. For a part, store the part's number, description, units on hand, item class, the number of the warehouse in which the part is located, and the price. All units of a particular part are stored in the same warehouse.

4. For an order, store the order number, order date, the number and name of the customer that placed the order, and the number of the sales rep who represents that customer.

5. For each line item within an order, store the part number and description, the number ordered, and the quoted price. The analyst also obtained the following information concerning orders:
   a. There is only one customer per order.
   b. On a given order, there is at most one line item for a given part. For example, part DR93 cannot appear on several lines within the same order.
   c. The quoted price might differ from the actual price, in cases in which the sales rep offered a discount for a certain part on a specific order.

Database Design Process Example

The following steps apply the design process to the requirements for Premiere Products to produce the appropriate database design:

1. There appear to be four entities: reps, customers, parts, and orders. The names assigned to these entities are REP, CUSTOMER, PART, and ORDERS, respectively.

2. From the collection of entities, review the data and determine the unique identifier for each entity. For the REP, CUSTOMER, PART, and ORDERS entities, the unique identifiers are the rep number, the customer number, the part number, and the order number, respectively. These unique identifiers were named REP_NUM, CUSTOMER_NUM, PART_NUM, and ORDER_NUM, respectively.

3. The attributes mentioned in the first requirement all refer to sales reps. The specific attributes mentioned in the requirement are the sales rep's number, name, street address, city, state, zip code, total commission, and commission rate. Assigning appropriate names to these attributes produces the following list:

```
REP_NUM
LAST_NAME
FIRST_NAME
STREET
CITY
STATE
ZIP
COMMISSION
RATE
```

The attributes mentioned in the second requirement refer to customers. The specific attributes are the customer's number, name, street address, city, state, zip code, balance, and credit limit. The requirement also mentions the number, first name, and last name of the sales rep who represents this customer. Assigning appropriate names to these attributes produces the following list:

```
CUSTOMER_NUM
CUSTOMER_NAME
STREET
CITY
STATE
ZIP
BALANCE
CREDIT_LIMIT
REP_NUM
LAST_NAME
FIRST_NAME
```

There are attributes named STREET, CITY, STATE, and ZIP for sales reps as well as attributes named STREET, CITY, STATE, and ZIP for customers. To distinguish these attributes in the final collection, the name of the attribute is followed by the name of the corresponding entity. For example, the street for a sales rep is STREET (REP) and the street for a customer is STREET (CUSTOMER).

The attributes mentioned in the third requirement refer to parts. The specific attributes are the part's number, description, units on hand, item class, the number of the warehouse in which the part is located, and the price. Assigning appropriate names to these attributes produces the following list:

```
PART_NUM
DESCRIPTION
ON_HAND
CLASS
WAREHOUSE
PRICE
```

The attributes mentioned in the fourth requirement refer to orders. The specific attributes include the order number, order date, the number and name of the customer that placed the order, and the number of the sales rep who represents the customer. Assigning appropriate names to these attributes produces the following list:

```
ORDER_NUM
ORDER_DATE
CUSTOMER_NUM
CUSTOMER_NAME
REP_NUM
```

The specific attributes associated with the statement in the requirements concerning line items are the order number (to determine the order to which the line item corresponds), part number, description, the number ordered, and the quoted price. If the quoted price must be the same as the price, you could simply call it PRICE. According to requirement 5c, however, the quoted price might differ from the price. Thus, you must add the quoted price to the list. Assigning appropriate names to these attributes produces the following list:

```
ORDER_NUM
PART_NUM
DESCRIPTION
NUM_ORDERED
QUOTED_PRICE
```

The complete list grouped by entity is as follows:

REP
```
REP_NUM
LAST_NAME
FIRST_NAME
STREET (REP)
CITY (REP)
STATE (REP)
ZIP (REP)
COMMISSION
RATE
```

CUSTOMER
```
CUSTOMER_NUM
CUSTOMER_NAME
STREET (CUSTOMER)
CITY (CUSTOMER)
STATE (CUSTOMER)
ZIP (CUSTOMER)
BALANCE
CREDIT_LIMIT
REP_NUM
LAST_NAME
FIRST_NAME
```

PART
```
PART_NUM
DESCRIPTION
ON_HAND
CLASS
WAREHOUSE
PRICE
```

ORDER
ORDER_NUM
ORDER_DATE
CUSTOMER_NUM
CUSTOMER_NAME
REP_NUM

For line items within an order
ORDER_NUM
PART_NUM
DESCRIPTION
NUM_ORDERED
QUOTED_PRICE

4. The fact that the unique identifier for sales reps is the rep number gives the following functional dependencies:

REP_NUM ➝ LAST_NAME, FIRST_NAME, STREET (REP), CITY (REP),
        STATE (REP), ZIP (REP), COMMISSION, RATE

   This notation indicates that the LAST_NAME, FIRST_NAME, STREET (REP), CITY (REP), STATE (REP), ZIP (REP), COMMISSION, and RATE are all functionally dependent on REP_NUM.

   The fact that the unique identifier for customers is the customer number gives the following functional dependencies:

CUSTOMER_NUM ➝ CUSTOMER_NAME, STREET (CUSTOMER),
        CITY (CUSTOMER), STATE (CUSTOMER), ZIP (CUSTOMER),
        BALANCE, CREDIT_LIMIT, REP_NUM,
        LAST_NAME, FIRST_NAME

Q & A

Question: Do you really need to include the last name and first name of a sales rep in the list of attributes determined by the customer number?

Answer: There is no need to include them in this list, because they both can be determined from the sales rep number and are already included in the list of attributes determined by REP_NUM.

   Thus, the functional dependencies for the CUSTOMER entity are as follows:

CUSTOMER_NUM ➝ CUSTOMER_NAME, STREET (CUSTOMER),
        CITY (CUSTOMER), STATE (CUSTOMER), ZIP (CUSTOMER),
        BALANCE, CREDIT_LIMIT, REP_NUM

   The fact that the unique identifier for parts is the part number gives the following functional dependencies:

PART_NUM ➝ DESCRIPTION, ON_HAND, CLASS, WAREHOUSE, PRICE

   The fact that the unique identifier for orders is the order number, gives the following functional dependencies:

ORDER_NUM ➝ ORDER_DATE, CUSTOMER_NUM, CUSTOMER_NAME, REP_NUM

Question: Do you really need to include the name of a customer and the number of the customer's rep in the list of attributes determined by the order number?
Answer: There is no need to include the customer name and the rep number in this list, because you can determine them from the customer number and they are already included in the list of attributes determined by CUSTOMER_NUM.

Thus, the functional dependencies for the ORDERS entity are as follows:

```
ORDER_NUM  ➜  ORDER_DATE, CUSTOMER_NUM
```

The final attributes to be examined are those associated with the line items within the order: PART_NUM, DESCRIPTION, NUM_ORDERED, and QUOTED_PRICE.

Question: Why aren't NUM_ORDERED and QUOTED_PRICE included in the list of attributes determined by the order number?
Answer: To uniquely identify a particular value for NUM_ORDERED or QUOTED_PRICE, ORDER_NUM alone is not sufficient. It requires the combination of ORDER_NUM and PART_NUM.

The following shorthand representation indicates that the combination of ORDER_NUM and PART_NUM functionally determines NUM_ORDERED and QUOTED_PRICE:

```
ORDER_NUM, PART_NUM  ➜  NUM_ORDERED, QUOTED_PRICE
```

Question: Does DESCRIPTION need to be included in this list?
Answer: No, because DESCRIPTION can be determined by the PART_NUMBER alone, and it already appears in the list of attributes dependent on the PART_NUM.

The complete list of functional dependencies is as follows:

```
REP_NUM  ➜  LAST_NAME, FIRST_NAME, STREET (REP), CITY (REP),
     STATE (REP), ZIP(REP), COMMISSION, RATE
CUSTOMER_NUM  ➜  CUSTOMER_NAME, STREET (CUSTOMER),
     CITY (CUSTOMER), STATE (CUSTOMER), ZIP (CUSTOMER),
     BALANCE, CREDIT_LIMIT, REP_NUM
PART_NUM  ➜  DESCRIPTION, ON_HAND, CLASS, WAREHOUSE, PRICE
ORDER_NUM  ➜  ORDER_DATE, CUSTOMER_NUM
ORDER_NUM, PART_NUM  ➜  NUM_ORDERED, QUOTED_PRICE
```

5. Using the functional dependencies, you can create tables with the attribute(s) to the left of the arrow being the primary key and the items to the right of the arrow being the other columns. For relations corresponding to those entities identified in Step 1, you can simply use the name you already determined. Because you did not identify any entity that had a unique identifier that was the combination of ORDER_NUM and PART_NUM, you need to assign a name to the table whose primary key consists of these two columns. Because this table represents the individual lines within an order, the name ORDER_LINE is a good choice. The final collection of tables is as follows:

```
REP (REP_NUM, LAST_NAME, FIRST_NAME, STREET,
        CITY, STATE, ZIP, COMMISSION, RATE)
CUSTOMER (CUSTOMER_NUM, CUSTOMER_NAME, STREET,
        CITY, STATE, ZIP, BALANCE, CREDIT_LIMIT,
        REP_NUM)
PART (PART_NUM, DESCRIPTION, ON_HAND, CLASS,
        WAREHOUSE, PRICE)
ORDERS (ORDER_NUM, ORDER_DATE, CUSTOMER_NUM)
ORDER_LINE (ORDER_NUM, PART_NUM, NUM_ORDERED,
        QUOTED_PRICE)
```

6. Examining the tables and identifying common columns gives the following list of relationships between the tables:

    a. The CUSTOMER and REP tables are related using the REP_NUM columns. Because the REP_NUM column is the primary key for the REP table, this indicates a one-to-many relationship between REP and CUSTOMER (one rep to many customers).

    b. The ORDERS and CUSTOMER tables are related using the CUSTOMER_NUM columns. Because the CUSTOMER_NUM column is the primary key for the CUSTOMER table, this indicates a one-to-many relationship between CUSTOMER and ORDERS (one customer to many orders).

    c. The ORDER_LINE and ORDERS tables are related using the ORDER_NUM columns. Because the ORDER_NUM column is the primary key for the ORDERS table, this indicates a one-to-many relationship between ORDERS and ORDER_LINE (one order to many order lines).

    d. The ORDER_LINE and PART tables are related using the PART_NUM columns. Because the PART_NUM column is the primary key for the PART table, this indicates a one-to-many relationship between PART and ORDER_LINE (one part to many order lines).

NORMALIZATION

After creating the database design, you must analyze it to make sure it is free of potential problems. To do so, you follow a process called **normalization**, in which you identify the existence of potential problems, such as data duplication and redundancy, and implement ways to correct these problems.

The goal of normalization is to convert **unnormalized relations** (that is, tables that satisfy the definition of a relation except that they might contain repeating groups) into various types of **normal forms**. A table in a particular normal form possesses a certain desirable collection of properties. Although there are several normal forms, the most common are first normal form, second normal form, and third normal form. Normalization is a process in which a table that is in first normal form is better than a table that is not in first normal form, a table that is in second normal form is better than one that is in first normal form, and so on. The goal of this process is to allow you to take a table or collection of tables and produce a new collection of tables that represents the same information but is free of problems.

First Normal Form

According to the definition of a relation, a relation (table) cannot contain a repeating group in which multiple entries exist on a single row. However, in the database design process, you might create a table that has all the other properties of a relation, but contains a repeating group. Removing repeating groups is the starting point when converting an unnormalized collection of data into a table that is in first normal form. A table (relation) is in **first normal form (1NF)** if it does not contain a repeating group.

For example, in the design process you might create the following ORDERS table, in which there is a repeating group consisting of PART_NUM and NUM_ORDERED. The notation for this table is as follows:

```
ORDERS (ORDER_NUM, ORDER_DATE, (PART_NUM, NUM_ORDERED) )
```

This notation describes a table named ORDERS that consists of a primary key, ORDER_NUM, and a column named ORDER_DATE. The inner parentheses indicate a repeating group that contains two columns, PART_NUM and NUM_ORDERED. This table contains one row per order with values in the PART_NUM and NUM_ORDERED columns for each order with the number ORDER_NUM and placed on ORDER_DATE. Figure 2-7 shows a single order with multiple combinations of a part number and a corresponding number of units ordered.

ORDERS

ORDER_NUM	ORDER_DATE	PART_NUM	NUM_ORDERED
21608	10/20/2007	AT94	11
21610	10/20/2007	DR93	1
		DW11	1
21613	10/21/2007	KL62	4
21614	10/21/2007	KT03	2
21617	10/23/2007	BV06	2
		CD52	4
21619	10/23/2007	DR93	1
21623	10/23/2007	KV29	2

FIGURE 2-7 Unnormalized order data

To convert the table to first normal form, you remove the repeating group as follows:

ORDERS (<u>ORDER_NUM</u>, ORDER_DATE, <u>PART_NUM</u>, NUM_ORDERED)

Figure 2-8 shows the table in first normal form.

ORDERS

ORDER_NUM	ORDER_DATE	PART_NUM	NUM_ORDERED
21608	10/20/2007	AT94	11
21610	10/20/2007	DR93	1
21610	10/20/2007	DW11	1
21613	10/21/2007	KL62	4
21614	10/21/2007	KT03	2
21617	10/23/2007	BV06	2
21617	10/23/2007	CD52	4
21619	10/23/2007	DR93	1
21623	10/23/2007	KV29	2

FIGURE 2-8 Order data converted to first normal form

In Figure 2-7, the second row indicates that part DR93 and part DW11 are both present on order 21610. In Figure 2-8, this information is represented by *two* rows, the second and third. The primary key for the unnormalized ORDERS table was the ORDER_NUM column alone. The primary key for the normalized table is now the combination of the ORDER_NUM and PART_NUM columns.

When you convert an unnormalized table to a table in first normal form, the primary key of the table in first normal form is usually the primary key of the unnormalized table concatenated with the key for the repeating group, which is the column in the repeating group that distinguishes one occurrence of the repeating group from another within a given row in the table. In the ORDERS table, PART_NUM was the key to the repeating group and ORDER_NUM was the primary key for the table. When converting the unnormalized data to first normal form, the primary key becomes the concatenation of the ORDER_NUM and PART_NUM columns.

Second Normal Form

The following ORDERS table is in first normal form, because it does not contain a repeating group:

ORDERS (<u>ORDER_NUM</u>, ORDER_DATE, <u>PART_NUM</u>, DESCRIPTION,
    NUM_ORDERED, QUOTED_PRICE)

The table contains the following functional dependencies:

```
ORDER_NUM ⟶ ORDER_DATE
PART_NUM ⟶ DESCRIPTION
ORDER_NUM, PART_NUM ⟶ NUM_ORDERED, QUOTED_PRICE
```

This notation indicates that ORDER_NUM alone determines ORDER_DATE, and PART_NUM alone determines DESCRIPTION, but it requires *both* an ORDER_NUM *and a* PART_NUM to determine either NUM_ORDERED or QUOTED_PRICE. Consider the sample of this table shown in Figure 2-9.

ORDERS

ORDER_ NUM	ORDER_ DATE	PART_ NUM	DESCRIPTION	NUM_ ORDERED	QUOTED_ PRICE
21608	10/20/2007	AT94	Iron	11	$21.95
21610	10/20/2007	DR93	Gas Range	1	$495.00
21610	10/20/2007	DW11	Washer	1	$399.99
21613	10/21/2007	KL62	Dryer	4	$329.95
21614	10/21/2007	KT03	Dishwasher	2	$595.00
21617	10/23/2007	BV06	Home Gym	2	$12.95
21617	10/23/2007	CD52	Microwave Oven	4	$150.00
21619	10/23/2007	DR93	Gas Range	1	$495.00
21623	10/23/2007	KV29	Treadmill	2	$325.99

FIGURE 2-9 Sample ORDERS table

Although the ORDERS table is in first normal form (there are no repeating groups), problems exist within the table that require you to restructure it.

The description of a specific part, DR93 for example, occurs two times in the table. This duplication (formally called **redundancy**) causes several problems. It is certainly wasteful of space, but that is not nearly as serious as some of the other problems. These other problems are called **update anomalies** and they fall into four categories:

1. **Update:** A change to the description of part DR93 requires not one change to the table, but two—you must change each row on which part DR93 appears. Updating the part description more than once makes the update process much more cumbersome and time consuming.
2. **Inconsistent data:** There is nothing about the design that prohibits part DR93 from having two *different* descriptions in the database. In fact, if part DR93 occurs on 20 rows in the table, it is possible for this part to have 20 different descriptions in the database.

3. **Additions:** If you try to add a new part and its description to the database, you will face a real problem. Because the primary key for the ORDERS table consists of both an ORDER_NUM and a PART_NUM, you need values for both of these columns to add a new row to the table. If you add a part to the table that does not yet have any orders, what do you use for an ORDER_NUM? The only solution is to create a dummy ORDER_NUM and then replace it with a real ORDER_NUM once an order for this part is actually received. Certainly this is not an acceptable solution.

4. **Deletions:** If you delete order 21608 from the database and it is the only order that contains part AT94, deleting the order also deletes all information about part AT94. For example, you would no longer know that part AT94 is an iron.

These problems occur because you have a column, DESCRIPTION, that is dependent on only a portion of the primary key, PART_NUM, and *not* on the complete primary key. This situation leads to the definition of second normal form. Second normal form represents an improvement over first normal form because it eliminates update anomalies in these situations. A table (relation) is in **second normal form** (**2NF**) if it is in first normal form and no **nonkey column** (that is, a column that is not part of the primary key) is dependent on only a portion of the primary key.

N O T E

If the primary key of a table contains only a single column, the table is automatically in second normal form.

You can identify the fundamental problem with the ORDERS table: It is not in second normal form. Although it is important to identify the problem, what you really need is a method to *correct* it; you want to be able to convert tables to second normal form. First, take each subset of the set of columns that make up the primary key, and begin a new table with this subset as its primary key. For the ORDERS table, the new design is:

```
(ORDER_NUM,
(PART_NUM,
(ORDER_NUM, PART_NUM,
```

Next, place each of the other columns with the appropriate primary key; that is, place each one with the minimal collection of columns on which it depends. For the ORDERS table, add the new columns as follows:

```
(ORDER_NUM, ORDER_DATE)
(PART_NUM, DESCRIPTION)
(ORDER_NUM, PART_NUM, NUM_ORDERED, QUOTED_PRICE)
```

Each of these new tables is given a descriptive name based on the meaning and contents of the table, such as ORDERS, PART, and ORDER_LINE. Figure 2-10 shows samples of the tables involved.

ORDERS

ORDER_NUM	ORDER_DATE	PART_NUM	DESCRIPTION	NUM_ORDERED	QUOTED_PRICE
21608	10/20/2007	AT94	Iron	11	$21.95
21610	10/20/2007	DR93	Gas Range	1	$495.00
21610	10/20/2007	DW11	Washer	1	$399.99
21613	10/21/2007	KL62	Dryer	4	$329.95
21614	10/21/2007	KT03	Dishwasher	2	$595.00
21617	10/23/2007	BV06	Home Gym	2	$12.95
21617	10/23/2007	CD52	Microwave Oven	4	$150.00
21619	10/23/2007	DR93	Gas Range	1	$495.00
21623	10/23/2007	KV29	Treadmill	2	$325.99

ORDERS

ORDER_NUM	ORDER_DATE
21608	10/20/2007
21610	10/20/2007
21613	10/21/2007
21614	10/21/2007
21617	10/23/2007
21619	10/23/2007
21623	10/23/2007

PART

PART_NUM	DESCRIPTION
AT94	Iron
BV06	Home Gym
CD52	Microwave Oven
DL71	Cordless Drill
DR93	Gas Range
DW11	Washer
FD21	Stand Mixer
KL62	Dryer
KT03	Dishwasher
KV29	Treadmill

ORDER_LINE

ORDER_NUM	PART_NUM	NUM_ORDERED	QUOTED_PRICE
21608	AT94	11	$21.95
21610	DR93	1	$495.00
21610	DW11	1	$399.99
21613	KL62	4	$329.95
21614	KT03	2	$595.00
21617	BV06	2	$12.95
21617	CD52	4	$150.00
21619	DR93	1	$495.00
21623	KV29	2	$325.99

FIGURE 2-10   ORDERS table converted to second normal form

In Figure 2-10, converting the original ORDERS table to a new ORDERS table, a PART table, and an ORDER_LINE table eliminates the update anomalies. A description appears only once for each part, so you do not have the redundancy that existed in the original table design. Changing the description of part DR93 from Gas Range to Deluxe Range, for example, is now a simple process involving a single change. Because the description for a part occurs in a single place, it is not possible to have multiple descriptions for a single part in the database at the same time.

To add a new part and its description, you create a new row in the PART table, regardless of whether that part has pending or actual orders. Also, deleting order 21608 does not delete part number AT94 from the database because it still exists in the PART table. Finally, you have not lost any information by converting the ORDERS table to second normal form. You can reconstruct the data in the original table from the data in the new tables.

Third Normal Form

Problems can still exist with tables that are in second normal form. For example, suppose that you create the following CUSTOMER table:

CUSTOMER (CUSTOMER_NUM, CUSTOMER_NAME, BALANCE, CREDIT_LIMIT,
    REP_NUM, LAST_NAME, FIRST_NAME)

This table has the following functional dependencies:

CUSTOMER_NUM ➝ CUSTOMER_NAME, BALANCE, CREDIT_LIMIT, REP_NUM,
    LAST_NAME, FIRST_NAME
REP_NUM ➝ LAST_NAME, FIRST_NAME

CUSTOMER_NUM determines all the other columns. In addition, REP_NUM determines LAST_NAME and FIRST_NAME.

If the primary key of a table is a single column, the table is automatically in second normal form. (If the table were not in second normal form, some column would be dependent on only a *portion* of the primary key, which is impossible when the primary key is just one column.) Thus, the CUSTOMER table is in second normal form.

Although this table is in second normal form, Figure 2-11 shows that it still possesses update problems similar to those identified for the ORDERS table shown in Figure 2-9. In Figure 2-11, the sales rep name occurs many times in the table.

CUSTOMER

CUSTOMER_ NUM	CUSTOMER_NAME	BALANCE	CREDIT_ LIMIT	REP_ NUM	LAST_ NAME	FIRST_ NAME
148	Al's Appliance and Sport	$6,550.00	$7,500.00	20	Kaiser	Valerie
282	Brookings Direct	$431.50	$10,000.00	35	Hull	Richard
356	Ferguson's	$5,785.00	$7,500.00	65	Perez	Juan
408	The Everything Shop	$5,285.25	$5,000.00	35	Hull	Richard
462	Bargains Galore	$3,412.00	$10,000.00	65	Perez	Juan
524	Kline's	$12,762.00	$15,000.00	20	Kaiser	Valerie
608	Johnson's Department Store	$2,106.00	$10,000.00	65	Perez	Juan
687	Lee's Sport and Appliance	$2,851.00	$5,000.00	35	Hull	Richard
725	Deerfield's Four Seasons	$248.00	$7,500.00	35	Hull	Richard
842	All Season	$8,221.00	$7,500.00	20	Kaiser	Valerie

FIGURE 2-11 Sample CUSTOMER table

The redundancy of including a sales rep number and name in the CUSTOMER table results in the same set of problems that existed for the ORDERS table. In addition to the problem of wasted space, you have the following update anomalies:

1. **Updates:** Changing the sales rep name requires changes to multiple rows in the table.
2. **Inconsistent data:** The design does not prohibit multiple iterations of sales rep names in the database. For example, a sales rep might represent 20 customers and his name might be entered 20 different ways in the table.
3. **Additions:** To add sales rep 87 (Emily Daniels) to the database, she must represent at least one customer. If Emily does not yet represent any customers, you either cannot record the fact that her name is Emily Daniels or you must create a fictitious customer for her to represent until she represents an actual customer. Neither of these solutions is desirable.
4. **Deletions:** If you delete all the customers of sales rep 35 from the database, you will also lose all information about sales rep 35.

These update anomalies are due to the fact that REP_NUM determines LAST_NAME and FIRST_NAME, but REP_NUM is not the primary key. As a result, the same REP_NUM and consequently the same LAST_NAME and FIRST_NAME can appear on many different rows.

You have seen that tables in second normal form represent an improvement over tables in first normal form, but to eliminate problems with tables in second normal form, you need an even better strategy for creating tables. Third normal form provides that strategy. Before looking at third normal form, however, you need to become familiar with the special name that is given to any column that determines another column (like REP_NUM in the CUSTOMER table). Any column (or collection of columns) that determines another column is called a **determinant**. A table's primary key is a determinant. In fact, by definition, any candidate key is a determinant. (Remember that a candidate key is a column or collection of columns that could function as the primary key.) In Figure 2-11, REP_NUM is a determinant, but it is not a candidate key, and that is the problem.

A table is in **third normal form (3NF)** if it is in second normal form and if the only determinants it contains are candidate keys.

NOTE

The definition given for third normal form is not the original definition. This more recent definition, which is preferable to the original, is often referred to as **Boyce-Codd normal form (BCNF)** when it is important to make a distinction between this definition and the original definition. This text does not make such a distinction but will take this to be the definition of third normal form.

Now you have identified the problem with the CUSTOMER table: It is not in third normal form. There are several steps for converting tables to third normal form.

First, for each determinant that is not a candidate key, remove from the table the columns that depend on this determinant (but do not remove the determinant). Next, create a new table containing all the columns from the original table that depend on this determinant. Finally, make the determinant the primary key of this new table.

In the CUSTOMER table, for example, remove LAST_NAME and FIRST_NAME because they depend on the determinant REP_NUM, which is not a candidate key. A new table is formed, consisting of REP_NUM as the primary key, and the columns LAST_NAME and FIRST_NAME, as follows:

```
CUSTOMER (CUSTOMER_NUM, CUSTOMER_NAME, BALANCE, CREDIT_LIMIT,
     REP_NUM)
```

and

```
REP (REP_NUM, LAST_NAME, FIRST_NAME)
```

Figure 2-12 shows the original CUSTOMER table and the tables created when converting the original table to third normal form.

CUSTOMER

CUSTOMER_NUM	CUSTOMER_NAME	BALANCE	CREDIT_LIMIT	REP_NUM	LAST_NAME	FIRST_NAME
148	Al's Appliance and Sport	$6,550.00	$7,500.00	20	Kaiser	Valerie
282	Brookings Direct	$431.50	$10,000.00	35	Hull	Richard
356	Ferguson's	$5,785.00	$7,500.00	65	Perez	Juan
408	The Everything Shop	$5,285.25	$5,000.00	35	Hull	Richard
462	Bargains Galore	$3,412.00	$10,000.00	65	Perez	Juan
524	Kline's	$12,762.00	$15,000.00	20	Kaiser	Valerie
608	Johnson's Department Store	$2,106.00	$10,000.00	65	Perez	Juan
687	Lee's Sport and Appliance	$2,851.00	$5,000.00	35	Hull	Richard
725	Deerfield's Four Seasons	$248.00	$7,500.00	35	Hull	Richard
842	All Season	$8,221.00	$7,500.00	20	Kaiser	Valerie

CUSTOMER

CUSTOMER_NUM	CUSTOMER_NAME	BALANCE	CREDIT_LIMIT	REP_NUM
148	Al's Appliance and Sport	$6,550.00	$7,500.00	20
282	Brookings Direct	$431.50	$10,000.00	35
356	Ferguson's	$5,785.00	$7,500.00	65
408	The Everything Shop	$5,285.25	$5,000.00	35
462	Bargains Galore	$3,412.00	$10,000.00	65
524	Kline's	$12,762.00	$15,000.00	20
608	Johnson's Department Store	$2,106.00	$10,000.00	65
687	Lee's Sport and Appliance	$2,851.00	$5,000.00	35
725	Deerfield's Four Seasons	$248.00	$7,500.00	35
842	All Season	$8,221.00	$7,500.00	20

REP

REP_NUM	LAST_NAME	FIRST_NAME
20	Kaiser	Valerie
35	Hull	Richard
65	Perez	Juan

FIGURE 2-12 CUSTOMER table converted to third normal form

Has this new design for the CUSTOMER table corrected all of the previously identified problems? A sales rep's name appears only once, thus avoiding redundancy and simplifying the process of changing a sales rep's name. This design prohibits a sales rep from having different names in the database. To add a new sales rep to the database, you add a row to the REP table; it is not necessary for a new rep to represent a customer. Finally, deleting all the customers of a given sales rep will not remove the sales rep's record from the REP table, retaining the sales rep's name in the database. You can reconstruct all the data in the original table from the data in the new collection of tables. All previously mentioned problems have indeed been solved.

Question: Convert the following table to third normal form. In this table, STUDENT_NUM determines STUDENT_NAME, NUM_CREDITS, ADVISOR_NUM, and ADVISOR_NAME. ADVISOR_NUM determines ADVISOR_NAME. COURSE_NUM determines DESCRIPTION. The combination of a STUDENT_NUM and a COURSE_NUM determines GRADE.

```
STUDENT (STUDENT_NUM, STUDENT_NAME, NUM_CREDITS, ADVISOR_NUM,
    ADVISOR_NAME, (COURSE_NUM, DESCRIPTION, GRADE) )
```

Answer: Complete the following steps:

Step 1. Remove the repeating group to convert the table to first normal form, as follows:

```
STUDENT (STUDENT_NUM, STUDENT_NAME, NUM_CREDITS, ADVISOR_NUM,
    ADVISOR_NAME, COURSE_NUM, DESCRIPTION, GRADE)
```

The STUDENT table is now in first normal form because it has no repeating groups. It is not, however, in second normal form because STUDENT_NAME is dependent only on STUDENT_NUM, which is only a portion of the primary key.

Step 2. Convert the STUDENT table to second normal form. First, for each subset of the primary key, start a table with that subset as its key yielding the following:

```
(STUDENT_NUM,
(COURSE_NUM,
(STUDENT_NUM, COURSE_NUM,
```

Next, place the rest of the columns with the smallest collection of columns on which they depend, as follows:

```
(STUDENT_NUM, STUDENT_NAME, NUM_CREDITS, ADVISOR_NUM, ADVISOR_NAME)
(COURSE_NUM, DESCRIPTION)
(STUDENT_NUM, COURSE_NUM, GRADE)
```

Finally, assign names to each of the new tables:

```
STUDENT (STUDENT_NUM, STUDENT_NAME, NUM_CREDITS, ADVISOR_NUM, ADVISOR_NAME)
COURSE (COURSE_NUM, DESCRIPTION)
STUDENT_COURSE (STUDENT_NUM, COURSE_NUM, GRADE)
```

Although these tables are all in second normal form, the COURSE and GRADE tables are also in third normal form. The STUDENT table is not in third normal form, however, because it contains a determinant (ADVISOR_NUM) that is not a candidate key.

Step 3: Convert the STUDENT table to third normal form by removing the column that depends on the determinant ADVISOR_NUM and placing it in a separate table, as follows:

```
(STUDENT_NUM, STUDENT_NAME, NUM_CREDITS, ADVISOR_NUM)
(ADVISOR_NUM, ADVISOR_NAME)
```

Step 4: Name the tables and put the entire collection together, as follows:

```
STUDENT (STUDENT_NUM, STUDENT_NAME, NUM_CREDITS, ADVISOR_NUM)
ADVISOR (ADVISOR_NUM, ADVISOR_NAME)
COURSE (COURSE_NUM, DESCRIPTION)
STUDENT_COURSE (STUDENT_NUM, COURSE_NUM, GRADE)
```

DIAGRAMS FOR DATABASE DESIGN

For many people, an illustration of the structure of the database is quite useful. A popular type of illustration used to represent the structure of a database is the **entity-relationship (E-R) diagram**. In an E-R diagram, a rectangle represents an entity (table). One-to-many relationships between entities are drawn as lines between the corresponding rectangles.

Several different styles of E-R diagrams are used to diagram a database design. In the version shown in Figure 2-13, an arrowhead indicates the "many" side of the relationship between tables. In the relationship between the REP and CUSTOMER tables, for example, the arrow points from the REP table to the CUSTOMER table, indicating that one sales rep is related to many customers. The ORDER_LINE table has two one-to-many relationships, as indicated by the line from the ORDERS table to the ORDER_LINE table and the line from the PART table to the ORDER_LINE table.

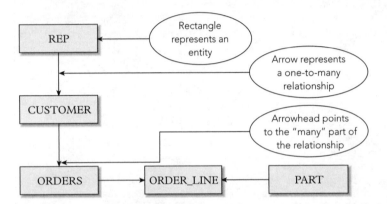

FIGURE 2-13 E-R diagram for the Premiere Products database with rectangles and arrows

NOTE

In this style of E-R diagram, you can put the rectangles in any position to represent the entities and relationships. The important thing is that the arrows connect the appropriate rectangles.

Another style of E-R diagram is to represent the "many" side of a relationship between tables with a crow's foot, as shown in Figure 2-14.

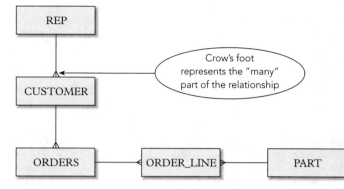

FIGURE 2-14 E-R diagram for the Premiere Products database with a crow's foot

The E-R diagram shown in Figure 2-15 represents the original style of E-R diagrams. In this style, relationships are indicated in diamonds that describe the relationship. The relationship between the REP and CUSTOMER tables, for example, is named REPRESENTS, reflecting the fact that a sales rep represents a customer. The relationship between the CUSTOMER and ORDERS table is named PLACED, reflecting the fact that customers place orders. The relationship between the ORDERS and ORDER_LINE tables is named CONTAINS, reflecting the fact that an order contains order lines. The relationship between the PART and ORDER_LINE tables is named IS_ON, reflecting the fact that a given part is on many orders. In this style of E-R diagram, the number 1 indicates the "one" side of the relationship and the letter "n" represents the "many" side of the relationship.

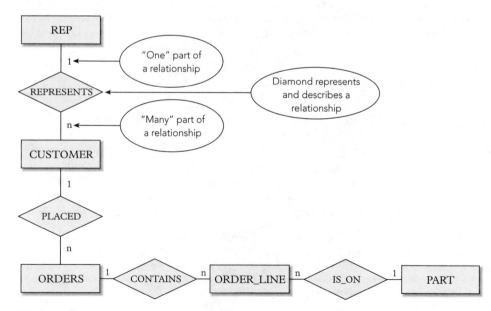

FIGURE 2-15 E-R diagram for the Premiere Products database with named relationships

Chapter Summary

An entity is a person, place, thing, or event. An attribute is a property of an entity. A relationship is an association between entities.

A relation is a two-dimensional table in which the entries in the table contain only single values, each column has a distinct name, all values in a column match this name, the order of the rows and columns is immaterial, and each row contains unique values. A relational database is a collection of relations.

Column B is functionally dependent on another column, A (or possibly a collection of columns), if a value for A determines a single value for B at any one time.

Column A (or a collection of columns) is the primary key for a relation (table), R, if *all* columns in R are functionally dependent on A and no subcollection of the columns in A (assuming A is a collection of columns and not just a single column) also has property 1.

To design a database to satisfy a particular set of requirements, first read through the requirements and identify the entities (objects) involved. Give names to the entities and identify the unique identifiers for these entities. Next, identify the attributes for all the entities and the functional dependencies that exist among the attributes, and then use the functional dependencies to identify the tables and columns. Finally, identify any relationships between tables by looking at matching columns.

A table (relation) is in first normal form (1NF) if it does not contain a repeating group. To convert an unnormalized table to first normal form, remove the repeating group and expand the primary key to include the original primary key along with the key to the repeating group.

A table (relation) is in second normal form (2NF) if it is in first normal form and no nonkey column (that is, a column that is not part of the primary key) is dependent on only a portion of the primary key. To convert a table in first normal form to a collection of tables in second normal form, take each subset of the set of columns that make up the primary key, and begin a new table with this subset as its primary key. Next, place each of the other columns with the appropriate primary key; that is, place each one with the minimal collection of columns on which it depends. Finally, give each of these new tables a name that is descriptive of the meaning and contents of the table.

A table is in third normal form (3NF) if it is in second normal form and if the only determinants (columns on which at least one other column depends) it contains are candidate keys (columns that could function as the primary key). To convert a table in second normal form to a collection of tables in third normal form, first, for each determinant that is not a candidate key, remove from the table the columns that depend on this determinant (but don't remove the determinant). Next, create a new table containing all the columns from the original table that depend on this determinant. Finally, make the determinant the primary key of this new table.

An entity-relationship (E-R) diagram is an illustration that represents the design of a database. There are several common styles of illustrating database design that use shapes to represent entities and connectors to illustrate the relationships between those entities.

KEY TERMS

attribute

Boyce-Codd normal form (BCNF)

candidate key

concatenation

database design

determinant

entity

entity-relationship (E-R) diagram

field

first normal form (1NF)

functionally dependent

functionally determine

nonkey column

normal form

normalization

one-to-many relationship

primary key

qualify

record

redundancy

relation

relational database

relationship

repeating group

second normal form (2NF)

third normal form (3NF)

tuple

unnormalized relation

update anomaly

REVIEW QUESTIONS

1. What is an entity?

2. What is an attribute?

3. What is a relationship? What is a one-to-many relationship?

4. What is a repeating group?

5. What is a relation?

6. What is a relational database?

7. Describe the shorthand representation of the structure of a relational database. Illustrate this technique by representing the database for Henry Books as shown in Chapter 1.

8. How do you qualify the name of a field, and when do you need to do this?

9. What does it mean for a column to be functionally dependent on another column?

10. What is a primary key? What is the primary key for each of the tables in the Henry Books database shown in Chapter 1?

11. A database at a college must support the following requirements:

    a. For a department, store its number and name.

    b. For an advisor, store his or her number, last name, first name, and the department number to which the advisor is assigned.

    c. For a course, store its code and description (for example, MTH110, Algebra).

    d. For a student, store his or her number, first name, and last name. For each course the student takes, store the course code, the course description, and the grade earned.

Also, store the number and name of the student's advisor. Assume that an advisor might advise any number of students but that each student has just one advisor.

Design the database for the preceding set of requirements. Use your own experience to determine any functional dependencies. List the tables, columns, and relationships. In addition, represent your design with an E-R diagram.

12. Define first normal form.

13. Define second normal form. What types of problems are encountered in tables that are not in second normal form?

14. Define third normal form. What types of problems are encountered in tables that are not in third normal form?

15. Using the functional dependencies you determined in Question 11, convert the following table to an equivalent collection of tables that is in third normal form.

```
STUDENT (STUDENT_NUM, STUDENT_LAST_NAME, STUDENT_FIRST_NAME,
        ADVISOR_NUM, ADVISOR_LAST_NAME, ADVISOR_FIRST_NAME,
        (COURSE_CODE, DESCRIPTION, GRADE) )
```

EXERCISES

Premiere Products

Answer each of the following questions using the Premiere Products data shown in Figure 2-1. No computer work is required.

1. Indicate the changes (using the shorthand representation) that you would need to make to the current design of the Premiere Products database to support the following requirements. A customer is not necessarily represented by a single sales rep, but can be represented by several sales reps. When a customer places an order, the sales rep who gets the commission on the order must be in the collection of sales reps who represent the customer.

2. Indicate the changes (using the shorthand representation) that you would need to make to the Premiere Products database design to support the following requirements. There is no relationship between customers and sales reps. When a customer places an order, any sales rep can process the order. On the order, you need to identify both the customer placing the order and the sales rep responsible for the order. Draw an E-R diagram for the new design.

3. Indicate the changes (using the shorthand representation) that you would need to make to the Premiere Products database design in the event that the original Requirement 3 is changed as follows. For a part, store the part's number, description, item class, and price. In addition, for each warehouse in which the part is located, store the number of the warehouse, the description of the warehouse, and the number of units of the part stored in the warehouse. Draw an E-R diagram for the new design.

4. Using your knowledge of Premiere Products, determine the functional dependencies that exist in the following table. After determining the functional dependencies, convert this table to an equivalent collection of tables that are in third normal form.

```
PART (PART_NUM, DESCRIPTION, ON_HAND, CLASS, WAREHOUSE, PRICE,
      (ORDER_NUM, ORDER_DATE, CUSTOMER_NUM, CUSTOMER_NAME,
      NUM_ORDERED, QUOTED_PRICE) )
```

Henry Books

Answer each of the following questions using the Henry Books data shown in Figures 1-4 through 1-7 in Chapter 1. No computer work is required.

1. Ray Henry is considering expanding the activities at his book stores to include movies. He has some ideas for how he wants to do this and he needs you to help with database design activities to address these ideas. In particular, he would like you to design a database for him. He is interested in movies and wants to store information about movies, stars, and directors in a database. He needs to be able to satisfy the following requirements:

    a. For each director, list his or her number, name, the year he or she was born, and, if he or she is deceased, the year of death.

    b. For each movie, list its number, title, the year the movie was made, and its type.

    c. For each movie, list its number, title, the number and name of its director, the critics' rating, the MPAA rating, the number of awards for which the movie was nominated, and the number of awards the movie won.

    d. For each movie star, list his or her number, name, birthplace, the year he or she was born, and, if he or she is deceased, the year of death.

    e. For each movie, list its number and title, along with the number and name of all the stars who appear in it.

    f. For each movie star, list his or her number and name, along with the number and name of all the movies in which he or she stars.

    List the tables, columns, and relationships. In addition, represent your design with an E-R diagram.

2. Determine the functional dependencies that exist in the following table, and then convert this table to an equivalent collection of tables that are in third normal form.

```
BOOK (BOOK_CODE, TITLE, TYPE, PRICE (AUTHOR_NUM, AUTHOR_LAST,
      AUTHOR_FIRST) )
```

3. Determine the functional dependencies that exist in the following table, and then convert this table to an equivalent collection of tables that are in third normal form.

```
BOOK (BOOK_CODE, TITLE, TYPE, PRICE, PUB_CODE, PUBLISHER_NAME,
      CITY)
```

Alexamara Marina Group

Answer each of the following questions using the Alexamara Marina Group data shown in Figures 1-8 through 1-12 in Chapter 1. No computer work is required.

1. Design a database that can satisfy the following requirements:

   a. For each marina, list the number, name, address, city, state, and zip code.

   b. For each boat owner, list the number, last name, first name, address, city, state, and zip code.

   c. For each marina, list all the slips in the marina. For each slip, list the length of the slip, the annual rental fee, the name and type of the boat occupying the slip, and the boat owner's number, last name, and first name.

   d. For each possible service category, list the category number and description. In addition, for each service request in a category, list the marina number, and slip number for the boat receiving the service, the estimated hours for the service, the hours already spent on the service, and the next date that is scheduled for the particular service.

   e. For each service request, list the marina number, slip number, category description, description of the particular service, and a description of the current status of the service.

   List the tables, columns, and relationships. In addition, represent your design with an E-R diagram.

2. Determine the functional dependencies that exist in the following table, and then convert this table to an equivalent collection of tables that are in third normal form.

   ```
   MARINA (MARINA_NUM, NAME, (SLIP_NUM, LENGTH, RENTAL_FEE,
         BOAT_NAME) )
   ```

3. Determine the functional dependencies that exist in the following table, and then convert this table to an equivalent collection of tables that are in third normal form.

   ```
   MARINA_SLIP (ID, MARINA_NUM, SLIP_NUM, LENGTH, RENTAL_FEE,
         BOAT_NAME, BOAT_TYPE, OWNER_NUM, LAST_NAME, FIRST_NAME)
   ```

CHAPTER 3

AN INTRODUCTION TO SQL

LEARNING OBJECTIVES

Objectives

- Start MySQL and learn how to use the MySQL Reference Manual
- Create a database
- Change (activate) a database
- Create tables using MySQL
- Create and run SQL commands in MySQL
- Identify and use data types to define columns in tables
- Understand and use nulls
- Add rows to tables
- View table data
- Correct errors in a database
- Save SQL commands and results to a file
- Describe a table's layout using MySQL

INTRODUCTION

You already might be an experienced user of a database management system (DBMS). You might find a DBMS at your school's library, at a site on the Internet, or in any other place where you retrieve data using a computer. In this chapter, you will begin your study of **Structured Query Language (SQL)**, which is one of the most popular and widely used languages for retrieving and manipulating database data. You will be using a specific version of SQL that the MySQL DBMS understands as you complete the chapters in this text.

In the mid-1970s, SQL was developed as the data manipulation language for IBM's prototype relational model DBMS, System R, under the name SEQUEL at IBM's San Jose research facilities. In 1980, the language was renamed SQL (but still pronounced "sequel" although the equally popular pronunciation of "S-Q-L" ["ess-cue-ell"] is used in this text) to avoid confusion with an unrelated hardware product named SEQUEL. Most DBMSs use a version of SQL as their data manipulation language.

In this chapter, you will learn the basics of working in MySQL. You will learn how to assign data types to columns in a database. You also will learn about a special type of value, called a null value, and learn how to handle these values during database creation. You will learn how to load a database by creating tables and adding data to them. Finally, you will learn how to describe a table's layout using MySQL.

INTRODUCTION TO MYSQL

This section gives some background information on working with MySQL, including obtaining help and accessing the reference manual that is installed with MySQL.

Starting MySQL

The exact way you start MySQL depends on the operating environment in which you are working. In a Windows XP installation of MySQL 4.1, for example, you would do the following:

STARTING MYSQL

- Click the Start button.
- Point to All Programs.
- Point to MySQL on the All Programs menu.
- Point to MySQL Server 4.1 on the MySQL submenu.
- Click MySQL Command Line Client on the MySQL Server 4.1 submenu to start the MySQL Command Line Client.

When the MySQL Command Line Client window opens, enter your password, and then press the Enter key. A message appears, followed by an indication of how to obtain help, and then the mysql> prompt appears as shown in Figure 3-1. To work in MySQL, you type commands at this prompt.

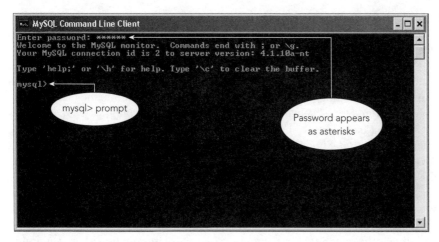

FIGURE 3-1 MySQL Command Line Client window

Obtaining Help in MySQL

The simplest way to obtain help in MySQL is to type \h at the mysql> prompt, as shown in Figure 3-2.

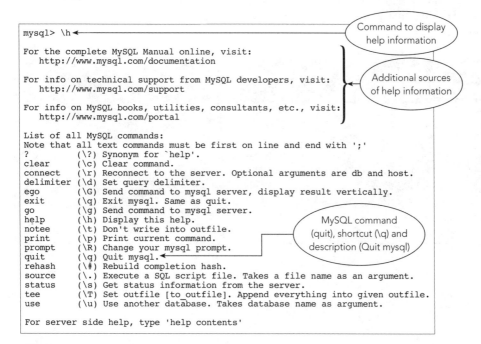

FIGURE 3-2 Obtaining help in MySQL

MySQL displays a list of commands, the shortcuts for those commands, and a description of the commands. The shortcut for the quit command, for example, is \q and the description for this command is "Quit mysql." Thus, to quit MySQL, you could type the word "quit" or \q at the command prompt.

You also can get help about many other SQL commands by typing the word "help" followed by the name of the command. For example, to view a list of commands for which help is available, you would type "help contents" at the command prompt. MySQL responds by listing the following categories of help topics: Administration, Column Types, Data Definition, Data Manipulation, Functions, Geographic Features, and Transactions. To access help for one of these categories, you type the word "help" followed by the category in which you are interested. For example, to view all the help topics in the Data Manipulation category, type "help Data Manipulation" at the command prompt. MySQL displays a list of all the help topics in the Data Manipulation category.

You also can use the help command to access help for a specific command directly, without going through the contents. For example, to get more information about the union command, you can type "help union" at the command prompt. MySQL responds by listing help information about the union command.

Using the MySQL Reference Manual to Get Help

To obtain more detailed help, you can access the MySQL Reference Manual. The exact way you access the MySQL Reference Manual depends on the operating environment in which you are working. In a Windows XP installation of MySQL 4.1, for example, you would do the following:

STARTING HELP FOR MYSQL IN WINDOWS XP

- Click the Start button.
- Point to All Programs.
- Point to MySQL on the All Programs menu.
- Point to MySQL Server 4.1 on the MySQL submenu.
- Click MySQL Manual - Table of Contents on the MySQL Server 4.1 submenu. A Web browser starts and opens the table of contents for the MySQL Reference Manual.

NOTE

If the MySQL Reference Manual does not appear on the MySQL submenu, you can access the online manual at *http://dev.mysql.com/doc/mysql/en/index.html.*

Figure 3-3 shows the table of contents for the MySQL Reference Manual.

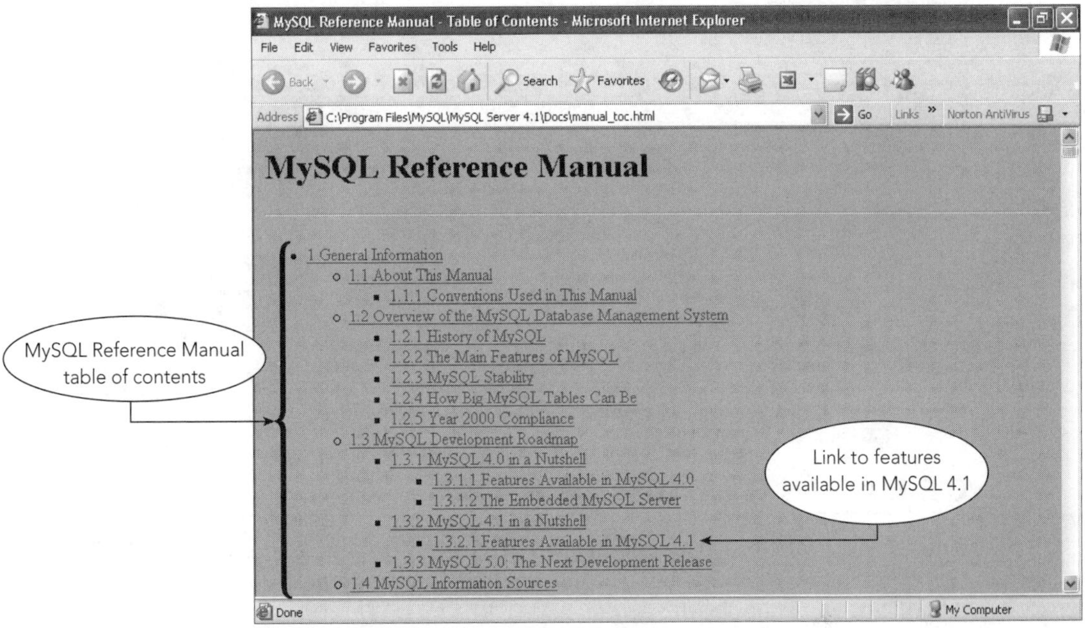

FIGURE 3-3 MySQL Reference Manual table of contents

You can browse the table of contents to find the topic you need and then click the link to view detailed information for the selected topic. If you click the Features Available in MySQL 4.1 link, for example, you would see the information shown in Figure 3-4. This information contains additional links that you can click to view more detailed information. For additional information on available MySQL documentation, visit the MySQL documentation page at *http://dev.mysql.com/doc/.*

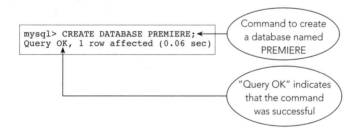

FIGURE 3-4 Information about MySQL 4.1 features

CREATING A DATABASE

Before creating tables, you must create a database by executing the **CREATE DATABASE** command followed by the name of the database. To create a database named PREMIERE, for example, the command is CREATE DATABASE PREMIERE; as shown in Figure 3-5. Notice that a semicolon ends the command; a semicolon signals the end of a command and is required in MySQL.

```
mysql> CREATE DATABASE PREMIERE;
Query OK, 1 row affected (0.06 sec)
```

Command to create a database named PREMIERE

"Query OK" indicates that the command was successful

FIGURE 3-5 Creating a database

The second line in the figure indicates that the command was successful. If there were a problem (for example, the database already existed), MySQL would display an error message about the problem.

CHANGING THE DEFAULT DATABASE

To work with a database, you must change the default database to the one you need to use. The **default database** is the database to which all subsequent commands pertain. To activate the default database, execute the **USE** command followed by the name of the database. For example, to change the default database to the Premiere Products database, the command is USE PREMIERE; as shown in Figure 3-6. Changing the default database also is known as activating or using a database.

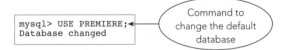

FIGURE 3-6 Changing (activating) the default database

NOTE

You only need to execute the CREATE DATABASE command once for a database. However, you must execute the USE command at the start of every session to activate the database. If you want to work with another database during a session, you need to execute another USE command to activate the new database.

CREATING A TABLE

Before you begin loading and accessing data in a table, you must describe the layout of each table that the database contains.

EXAMPLE 1

Describe the layout of the REP table to the DBMS.

You use the **CREATE TABLE** command to describe the layout of a table. The word TABLE is followed by the name of the table to be created and then by the names and data types of the columns that the table contains. The data type indicates the type of data that the column can contain (for example, characters, numbers, or dates) as well as the maximum number of characters or digits that the column can store.

The restrictions placed on table and column names are as follows:

1. The names cannot exceed 18 characters.
2. The names must start with a letter.
3. The names can contain letters, numbers, and underscores (_).
4. The names cannot contain spaces.

The appropriate SQL command for Example 1 is shown in Figure 3-7.

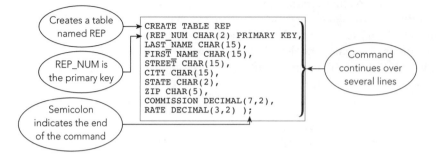

FIGURE 3-7   CREATE TABLE command for the REP table

This CREATE TABLE command, which uses the data definition features of SQL, describes a table named REP. The table contains nine columns: REP_NUM, LAST_NAME, FIRST_NAME, STREET, CITY, STATE, ZIP, COMMISSION, and RATE. The REP_NUM column can store two characters and is the primary key. The LAST_NAME column can store 15 characters, and the STATE column can store two characters. The COMMISSION column can store only numbers, and those numbers are limited to seven digits, including two decimal places. Similarly, the RATE column can store three numbers, including two decimal places. You can think of the SQL command in Figure 3-7 as creating an empty table with column headings for each column name.

In SQL, commands are free format; that is, no rule says that a particular word must begin in a particular position on the line. For example, you could have written the CREATE TABLE command shown in Figure 3-7 as follows:

```
CREATE TABLE REP (REP_NUM CHAR(2) PRIMARY KEY, LAST_NAME CHAR(15),
FIRST_NAME CHAR(15), STREET CHAR(15), CITY CHAR(15), STATE CHAR(2),
ZIP CHAR(5), COMMISSION DECIMAL(7,2), RATE DECIMAL(3,2) );
```

The manner in which the CREATE TABLE command shown in Figure 3-7 was written simply makes the command more readable. This text will strive for such readability when writing SQL commands.

NOTE

MySQL is not case sensitive; you can type commands using uppercase or lowercase letters. There is one exception to this rule, however. When you are inserting character values into a table, you must use the correct case.

RUNNING SQL COMMANDS

To enter a command in MySQL, such as the one shown in Figure 3-7, begin typing the command at the mysql> prompt. When you type a command that extends over several lines, such as the CREATE TABLE command shown in Figure 3-7, you can press the Enter key at the end of each line. MySQL moves the cursor to the next line and displays the continuation indicator (->). To finish a command, type a semicolon at the end of the last line of the command, and then press the Enter key. MySQL executes the command and indicates whether the command was successful, as shown in Figure 3-8.

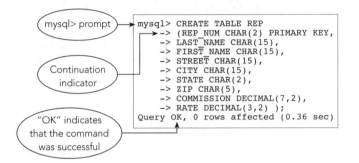

FIGURE 3-8   CREATE TABLE command in MySQL for the REP table

Because the command was successful, the REP table now exists in the default database (PREMIERE). The REP table does not yet contain any rows, however. You will learn how to add data to a table later in this chapter.

Editing SQL Commands

In MySQL, the most recent command you entered is stored in a special area of memory called the **statement history**. You can edit the command in the statement history by using the editing commands shown in Figure 3-9.

Activity	Key or key combination
Move up a line in the statement history	Up arrow
Move down a line in the statement history	Down arrow
Move left one character within a line	Left arrow
Move right one character within a line	Right arrow
Move to the beginning of a line	Ctrl+A
Move to the end of a line	Ctrl+E
Delete the previous character	Backspace
Delete the character under the cursor	Delete

FIGURE 3-9 MySQL editing commands

Suppose that you tried to create the REP table using the CREATE TABLE command shown in Figure 3-10, which contains several mistakes. Instead of displaying a message that the table was created successfully, MySQL displays an error message that identifies the lines in the command that contain problems. In reviewing the command, you see that CHAR is misspelled on line 4, that line 5 is missing a comma, that the CITY column was omitted, and that line 7 should be deleted.

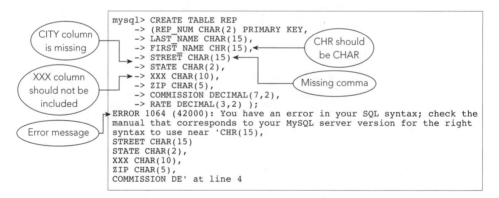

FIGURE 3-10 CREATE TABLE command for the REP table with errors

To begin the editing process, press the Up arrow key to move back through the lines in the command until the first line, CREATE TABLE REP, appears after the mysql> prompt. Because this line is correct, press the Enter key. MySQL moves the cursor to the second line and displays the continuation indicator (->). Press the Down arrow key to move to the second line, containing the REP_NUM column. Because this line also is correct, press the Enter key. Press the Down arrow key to move to the third line, containing the

LAST_NAME column, and then press the Enter key to indicate that it is correct. Move to the fourth line, containing the FIRST_NAME column; this line contains an error. Use the Left or Right arrow key as necessary to move the cursor to the R in CHR, and type the letter A to change CHR to CHAR. (If the A replaces the letter R so that you changed CHR to CHA, you are not in insert mode. Press the Insert key and then type the letter R.) When the line is correct, press the Enter key.

Move to the line containing the STREET column, type a comma at the end of the line, and then press the Enter key. You need to insert the line for the CITY column after the line containing the STREET column. Rather than moving to another line in the statement history, simply type the correct line (CITY CHAR(15),) and then press the Enter key. Move to the line containing the STATE column and press the Enter key to indicate that it is correct. Move to the line containing the ZIP column and press the Enter key to indicate that it is correct. In the process, you will move right through the line containing the XXX error. Because you did not press the Enter key for that line, it will not be part of the revised command. Move to the line containing the COMMISSION column and press the Enter key to indicate that it is correct. Move to the line containing the RATE column and press the Enter key to indicate that it is correct. Because this line ends with a semicolon, MySQL executes the revised command, which now is correct.

NOTE

If you try to execute a CREATE TABLE command for the same table more than once, MySQL displays an error message indicating that the table you are trying to create already exists. You will learn about making changes to existing tables later in this text.

Dropping a Table

After successfully creating a table, you might notice that you added a column that you do not need or that you assigned the wrong data type or column size to a column. Another way of correcting errors in a table is to delete (drop) the table and start over. For example, suppose your CREATE TABLE command contains a column named LST instead of LAST or defines a column as CHAR(5) instead of CHAR(15). Suppose you do not discover the error and you execute the command, creating a table with these problems. In this case, you can delete the entire table using the **DROP TABLE** command and then re-create the table using the correct CREATE TABLE command.

To drop a table, execute the DROP TABLE command, followed by the name of the table you want to delete and a semicolon. To delete the REP table, for example, you would enter the following command:

```
DROP TABLE REP;
```

Dropping a table also deletes any data that you entered into the table. It is a good idea to check your CREATE TABLE commands carefully before executing them and to correct any problems before adding data to them. Later in this text, you will learn how to change a table's structure without having to delete the entire table.

DATA TYPES

For each column in a table, you must specify the **data type**, that is, the type of data that the column stores. Figure 3-11 describes some common data types used in databases. For other data types that are available in MySQL, see Chapter 11 in the MySQL Reference Manual.

Data type	Description
CHAR(n)	Stores a character string n characters long. You use the CHAR data type for columns that contain letters and special characters and for columns containing numbers that will not be used in any calculations. Because neither sales rep numbers nor customer numbers will be used in any calculations, for example, the REP_NUM and CUSTOMER_NUM columns are both assigned the CHAR data type.
VARCHAR(n)	An alternative to CHAR that stores a character string up to n characters long. Unlike CHAR, all that is stored is the actual character string. If a character string 20 characters long is stored in a CHAR(30) column, for example, it will occupy 30 characters (20 characters plus 10 blank spaces). If it is stored in a VARCHAR(30) column, it will only occupy 20 characters. In general, tables that use VARCHAR instead of CHAR occupy less space, but will not process as rapidly during queries and updates. Both are legitimate choices. This text uses CHAR, but VARCHAR would work equally well.
DATE	Stores date data. In MySQL, dates are enclosed in single quotation marks and have the form YYYY-MM-DD (for example, '2007-10-15' is October 15, 2007).
DECIMAL(p,q)	Stores a decimal number p digits long with q of these digits being decimal places to the right of the decimal point. For example, the data type DECIMAL(5,2) represents a number with three places to the left and two places to the right of the decimal (for example, 100.00). You can use the contents of DECIMAL columns in calculations.
INT	Stores integers, which are numbers without a decimal part. The valid range is –2147483648 to 2147483647. You can use the contents of INT columns in calculations. If you follow the word INT with AUTO_INCREMENT, you create a column for which MySQL will automatically generate a new sequence number each time you add a new row. This would be the appropriate choice, for example, if you want to let the DBMS generate a value for a primary key.
SMALLINT	Stores integers, but uses less space than the INT data type. The valid range is –32768 to 32767. SMALLINT is a better choice than INT when you are certain that the column will store numbers within the indicated range. You can use the contents of SMALLINT columns in calculations.

FIGURE 3-11 Commonly used data types

NULLS

Occasionally, when you enter a new row into a table or modify an existing row, the values for one or more columns are unknown or unavailable. For example, you can add a customer's name and address to a table even though the customer does not have an assigned sales rep or an established credit limit. In other cases, some values might never be known—perhaps there is a customer that does not have a sales rep. In SQL, you handle this situation by using a special value to represent cases in which an actual value is unknown, unavailable, or not applicable. This special value is called a **null data value**, or simply a **null**. When creating a table, you can specify whether to allow nulls in the individual columns.

Q & A

Question: Should a user be allowed to enter null values for the primary key?
Answer: No. The primary key is supposed to uniquely identify a given row, and this would be impossible if nulls were allowed. For example, if you stored two customer records without values in the primary key column, you would have no way to tell them apart.

Implementation of Nulls

In SQL, you use the **NOT NULL** clause in a CREATE TABLE command to indicate columns that *cannot* contain null values. The default is to allow nulls; columns for which you do not specify NOT NULL can accept null values.

For example, suppose that the LAST_NAME and FIRST_NAME columns in the REP table cannot accept null values, but all other columns in the REP table can. The following CREATE TABLE command accomplishes this goal:

```
CREATE TABLE REP
(REP_NUM CHAR(2) PRIMARY KEY,
LAST_NAME CHAR(15) NOT NULL,
FIRST_NAME CHAR(15) NOT NULL,
STREET CHAR(15),
CITY CHAR(15),
STATE CHAR(2),
ZIP CHAR(5),
COMMISSION DECIMAL(7,2),
RATE DECIMAL(3,2) );
```

The system will reject any attempt to store a null value in either the LAST_NAME or FIRST_NAME column. The system will accept an attempt to store a null value in the STREET column, however, because the STREET column can accept null values. Because the primary key column cannot accept null values, you do not need to specify the REP_NUM column as NOT NULL.

ADDING ROWS TO A TABLE

After you have created a table in a database, you can load data into it by using the INSERT command.

The INSERT Command

The **INSERT** command adds rows to a table. You type INSERT INTO followed by the name of the table into which you are adding data. Then you type the **VALUES** command followed by the specific values to be inserted in parentheses. When adding rows to character columns, make sure you enclose the values in single quotation marks (for example, 'Kaiser'). You also must enter the values in the appropriate case, because character data is stored exactly as you enter it.

NOTE

You must enclose values in single quotation marks for any column whose type is character (CHAR) even if the data contains numbers. Because the ZIP column in the REP table has a CHAR data type, for example, you must enclose zip codes in single quotation marks, even though they are numbers.

NOTE

If you need to enter an apostrophe (single quotation mark) into a column, you type two single quotation marks. For example, to enter the name O'Toole in the LAST_NAME column, you would type 'O''Toole' as the value in the INSERT command.

EXAMPLE 2

Add sales rep 20 to the database.

The command for this example is shown in Figure 3-12. Note that the character strings ('20','Kaiser','Valerie', and so on) are enclosed in single quotation marks. After you execute the command, the first record is added to the REP table.

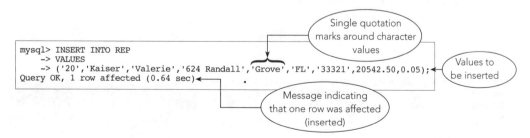

FIGURE 3-12 INSERT command for the first record in the REP table

EXAMPLE 3

Add sales reps 35 and 65 to the REP table.

You could enter and execute new INSERT commands to add the new rows to the table. However, an easier and faster way is to modify the previous INSERT command and execute it to add the record for the second sales rep and then modify and execute the INSERT command again for the third sales rep.

You can use the same editing techniques you previously learned to add the two additional rows instead of typing two new INSERT commands. You can use the Up arrow key to bring the line from the previous INSERT command to the mysql> prompt and then press the Enter key. Use the Down arrow key to bring the VALUES line in the command to the screen and then press the Enter key. Finally, use the Down arrow key to bring the line containing the values from the previous INSERT command to the screen, change the values to the ones for the new row you want to add, and then press the Enter key. Figure 3-13 shows the result of using this technique to add the second and third rows to the REP table.

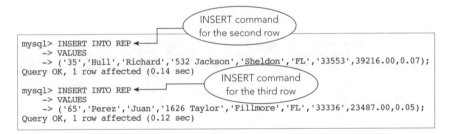

FIGURE 3-13   Modifying the INSERT command to add rows 2 and 3 to the REP table

The INSERT Command with Nulls

To enter a null value into a table, you use a special form of the INSERT command in which you identify the names of the columns that will accept non-null values, and then list only these non-null values after the VALUES command, as shown in Example 4.

EXAMPLE 4

Add sales rep 85 to the REP table. Her name is Tina Webb. All columns except REP_NUM, LAST_NAME, and FIRST_NAME are null.

In this case, you do not enter a value of null; you enter only the non-null values. To do so, you must indicate precisely which values you are entering by listing the corresponding columns as shown in Figure 3-14. The command shown in the figure indicates that you are entering data in only the REP_NUM, LAST_NAME, and FIRST_NAME columns and that you are *not* entering values in any other columns.

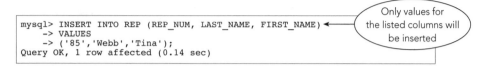

```
mysql> INSERT INTO REP (REP_NUM, LAST_NAME, FIRST_NAME)         Only values for
    -> VALUES                                                   the listed columns will
    -> ('85','Webb','Tina');                                    be inserted
Query OK, 1 row affected (0.14 sec)
```

FIGURE 3-14   Inserting a row in the REP table that contains null values

VIEWING TABLE DATA

To view the data in a table, you use the **SELECT** command, which is described in more detail in Chapters 4 and 5. There is a simple version, however, that you can use to display all the rows and columns in a table: It consists of the word SELECT, followed by an asterisk, followed by the word FROM and then the name of the table containing the data you want to view. Just as with other SQL commands, the command ends with a semicolon.

In MySQL, you type the command at the mysql> prompt and press the Enter key at the end of each line. When you type the semicolon at the end of the last line and press the Enter key, MySQL executes the command and displays its results, as shown in Figure 3-15.

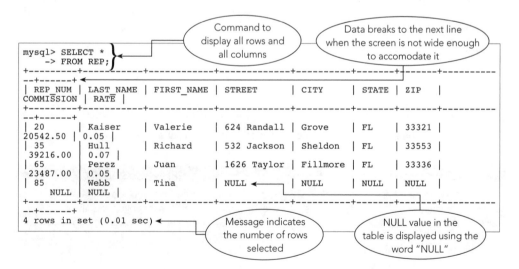

FIGURE 3-15   Using a SELECT command to view table data horizontally

The results in Figure 3-15 contain line breaks because the data is too wide to fit on the screen, making the output difficult to read. In many cases, the results will fit on the screen without any adjustments. In cases in which the data does not fit on the screen, you can display the data vertically instead of horizontally. To do so, replace the semicolon at the end of the command with a backslash (\) and the letter G, as shown in Figure 3-16.

```
                                    ┌─────────────────────┐
                                    │   Option to display  │
                           ┌────────│  the rows in the results │
                           │        │       vertically     │
                           │        └─────────────────────┘
mysql> SELECT *            │
    -> FROM REP\G ◄────────┘
*************************** 1. row ***************************
   REP_NUM: 20
 LAST_NAME: Kaiser
FIRST_NAME: Valerie
    STREET: 624 Randall
      CITY: Grove
     STATE: FL
       ZIP: 33321
COMMISSION: 20542.50
      RATE: 0.05
*************************** 2. row ***************************
   REP_NUM: 35
 LAST_NAME: Hull
FIRST_NAME: Richard
    STREET: 532 Jackson
      CITY: Sheldon
     STATE: FL
       ZIP: 33553
COMMISSION: 39216.00
      RATE: 0.07
*************************** 3. row ***************************
   REP_NUM: 65
 LAST_NAME: Perez
FIRST_NAME: Juan
    STREET: 1626 Taylor
      CITY: Fillmore
     STATE: FL
       ZIP: 33336
COMMISSION: 23487.00
      RATE: 0.05
*************************** 4. row ***************************
   REP_NUM: 85
 LAST_NAME: Webb
FIRST_NAME: Tina
    STREET: NULL
      CITY: NULL
     STATE: NULL
       ZIP: NULL
COMMISSION: NULL
      RATE: NULL
4 rows in set (0.00 sec)
```

FIGURE 3-16   Using a SELECT command to view table data vertically

NOTE

In Chapter 4, you will learn how to select specific columns that you want to include in the results. By selecting columns appropriately, you usually can ensure that the columns will fit on a single line when you view the results horizontally. Thus, you usually will not have to display the results vertically, as illustrated in Figure 3-16.

CORRECTING ERRORS IN THE DATABASE

After executing a SELECT command to view a table's data, you might find that you need to change the value in a column. You can use the **UPDATE** command shown in Figure 3-17 to change a value in a table. The first UPDATE command shown in the figure changes the last name in the row on which the sales rep number is 85 to Perry. The SELECT command displays the updated data.

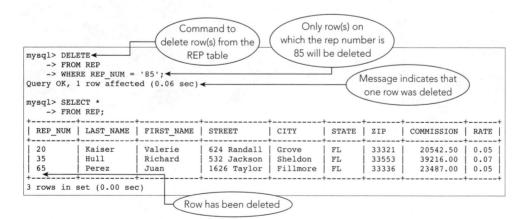

FIGURE 3-17   Using an UPDATE command to change a value

If you need to delete a row from a table, you can use the **DELETE** command. The DELETE command shown in Figure 3-18 deletes any row on which the sales rep number is 85. The SELECT command displays the updated data.

```
                           Command to              Only row(s) on
                       delete row(s) from the   which the rep number is
                           REP table              85 will be deleted
mysql> DELETE
    -> FROM REP
    -> WHERE REP_NUM = '85';
Query OK, 1 row affected (0.06 sec)                Message indicates that
                                                   one row was deleted
mysql> SELECT *
    -> FROM REP;
+---------+-----------+------------+-------------+----------+-------+-------+------------+------+
| REP_NUM | LAST_NAME | FIRST_NAME | STREET      | CITY     | STATE | ZIP   | COMMISSION | RATE |
+---------+-----------+------------+-------------+----------+-------+-------+------------+------+
| 20      | Kaiser    | Valerie    | 624 Randall | Grove    | FL    | 33321 | 20542.50   | 0.05 |
| 35      | Hull      | Richard    | 532 Jackson | Sheldon  | FL    | 33553 | 39216.00   | 0.07 |
| 65      | Perez     | Juan       | 1626 Taylor | Fillmore | FL    | 33336 | 23487.00   | 0.05 |
+---------+-----------+------------+-------------+----------+-------+-------+------------+------+
3 rows in set (0.00 sec)
                      Row has been deleted
```

FIGURE 3-18   Using a DELETE command to delete a row

An Introduction to SQL

Question: How do I correct errors in my data?

Answer: It depends on the type of error you need to correct. If you added a row that should not be in the table, use a DELETE command to remove it. If you forgot to add a row, you can use an INSERT command to add it. If you added a row that contains incorrect data, you can use an UPDATE command to make the necessary corrections. Alternatively, you could use a DELETE command to remove the row containing the error and then use an INSERT command to insert the correct row.

SAVING SQL COMMANDS

Saving SQL commands in a file lets you use the commands again without retyping them. A file containing SQL commands is called a **script file**. The exact manner in which you create and use script files depends on the SQL implementation that you are using.

In MySQL, you can use a text editor (such as Notepad) or a word processor (such as Microsoft Word) to create script files. (Be sure to save script files as text files with .txt filename extensions.) To run the command(s) in the file in MySQL, type the word SOURCE or a backslash and a period (\.) followed by the name of the file. For example, to run a script saved in a file named cre_cust.txt, you would type one of the following commands:

```
SOURCE cre_cust.txt
```

or

```
\. cre_cust.txt
```

NOTE

If you saved the script file in a folder other than the default folder for your DBMS, you must include the full path to the file with the filename. You use the forward slash (/) to specify the path. For example, if the file cre_cust.txt is located in a folder named Data on drive C, the command to run the script is:

```
SOURCE C:/Data/cre_cust.txt
```

or

```
\. C:/Data/cre_cust.txt
```

After you press the Enter key, MySQL executes the command(s) contained in the script file.

CREATING THE REMAINING DATABASE TABLES

To create the remaining tables in the Premiere Products database, you need to execute the appropriate CREATE TABLE and INSERT commands. You should save these commands as scripts so you can re-create your database, if necessary, by running the scripts.

Figure 3-19 shows the CREATE TABLE command for the CUSTOMER table. Notice that the CUSTOMER_NAME column is specified as NOT NULL. Additionally, the CUSTOMER_NUM column is the table's primary key, indicating that the CUSTOMER_NUM column is the unique identifier of rows within the table. With this column designated as the primary key, the DBMS will reject any attempt to store a customer number if that number already exists in the table.

```
CREATE TABLE CUSTOMER
(CUSTOMER_NUM CHAR(3) PRIMARY KEY,
CUSTOMER_NAME CHAR(35) NOT NULL,
STREET CHAR(15),
CITY CHAR(15),
STATE CHAR(2),
ZIP CHAR(5),
BALANCE DECIMAL(8,2),
CREDIT_LIMIT DECIMAL(8,2),
REP_NUM CHAR(2) );
```

FIGURE 3-19   CREATE TABLE command for the CUSTOMER table

After creating the CUSTOMER table, you can create another file containing the INSERT commands to add the customer rows to the table. When a script file contains more than one command, each command must end with a semicolon. Figure 3-20 shows the INSERT commands to load the CUSTOMER table with data. As noted previously, to enter an apostrophe (single quotation mark) in the value for a field, type two single quotation marks, as illustrated in the name in the first INSERT command (Al's Appliance and Sport) in Figure 3-20.

```
INSERT INTO CUSTOMER
VALUES
('148','Al''s Appliance and Sport','2837 Greenway','Fillmore','FL','33336',6550.00,7500.00,'20');
INSERT INTO CUSTOMER
VALUES
('282','Brookings Direct','3827 Devon','Grove','FL','33321',431.50,10000.00,'35');
INSERT INTO CUSTOMER
VALUES
('356','Ferguson''s','382 Wildwood','Northfield','FL','33146',5785.00,7500.00,'65');
INSERT INTO CUSTOMER
VALUES
('408','The Everything Shop','1828 Raven','Crystal','FL','33503',5285.25,5000.00,'35');
INSERT INTO CUSTOMER
VALUES
('462','Bargains Galore','3829 Central','Grove','FL','33321',3412.00,10000.00,'65');
INSERT INTO CUSTOMER
VALUES
('524','Kline''s','838 Ridgeland','Fillmore','FL','33336',12762.00,15000.00,'20');
INSERT INTO CUSTOMER
VALUES
('608','Johnson''s Department Store','372 Oxford','Sheldon','FL','33553',2106.00,10000.00,'65');
INSERT INTO CUSTOMER
VALUES
('687','Lee''s Sport and Appliance','282 Evergreen','Altonville','FL','32543',2851.00,5000.00,'35');
INSERT INTO CUSTOMER
VALUES
('725','Deerfield''s Four Seasons','282 Columbia','Sheldon','FL','33553',248.00,7500.00,'35');
INSERT INTO CUSTOMER
VALUES
('842','All Season','28 Lakeview','Grove','FL','33321',8221.00,7500.00,'20');
```

FIGURE 3-20   INSERT commands for the CUSTOMER table

Figures 3-21 through 3-26 show the scripts for the CREATE TABLE and INSERT commands for creating and inserting data into the ORDERS, PART, and ORDER_LINE tables in the Premiere Products database. Figure 3-21 contains the CREATE TABLE command for the ORDERS table.

```
CREATE TABLE ORDERS
(ORDER_NUM CHAR(5) PRIMARY KEY,
ORDER_DATE DATE,
CUSTOMER_NUM CHAR(3) );
```

FIGURE 3-21   CREATE TABLE command for the ORDERS table

Figure 3-22 contains the INSERT commands to load data into the ORDERS table. Notice the way that dates are entered.

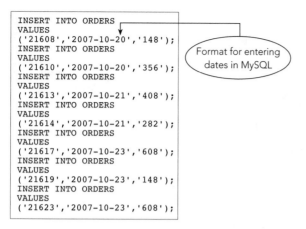

```
INSERT INTO ORDERS
VALUES
('21608','2007-10-20','148');
INSERT INTO ORDERS
VALUES
('21610','2007-10-20','356');
INSERT INTO ORDERS
VALUES
('21613','2007-10-21','408');
INSERT INTO ORDERS
VALUES
('21614','2007-10-21','282');
INSERT INTO ORDERS
VALUES
('21617','2007-10-23','608');
INSERT INTO ORDERS
VALUES
('21619','2007-10-23','148');
INSERT INTO ORDERS
VALUES
('21623','2007-10-23','608');
```

Format for entering dates in MySQL

FIGURE 3-22 INSERT commands for the ORDERS table

Figure 3-23 contains the CREATE TABLE command for the PART table.

```
CREATE TABLE PART
(PART_NUM CHAR(4) PRIMARY KEY,
DESCRIPTION CHAR(15),
ON_HAND DECIMAL(4,0),
CLASS CHAR(2),
WAREHOUSE CHAR(1),
PRICE DECIMAL(6,2) );
```

FIGURE 3-23 CREATE TABLE command for the PART table

Figure 3-24 contains the INSERT commands to load data into the PART table.

```
INSERT INTO PART
VALUES
('AT94','Iron',50,'HW','3',24.95);
INSERT INTO PART
VALUES
('BV06','Home Gym',45,'SG','2',794.95);
INSERT INTO PART
VALUES
('CD52','Microwave Oven',32,'AP','1',165.00);
INSERT INTO PART
VALUES
('DL71','Cordless Drill',21,'HW','3',129.95);
INSERT INTO PART
VALUES
('DR93','Gas Range',8,'AP','2',495.00);
INSERT INTO PART
VALUES
('DW11','Washer',12,'AP','3',399.99);
INSERT INTO PART
VALUES
('FD21','Stand Mixer',22,'HW','3',159.95);
INSERT INTO PART
VALUES
('KL62','Dryer',12,'AP','1',349.95);
INSERT INTO PART
VALUES
('KT03','Dishwasher',8,'AP','3',595.00);
INSERT INTO PART
VALUES
('KV29','Treadmill',9,'SG','2',1390.00);
```

FIGURE 3-24 INSERT commands for the PART table

Figure 3-25 contains the CREATE TABLE command for the ORDER_LINE table. Notice the way that the primary key is defined when it consists of more than one column.

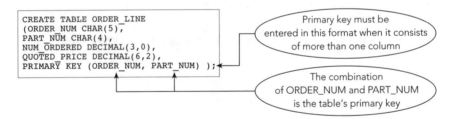

FIGURE 3-25 CREATE TABLE command for the ORDER_LINE table

Figure 3-26 contains the INSERT commands to load data into the ORDER_LINE table.

```
INSERT INTO ORDER_LINE
VALUES
('21608','AT94',11,21.95);
INSERT INTO ORDER_LINE
VALUES
('21610','DR93',1,495.00);
INSERT INTO ORDER_LINE
VALUES
('21610','DW11',1,399.99);
INSERT INTO ORDER_LINE
VALUES
('21613','KL62',4,329.95);
INSERT INTO ORDER_LINE
VALUES
('21614','KT03',2,595.00);
INSERT INTO ORDER_LINE
VALUES
('21617','BV06',2,794.95);
INSERT INTO ORDER_LINE
VALUES
('21617','CD52',4,150.00);
INSERT INTO ORDER_LINE
VALUES
('21619','DR93',1,495.00);
INSERT INTO ORDER_LINE
VALUES
('21623','KV29',2,1290.00);
```

FIGURE 3-26 INSERT commands for the ORDER_LINE table

DESCRIBING A TABLE

The CREATE TABLE command defines a table's structure by listing its columns, data types, and column lengths. The CREATE TABLE command also indicates which columns cannot accept nulls. When you work with a table, you might not have access to the CREATE TABLE command that was used to create it. For example, another programmer might have created the table, or perhaps you created the table several months ago but did not save the command. You still might want to examine the table's structure to see the details about the columns in the table. Each DBMS provides a method to examine a table's structure.

In MySQL, you can use the **SHOW COLUMNS** command to list all the columns in a table. Figure 3-27 shows the SHOW COLUMNS command and result for the REP table.

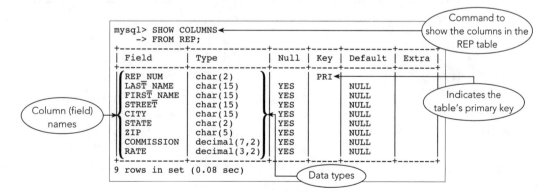

FIGURE 3-27 SHOW COLUMNS command for the REP table

Chapter Summary

The manner in which you start MySQL depends on your environment. In a Windows XP installation, click the Start button, point to All Programs, point to MySQL, point to MySQL Server 4.1, and then click MySQL Command Line Client. If necessary, enter your password.

To obtain help in MySQL, type \h or the word "help" at the mysql> prompt and then press the Enter key.

The manner in which you access the MySQL Reference Manual depends on the operating system you are using. In a Windows XP installation, click the Start button, point to All Programs, point to MySQL, point to MySQL Server 4.1, and then click MySQL Manual - Table of Contents.

To create a database, use the CREATE DATABASE command.

To make a database the default database, use the USE DATABASE command.

Use the CREATE TABLE command to create a table by typing the table name and then listing within a single set of parentheses the columns in the table.

Use the DROP TABLE command to delete a table and all its data from the database.

Some commonly used data types in MySQL are INT, SMALLINT, DECIMAL, CHAR, VARCHAR, and DATE.

A null data value (or null) is a special value that is used when the actual value for a column is unknown, unavailable, or not applicable.

Use the NOT NULL clause in a CREATE TABLE command to identify columns that cannot accept null values.

Use the INSERT command to load data into a table.

Use the SELECT command to view the data in a table.

Use the UPDATE command to change the value in a column.

Use the DELETE command to delete a row in a table.

You can use the SHOW COLUMNS command to display a table's structure and layout.

Key Terms

CREATE DATABASE	null data value
CREATE TABLE	script file
data type	SELECT
default database	SHOW COLUMNS
DELETE	Structured Query Language (SQL)
DROP TABLE	statement history
INSERT	UPDATE
NOT NULL	USE
null	VALUES

Review Questions

1. How do you start MySQL?
2. How do you obtain help in MySQL? How can you use the MySQL Reference Manual?
3. How do you create a database in MySQL?
4. What is the default database? How do you change the default database?
5. How do you create a table in MySQL?
6. How do you delete a table in MySQL?
7. What are the common data types used to define columns in MySQL?
8. What is a null value? How do you identify columns that cannot accept null values?
9. Which command do you use to add a row to a table?
10. Which command do you use to view the data in a table?
11. Which command do you use to change the value in a column in a table?
12. Which command do you use to delete rows from a table?
13. How do you display the layout of a table in MySQL?

Exercises

Note: To print a copy of your commands and results, first save the commands and results in a file. To do so, execute a command consisting of the word TEE or a slash and the letter T (\T) followed by the name of the file. All the commands (and their results) that you enter from that point will be saved in the file that you named. For example, to save the commands and results to a file named CHAPTER3.TXT on drive A, execute either of the following commands before beginning your work:

```
TEE A:CHAPTER3.TXT
```

or

```
\T A:CHAPTER3.TXT
```

If you are using a USB device to save your work, replace the A: with the drive letter for the USB device. When you have finished entering and running your commands, start any program that can open text files (such as Notepad or WordPad), open the file that you saved, and print it using the Print command on the File menu.

Premiere Products

Use MySQL and Figure 2-1 in Chapter 2 to complete the following exercises.

1. Execute the CREATE TABLE commands to create the tables in the Premiere Products database. (The CREATE TABLE commands you need are shown in Figures 3-8, 3-19, 3-21, 3-23, and 3-25.)
2. Add the sales reps shown in Figure 2-1 to the REP table using INSERT commands.
3. Add the customers shown in Figure 2-1 to the CUSTOMER table.

4. Add the orders shown in Figure 2-1 to the ORDERS table.

5. Add the part data shown in Figure 2-1 to the PART table.

6. Add the order line information shown in Figure 2-1 to the ORDER_LINE table.

Henry Books

Use MySQL and Figures 1-4 through 1-7 in Chapter 1 to complete the following exercises.

1. Use the appropriate CREATE TABLE commands to create the tables in the Henry Books database. The information you need appears in Figure 3-28.

2. Add the branch information shown in Figure 1-4 (in Chapter 1) to the BRANCH table using INSERT commands.

3. Add the publisher information shown in Figure 1-4 to the PUBLISHER table.

4. Add the author information shown in Figure 1-5 to the AUTHOR table.

5. Add the book information shown in Figure 1-6 to the BOOK table. In the PAPERBACK column, enter Y when the entry in Figure 1-6 is Yes and N when the entry is No.

6. Add the author and book information shown in Figure 1-7 to the WROTE table.

7. Add the inventory information shown in Figure 1-7 to the INVENTORY table.

BRANCH

Column	Type	Length	Decimal places	Nulls allowed?	Description
BRANCH_NUM	DECIMAL	2	0	No	Branch number (primary key)
BRANCH_NAME	CHAR	50			Branch name
BRANCH_LOCATION	CHAR	50			Branch location
NUM_EMPLOYEES	DECIMAL	2	0		Number of employees

PUBLISHER

Column	Type	Length	Decimal places	Nulls allowed?	Description
PUBLISHER_CODE	CHAR	3		No	Publisher code (primary key)
PUBLISHER_NAME	CHAR	25			Publisher name
CITY	CHAR	20			Publisher city

FIGURE 3-28 Table layouts for the Henry Books database

AUTHOR

Column	Type	Length	Decimal places	Nulls allowed?	Description
AUTHOR_NUM	DECIMAL	2	0	No	Author number (primary key)
AUTHOR_LAST	CHAR	12			Author last name
AUTHOR_FIRST	CHAR	10			Author first name

BOOK

Column	Type	Length	Decimal places	Nulls allowed?	Description
BOOK_CODE	CHAR	4		No	Book code (primary key)
TITLE	CHAR	40			Book title
PUBLISHER_CODE	CHAR	3			Publisher code
TYPE	CHAR	3			Book type
PRICE	DECIMAL	4	2		Book price
PAPERBACK	CHAR	1			Paperback (Y, N)

WROTE

Column	Type	Length	Decimal places	Nulls allowed?	Description
BOOK_CODE	CHAR	4		No	Book code (primary key)
AUTHOR_NUM	DECIMAL	2	0	No	Author number (primary key)
SEQUENCE	DECIMAL	1	0		Sequence number

INVENTORY

Column	Type	Length	Decimal places	Nulls allowed?	Description
BOOK_CODE	CHAR	4		No	Book code (primary key)
BRANCH_NUM	DECIMAL	2	0	No	Branch number (primary key)
ON_HAND	DECIMAL	2	0		Units on hand

FIGURE 3-28   Table layouts for the Henry Books database (continued)

Alexamara Marina Group

Use MySQL and Figures 1-8 through 1-12 in Chapter 1 to complete the following exercises.

1. Use the appropriate CREATE TABLE commands to create the tables in the Alexamara Marina Group database. The information you need appears in Figure 3-29.

2. Add the marina information in Figure 1-8 to the MARINA table using INSERT commands.

3. Add the owner information in Figure 1-9 to the OWNER table using INSERT commands.

4. Add the slip information in Figure 1-10 to the MARINA_SLIP table using INSERT commands.

5. Add the service category information in Figure 1-11 to the SERVICE_CATEGORY table using INSERT commands.

6. Add the service request information in Figure 1-12 to the SERVICE_REQUEST table using INSERT commands. (*Hint:* The values for next service dates on some rows are null. To enter a null value, you can use the type of INSERT command illustrated in Example 4. Alternatively, you might find it simpler to enter a date that does not occur on any other row (such as December 31, 2010) for the dates that should be null. Once you have added all rows, you can change this date to null on any row on which it occurs. To do so in MySQL, use the following command:

```
UPDATE SERVICE_REQUEST
SET NEXT_SERVICE_DATE = NULL
WHERE NEXT_SERVICE_DATE = '2010-12-31';
```

MARINA

Column	Type	Length	Decimal places	Nulls allowed?	Description
MARINA_NUM	CHAR	4		No	Marina number (primary key)
NAME	CHAR	20			Marina name
ADDRESS	CHAR	15			Marina street address
CITY	CHAR	15			Marina city
STATE	CHAR	2			Marina state
ZIP	CHAR	5			Marina zip code

FIGURE 3-29 Table layouts for the Alexamara Marina Group database

OWNER

Column	Type	Length	Decimal places	Nulls allowed?	Description
OWNER_NUM	CHAR	4		No	Owner number (primary key)
LAST_NAME	CHAR	50			Owner last name
FIRST_NAME	CHAR	20			Owner first name
ADDRESS	CHAR	15			Owner street address
CITY	CHAR	15			Owner city
STATE	CHAR	2			Owner state
ZIP	CHAR	5			Owner zip code

MARINA_SLIP

Column	Type	Length	Decimal places	Nulls allowed?	Description
SLIP_ID	DECIMAL	4	0	No	Slip ID (primary key)
MARINA_NUM	CHAR	4			Marina number
SLIP_NUM	CHAR	4			Slip number in the marina
LENGTH	DECIMAL	4	0		Length of slip (in feet)
RENTAL_FEE	DECIMAL	8	2		Annual rental fee for the slip
BOAT_NAME	CHAR	50			Name of boat currently in the slip
BOAT_TYPE	CHAR	50			Type of boat currently in the slip
OWNER_NUM	CHAR	4			Number of boat owner renting the slip

SERVICE_CATEGORY

Column	Type	Length	Decimal places	Nulls allowed?	Description
CATEGORY_NUM	DECIMAL	4	0	No	Category number (primary key)
CATEGORY_DESCRIPTION	CHAR	255			Category description

FIGURE 3-29 Table layouts for the Alexamara Marina Group database (continued)

SERVICE_REQUEST

Column	Type	Length	Decimal places	Nulls allowed?	Description
SERVICE_ID	DECIMAL	4	0	No	Service ID (primary key)
SLIP_ID	DECIMAL	4	0		Slip ID of the boat for which service is requested
CATEGORY_NUM	DECIMAL	4	0		Category number of the requested service
DESCRIPTION	CHAR	255			Description of specific service requested for boat
STATUS	CHAR	255			Description of status of service request
EST_HOURS	DECIMAL	4	2		Estimated number of hours required to complete the service
SPENT_HOURS	DECIMAL	4	2		Hours already spent on the service
NEXT_SERVICE_DATE	DATE				Next scheduled date for work on this service (or null if no next service date is specified)

FIGURE 3-29 Table layouts for the Alexamara Marina Group database (continued)

CHAPTER 4

SINGLE-TABLE QUERIES

LEARNING OBJECTIVES

Objectives

- Retrieve data from a database using SQL commands
- Use compound conditions in queries
- Use computed columns in queries
- Use the SQL LIKE operator
- Use the SQL IN operator
- Sort data using the ORDER BY clause
- Sort data using multiple keys and in ascending and descending order
- Use SQL aggregate functions
- Use subqueries
- Group data using the GROUP BY clause
- Select individual groups of data using the HAVING clause
- Retrieve columns with null values

INTRODUCTION

In this chapter, you will learn about the SQL SELECT command that is used to retrieve data in a database.

You will examine ways to sort data and use SQL functions to count rows and calculate totals. You also will

learn about a special feature of SQL that lets you nest SELECT commands by placing one SELECT

command inside another. Finally, you will learn how to group rows that have matching values in some

column.

CONSTRUCTING SIMPLE QUERIES

One of the most important features of a database management system is its ability to answer a wide variety of questions concerning the data in a database. When you need to find data that answers a specific question, you use a query. A **query** is a question represented in a way that the DBMS can understand.

In MySQL, you use the SELECT command to query a database. The basic form of the SELECT command is SELECT-FROM-WHERE. After you type the word SELECT, you list the columns that you want to include in the query results. This portion of the command is called the **SELECT clause**. Next, you type the word FROM followed by the name of the table that contains the data you need to query. This portion of the command is called the **FROM clause**. Finally, after the word WHERE, you list any conditions (restrictions) that apply to the data you want to retrieve. This optional portion of the command is called the **WHERE clause**. For example, if you need to retrieve the rows for only those customers with credit limits of $7,500, include a condition in the WHERE clause specifying that the value in the CREDIT_LIMIT column must be $7,500 (CREDIT_LIMIT = 7500).

There are no special formatting rules in MySQL. In this text, the FROM clause and the WHERE clause (when it is used) appear on separate lines only to make the commands more readable and understandable.

Retrieving Certain Columns and All Rows

You can write a command to retrieve specified columns and all rows from a table, as illustrated in Example 1.

EXAMPLE 1

List the number, name, and balance for all customers.

Because you need to list *all* customers, you do not need to include a WHERE clause; you do not need to put any restrictions on the data to retrieve. You simply list the columns to be included (CUSTOMER_NUM, CUSTOMER_NAME, and BALANCE) in the SELECT clause and the name of the table (CUSTOMER) in the FROM clause. The query and its results appear in Figure 4-1.

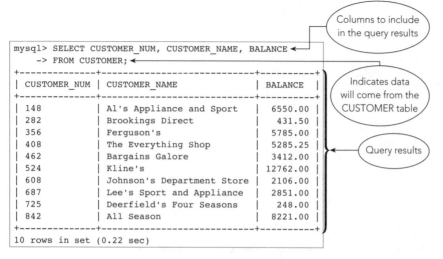

```
mysql> SELECT CUSTOMER_NUM, CUSTOMER_NAME, BALANCE
    -> FROM CUSTOMER;
+--------------+---------------------------+----------+
| CUSTOMER_NUM | CUSTOMER_NAME             | BALANCE  |
+--------------+---------------------------+----------+
| 148          | Al's Appliance and Sport  |  6550.00 |
| 282          | Brookings Direct          |   431.50 |
| 356          | Ferguson's                |  5785.00 |
| 408          | The Everything Shop       |  5285.25 |
| 462          | Bargains Galore           |  3412.00 |
| 524          | Kline's                   | 12762.00 |
| 608          | Johnson's Department Store |  2106.00 |
| 687          | Lee's Sport and Appliance |  2851.00 |
| 725          | Deerfield's Four Seasons  |   248.00 |
| 842          | All Season                |  8221.00 |
+--------------+---------------------------+----------+
10 rows in set (0.22 sec)
```

Columns to include in the query results

Indicates data will come from the CUSTOMER table

Query results

FIGURE 4-1 SELECT command to select certain columns in the CUSTOMER table

Retrieving All Columns and All Rows

You can use the same type of command illustrated in Example 1 to retrieve all columns and all rows from a table. As Example 2 illustrates, however, you can use a shortcut to accomplish this task.

EXAMPLE 2

List the complete PART table.

Instead of listing every column in the SELECT clause, you can use an asterisk (*) to indicate that you want to include all columns. The result lists all columns in the order in which you described them to the system when you created the table. If you want the columns listed in a different order, type the column names in the order in which you want them to appear in the query results. In this case, assuming that the default order is appropriate, you can use the query shown in Figure 4-2.

FIGURE 4-2 SELECT command to select all columns from the PART table

Using a WHERE Clause

You use the WHERE clause to retrieve rows that satisfy some condition, as shown in Example 3.

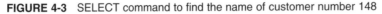

EXAMPLE 3

What is the name of customer number 148?

You can use the WHERE clause to restrict the query output to customer number 148, as shown in Figure 4-3. Because CUSTOMER_NUM is a character column, the value 148 is enclosed in single quotation marks. In addition, because the CUSTOMER_NUM column is the primary key of the CUSTOMER table, there can be only one customer whose number matches the number in the WHERE clause.

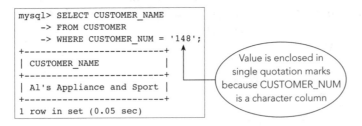

FIGURE 4-3 SELECT command to find the name of customer number 148

The condition in the preceding WHERE clause is called a simple condition. A **simple condition** has the form column name, comparison operator, and then either another column name or a value. Figure 4-4 lists the comparison operators that you can use in MySQL. Notice that there are two versions of the "not equal to" operator: < > and !=.

Comparison operator	Description
=	Equal to
<	Less than
>	Greater than
<=	Less than or equal to
>=	Greater than or equal to
< >	Not equal to
!=	Not equal to

FIGURE 4-4   Comparison operators used in MySQL commands

NOTE

Although MySQL supports both versions of the "not equal to" operator, some SQL implementations only support one version.

EXAMPLE 4

Find the number and name of each customer located in the city of Grove.

The only difference between this example and the previous one is that in Example 3, there could not be more than one row in the answer because the condition involved the table's primary key. In Example 4, the condition involves a column that is *not* the table's primary key. Because there is more than one customer located in the city of Grove, the results can and do contain more than one row, as shown in Figure 4-5.

```
mysql> SELECT CUSTOMER_NUM, CUSTOMER_NAME
    -> FROM CUSTOMER
    -> WHERE CITY = 'Grove';              Condition
+--------------+------------------+
| CUSTOMER_NUM | CUSTOMER_NAME    |
+--------------+------------------+
| 282          | Brookings Direct |
| 462          | Bargains Galore  |
| 842          | All Season       |
+--------------+------------------+
3 rows in set (0.00 sec)
```

FIGURE 4-5   SELECT command to find all customers located in Grove

NOTE

In Example 4, using the clause WHERE CITY = 'grove' would retrieve exactly the same results. In other SQL implementations, however, no rows would be retrieved because "Grove" is considered to be different from "grove." In MySQL, you can retrieve character data that matches the case used in the WHERE clause by using the BINARY keyword. For example, in Example 4, the clause WHERE BINARY CITY = 'grove' would retrieve no rows because the values in the table are stored as "Grove."

EXAMPLE 5

Find the number, name, balance, and credit limit for all customers with balances that exceed their credit limits.

A simple condition also can involve a comparison of two columns. In Figure 4-6, the WHERE clause includes a comparison operator to select those rows in which the balance is greater than the credit limit.

```
mysql> SELECT CUSTOMER_NUM, CUSTOMER_NAME, BALANCE, CREDIT_LIMIT
    -> FROM CUSTOMER
    -> WHERE BALANCE > CREDIT_LIMIT;
+--------------+---------------------+---------+--------------+
| CUSTOMER_NUM | CUSTOMER_NAME       | BALANCE | CREDIT_LIMIT |
+--------------+---------------------+---------+--------------+
| 408          | The Everything Shop | 5285.25 |      5000.00 |
| 842          | All Season          | 8221.00 |      7500.00 |
+--------------+---------------------+---------+--------------+
2 rows in set (0.08 sec)
```

FIGURE 4-6 SELECT command to find all customers with balances that exceed their credit limits

Using Compound Conditions

The conditions you have seen so far are called simple conditions. The following examples require compound conditions. You form a **compound condition** by connecting two or more simple conditions with the AND, OR, and NOT operators. When the **AND** operator connects simple conditions, all the simple conditions must be true in order for the compound condition to be true. When the **OR** operator connects the simple conditions, the compound condition will be true whenever any one of the simple conditions is true. Preceding a condition by the **NOT** operator reverses the truth of the original condition. For example, if the original condition is true, the new condition will be false; if the original condition is false, the new one will be true.

EXAMPLE 6

List the descriptions of all parts that are located in warehouse 3 and for which there are more than 25 units on hand.

In Example 6, you need to retrieve those parts that meet *both* conditions—the warehouse number is equal to 3 *and* the number of units on hand is greater than 25. To find the answer, you form a compound condition using the AND operator, as shown in Figure 4-7. The query examines the data in the PART table and lists the parts that are located in warehouse 3 and for which there are more than 25 units on hand. When a WHERE clause uses the AND operator to connect simple conditions, it also is called an AND condition.

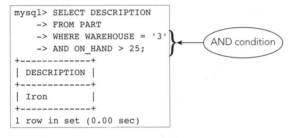

```
mysql> SELECT DESCRIPTION
    -> FROM PART
    -> WHERE WAREHOUSE = '3'
    -> AND ON_HAND > 25;
+-------------+
| DESCRIPTION |
+-------------+
| Iron        |
+-------------+
1 row in set (0.00 sec)
```

AND condition

FIGURE 4-7   SELECT command with an AND condition on separate lines

For readability, each of the simple conditions in the query shown in Figure 4-7 appears on a separate line. Some people prefer to put the conditions on the same line with parentheses around each simple condition, as shown in Figure 4-8. These two methods accomplish the same thing. In this text, simple conditions will appear on separate lines and without parentheses.

```
mysql> SELECT DESCRIPTION
    -> FROM PART
    -> WHERE (WAREHOUSE = '3') AND (ON_HAND > 25);
+-------------+
| DESCRIPTION |
+-------------+
| Iron        |
+-------------+
1 row in set (0.00 sec)
```

FIGURE 4-8   SELECT command with an AND condition on a single line

List the descriptions of all parts that are located in warehouse 3 or for which there are more than 25 units on hand.

In Example 7, you need to retrieve descriptions for those parts for which the warehouse number is equal to 3, *or* the number of units on hand is greater than 25, *or* both. To do this, you form a compound condition using the OR operator, as shown in Figure 4-9. When a WHERE clause uses the OR operator to connect simple conditions, it also is called an OR condition.

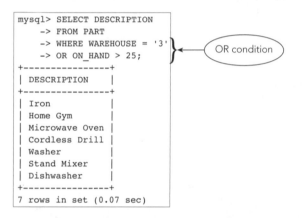

```
mysql> SELECT DESCRIPTION
    -> FROM PART
    -> WHERE WAREHOUSE = '3'
    -> OR ON_HAND > 25;
+-----------------+
| DESCRIPTION     |
+-----------------+
| Iron            |
| Home Gym        |
| Microwave Oven  |
| Cordless Drill  |
| Washer          |
| Stand Mixer     |
| Dishwasher      |
+-----------------+
7 rows in set (0.07 sec)
```

OR condition

FIGURE 4-9 SELECT command with an OR condition

List the descriptions of all parts that are not in warehouse 3.

For Example 8, you could use a simple condition and the "not equal to" operator (WHERE WAREHOUSE < > '3'). As an alternative, you could use the EQUAL operator (=) in the condition and precede the entire condition with the NOT operator, as shown in Figure 4-10. When a WHERE clause uses the NOT operator to connect simple conditions, it also is called a NOT condition.

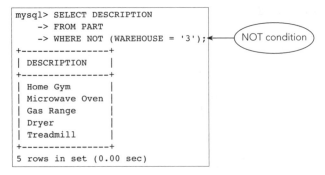

```
mysql> SELECT DESCRIPTION
    -> FROM PART
    -> WHERE NOT (WAREHOUSE = '3');      NOT condition
+----------------+
| DESCRIPTION    |
+----------------+
| Home Gym       |
| Microwave Oven |
| Gas Range      |
| Dryer          |
| Treadmill      |
+----------------+
5 rows in set (0.00 sec)
```

FIGURE 4-10   SELECT command with a NOT condition

You do not need to enclose the condition WAREHOUSE = '3' in parentheses, but doing so makes the command more readable.

Using the BETWEEN Operator

Example 9 requires a compound condition to determine the answer.

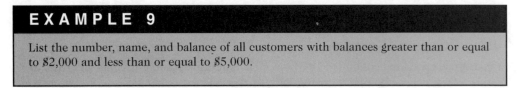

E X A M P L E   9

List the number, name, and balance of all customers with balances greater than or equal to $2,000 and less than or equal to $5,000.

You can use a WHERE clause and the AND operator as shown in Figure 4-11 to retrieve the data.

```
mysql> SELECT CUSTOMER_NUM, CUSTOMER_NAME, BALANCE
    -> FROM CUSTOMER
    -> WHERE BALANCE >= 2000
    -> AND BALANCE <= 5000;
+--------------+--------------------------+---------+
| CUSTOMER_NUM | CUSTOMER_NAME            | BALANCE |
+--------------+--------------------------+---------+
| 462          | Bargains Galore          | 3412.00 |
| 608          | Johnson's Department Store | 2106.00 |
| 687          | Lee's Sport and Appliance | 2851.00 |
+--------------+--------------------------+---------+
3 rows in set (0.00 sec)
```

FIGURE 4-11   SELECT command with an AND condition for a single column

An alternative to this approach uses the BETWEEN operator, as shown in Figure 4-12. The **BETWEEN** operator lets you specify a range of values in a condition.

```
mysql> SELECT CUSTOMER_NUM, CUSTOMER_NAME, BALANCE
    -> FROM CUSTOMER
    -> WHERE BALANCE BETWEEN 2000 AND 5000;
+--------------+----------------------------+---------+
| CUSTOMER_NUM | CUSTOMER_NAME              | BALANCE |
+--------------+----------------------------+---------+
| 462          | Bargains Galore            | 3412.00 |
| 608          | Johnson's Department Store | 2106.00 |
| 687          | Lee's Sport and Appliance  | 2851.00 |
+--------------+----------------------------+---------+
3 rows in set (0.08 sec)
```

FIGURE 4-12 SELECT command with a BETWEEN operator

The BETWEEN operator is not an essential feature of SQL; you have just seen that you can obtain the same result without it. Using the BETWEEN operator, however, does make certain SELECT commands simpler to construct.

NOTE

The BETWEEN operator is inclusive, meaning that a value equal to either value in the condition is selected. In the clause BETWEEN 2000 and 5000, for example, values of either 2,000 or 5,000 would make the condition true.

Using Computed Columns

You can use computed columns in SQL queries. A **computed column** does not exist in the database but can be computed using data in the existing columns. Computations can involve any arithmetic operator shown in Figure 4-13.

Arithmetic operator	Description
+	Addition
−	Subtraction
*	Multiplication
/	Division

FIGURE 4-13 Arithmetic operators

EXAMPLE 10

Find the number, name, and available credit (the credit limit minus the balance) for each customer.

There is no column for available credit in the Premiere Products database, but you can compute the available credit from two columns that are present: CREDIT_LIMIT and BALANCE. To compute the available credit, you use the expression CREDIT_LIMIT – BALANCE, as shown in Figure 4-14.

```
                              Computation              Computed
                                                       column
mysql> SELECT CUSTOMER_NUM, CUSTOMER_NAME, (CREDIT_LIMIT - BALANCE)
    -> FROM CUSTOMER;
+--------------+----------------------------+--------------------------+
| CUSTOMER_NUM | CUSTOMER_NAME              | (CREDIT_LIMIT - BALANCE) |
+--------------+----------------------------+--------------------------+
|     148      | Al's Appliance and Sport   |                   950.00 |
|     282      | Brookings Direct           |                  9568.50 |
|     356      | Ferguson's                 |                  1715.00 |
|     408      | The Everything Shop        |                  -285.25 |
|     462      | Bargains Galore            |                  6588.00 |
|     524      | Kline's                    |                  2238.00 |
|     608      | Johnson's Department Store |                  7894.00 |
|     687      | Lee's Sport and Appliance  |                  2149.00 |
|     725      | Deerfield's Four Seasons   |                  7252.00 |
|     842      | All Season                 |                  -721.00 |
+--------------+----------------------------+--------------------------+
10 rows in set (0.10 sec)
```

FIGURE 4-14   SELECT command with a computed column

The parentheses around the calculation (CREDIT_LIMIT – BALANCE) are not essential but improve readability.

You also can assign a name to a computed column by following the computation with the word AS and the desired name. The command in Figure 4-15, for example, assigns the name AVAILABLE_CREDIT to the computed column.

```
mysql> SELECT CUSTOMER_NUM, CUSTOMER_NAME, (CREDIT_LIMIT - BALANCE) AS
    -> AVAILABLE_CREDIT                        Name of computed column
    -> FROM CUSTOMER;
+--------------+----------------------------+------------------+
| CUSTOMER_NUM | CUSTOMER_NAME              | AVAILABLE_CREDIT |
+--------------+----------------------------+------------------+
|     148      | Al's Appliance and Sport   |           950.00 |
|     282      | Brookings Direct           |          9568.50 |
|     356      | Ferguson's                 |          1715.00 |
|     408      | The Everything Shop        |          -285.25 |
|     462      | Bargains Galore            |          6588.00 |
|     524      | Kline's                    |          2238.00 |
|     608      | Johnson's Department Store |          7894.00 |
|     687      | Lee's Sport and Appliance  |          2149.00 |
|     725      | Deerfield's Four Seasons   |          7252.00 |
|     842      | All Season                 |          -721.00 |
+--------------+----------------------------+------------------+
10 rows in set (0.00 sec)
```

FIGURE 4-15   SELECT command with a named computed column

EXAMPLE 11

Find the number, name, and available credit for each customer with at least $5,000 of available credit.

You also can use computed columns in comparisons, as shown in Figure 4-16.

```
mysql> SELECT CUSTOMER_NUM, CUSTOMER_NAME, (CREDIT_LIMIT - BALANCE) AS
    -> AVAILABLE_CREDIT
    -> FROM CUSTOMER
    -> WHERE (CREDIT_LIMIT - BALANCE) >= 5000;
+--------------+---------------------------+------------------+
| CUSTOMER_NUM | CUSTOMER_NAME             | AVAILABLE_CREDIT |
+--------------+---------------------------+------------------+
| 282          | Brookings Direct          |          9568.50 |
| 462          | Bargains Galore           |          6588.00 |
| 608          | Johnson's Department Store |         7894.00 |
| 725          | Deerfield's Four Seasons  |          7252.00 |
+--------------+---------------------------+------------------+
4 rows in set (0.00 sec)
```

FIGURE 4-16   SELECT command with a computation in the WHERE clause

Using the LIKE Operator

In most cases, the conditions in WHERE clauses involve exact matches, such as retrieving rows for each customer located in the city of Grove. In some cases, however, exact matches do not work. For example, you might know that the desired value contains only a certain collection of characters. In such cases, you use the LIKE operator with a wildcard symbol, as shown in Example 12. Rather than testing for equality, the **LIKE** operator uses one or more wildcard characters to test for a pattern match.

EXAMPLE 12

List the number, name, and complete address of each customer located on a street that contains the letters "Central."

All you know is that the addresses you want contain a certain collection of characters ("Central") somewhere in the STREET column, but you do not know where. In MySQL, the percent sign (%) is used as a wildcard to represent any collection of characters. As shown in Figure 4-17, the condition LIKE '%Central%' retrieves information for each customer whose street contains some collection of characters, followed by the letters "Central," followed potentially by some additional characters. Note that this query also would retrieve information for a customer whose address is "123 Centralia" because "Centralia" also contains the letters "Central."

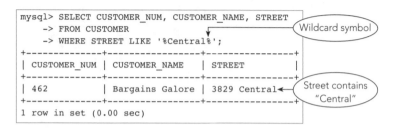

FIGURE 4-17 SELECT command with a LIKE operator and wildcards

Another wildcard symbol in MySQL is the underscore (_), which represents any individual character. For example, "T_m" represents the letter "T" followed by any single character, followed by the letter "m," and would retrieve rows that include the words Tim, Tom, or T3m.

NOTE

In a large database, you should use wildcards only when absolutely necessary. Searches involving wildcards can be extremely slow to process.

Using the IN Operator

An **IN clause**, which consists of the **IN** operator followed by a collection of values, provides a concise way of phrasing certain conditions, as Example 13 illustrates. You will see another use for the IN clause in more complex examples later in this chapter.

EXAMPLE 13

List the number, name, and credit limit for each customer with a credit limit of $5,000, $10,000, or $15,000.

In this query, you can use an IN clause to determine whether a credit limit is $5,000, $10,000, or $15,000. You could obtain the same answer by using the condition WHERE CREDIT_LIMIT = 5000 OR CREDIT_LIMIT = 10000 OR CREDIT_LIMIT = 15000. The approach shown in Figure 4-18 is simpler because the IN clause contains a collection of values: 5000, 10000, and 15000. The condition is true for those rows in which the value in the CREDIT_LIMIT column is in this collection.

```
mysql> SELECT CUSTOMER_NUM, CUSTOMER_NAME, CREDIT_LIMIT
    -> FROM CUSTOMER
    -> WHERE CREDIT_LIMIT IN (5000, 10000, 15000);
+--------------+---------------------------+--------------+
| CUSTOMER_NUM | CUSTOMER_NAME             | CREDIT_LIMIT |
+--------------+---------------------------+--------------+
| 282          | Brookings Direct          |     10000.00 |
| 408          | The Everything Shop       |      5000.00 |
| 462          | Bargains Galore           |     10000.00 |
| 524          | Kline's                   |     15000.00 |
| 608          | Johnson's Department Store |    10000.00 |
| 687          | Lee's Sport and Appliance |      5000.00 |
+--------------+---------------------------+--------------+
6 rows in set (0.00 sec)
```

List of values in the IN clause

FIGURE 4-18 SELECT command with an IN clause

SORTING

Recall that the order of rows in a table is immaterial to the DBMS. From a practical standpoint, this means that when you query a relational database, there is no defined order in which the results are displayed. Rows can be displayed in the order in which the data was originally entered, but even this is not certain. If the order in which the data is displayed is important, you can specifically request that the results appear in a desired order. In MySQL, you specify the results order by using the ORDER BY clause.

Using the ORDER BY Clause

You use the **ORDER BY clause** to list data in a specific order, as shown in Example 14.

EXAMPLE 14

List the number, name, and balance of each customer. Order (sort) the output in ascending (increasing) order by balance.

The column on which data is to be sorted is called a **sort key** or simply a **key**. In Example 14, you need to order the output by balance, so the sort key is the BALANCE column. To sort the output, use an ORDER BY clause followed by the sort key. If you do not specify a sort order, the default is ascending. The query appears in Figure 4-19.

```
mysql> SELECT CUSTOMER_NUM, CUSTOMER_NAME, BALANCE
    -> FROM CUSTOMER
    -> ORDER BY BALANCE;
+--------------+----------------------------+----------+
| CUSTOMER_NUM | CUSTOMER_NAME              | BALANCE  |
+--------------+----------------------------+----------+
| 725          | Deerfield's Four Seasons   |   248.00 |
| 282          | Brookings Direct           |   431.50 |
| 608          | Johnson's Department Store | 2106.00  |
| 687          | Lee's Sport and Appliance  | 2851.00  |
| 462          | Bargains Galore            | 3412.00  |
| 408          | The Everything Shop        | 5285.25  |
| 356          | Ferguson's                 | 5785.00  |
| 148          | Al's Appliance and Sport   | 6550.00  |
| 842          | All Season                 | 8221.00  |
| 524          | Kline's                    | 12762.00 |
+--------------+----------------------------+----------+
10 rows in set (0.07 sec)
```

Sort key

ORDER BY clause

Rows are sorted
in ascending order
by balance

FIGURE 4-19 SELECT command with an ORDER BY clause

Additional Sorting Options

Sometimes you might need to sort data using more than one key, as shown in Example 15.

EXAMPLE 15

List the number, name, and credit limit of each customer. Order the customers by name within descending credit limit. (In other words, sort the customers by credit limit in descending order. Within each group of customers that have a common credit limit, sort the customers by name in ascending order.)

Example 15 involves two new ideas: sorting on multiple keys—CREDIT_LIMIT and CUSTOMER_NAME—and sorting one of the keys in descending order. When you need to sort data on two columns, the more important column (in this case, CREDIT_LIMIT) is called the **major sort key** (or the **primary sort key**) and the less important column (in this case, CUSTOMER_NAME) is called the **minor sort key** (or the **secondary sort key**). To sort on multiple keys, you list the keys in order of importance in the ORDER BY clause. To sort in descending order, you follow the name of the sort key with the **DESC** operator, as shown in Figure 4-20.

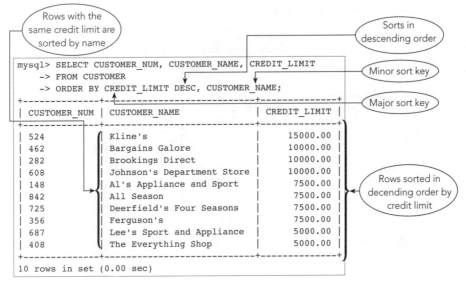

FIGURE 4-20 SELECT command to sort data using multiple sort keys

USING FUNCTIONS

MySQL uses special functions, called **aggregate functions**, to calculate sums, averages, counts, maximum values, and minimum values. These functions apply to *groups* of rows. They could apply to all the rows in a table (for example, calculating the average balance of all customers). They also could apply to those rows satisfying some particular condition (for example, the average balance of all customers of sales rep 20). The descriptions of the aggregate functions appear in Figure 4-21.

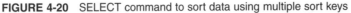

Function	Description
AVG	Calculates the average value in a column
COUNT	Determines the number of rows in a table
MAX	Determines the maximum value in a column
MIN	Determines the minimum value in a column
SUM	Calculates a total of the values in a column

FIGURE 4-21 MySQL aggregate functions

Using the COUNT Function

The **COUNT** function, as illustrated in Example 16, counts the number of rows in a table.

EXAMPLE 16

How many parts are in item class HW?

For this query, you need to determine the total number of rows in the PART table with the value HW in the CLASS column. You could count the part numbers in the query results, or the number of part descriptions, or the number of entries in any other column. It doesn't matter which column you choose because all columns should provide the same answer. Rather than arbitrarily selecting one column, most SQL implementations let you use the asterisk (*) to represent any column, as shown in Figure 4-22.

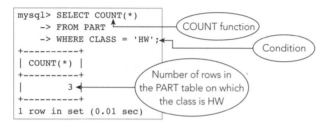

FIGURE 4-22   SELECT command to count rows

You also can count the number of rows in a query by selecting a specific column instead of using the asterisk, as follows:

```
SELECT COUNT(PART_NUM)
FROM PART
WHERE CLASS = 'HW';
```

Using the SUM Function

If you want to calculate the total of all customers' balances, you can use the **SUM** function, as illustrated in Example 17.

EXAMPLE 17

Find the total number of Premiere Products customers and the total of their balances.

When you use the SUM function, you must specify the column to total, and the column data type must be numeric. (How could you calculate a sum of names or addresses?) Figure 4-23 shows the query.

```
mysql> SELECT COUNT(*), SUM(BALANCE)
    -> FROM CUSTOMER;
+----------+--------------+
| COUNT(*) | SUM(BALANCE) |
+----------+--------------+
|       10 |     47651.75 |
+----------+--------------+
1 row in set (0.00 sec)
```

FIGURE 4-23   SELECT command to count rows and calculate a total

Using the AVG, MAX, and MIN Functions

Using the AVG, MAX, and MIN functions is similar to using SUM, except that different statistics are calculated. **AVG** calculates the average value in a numeric range, **MAX** calculates the maximum value in a numeric range, and **MIN** calculates the minimum value in a numeric range. Figure 4-24 shows the query to select the sum of all balances, the average balance, the maximum balance, and the minimum balance of all Premiere Products customers.

```
mysql> SELECT SUM(BALANCE), AVG(BALANCE), MAX(BALANCE), MIN(BALANCE)
    -> FROM CUSTOMER;
+--------------+--------------+--------------+--------------+
| SUM(BALANCE) | AVG(BALANCE) | MAX(BALANCE) | MIN(BALANCE) |
+--------------+--------------+--------------+--------------+
|     47651.75 |  4765.175000 |     12762.00 |       248.00 |
+--------------+--------------+--------------+--------------+
1 row in set (0.00 sec)
```

FIGURE 4-24   SELECT command with several functions

NOTE

When you use the SUM, AVG, MAX, or MIN functions, MySQL ignores any null value(s) in the column and eliminates them from the computations.

NOTE

Null values in numeric columns can produce strange results when statistics are computed. Suppose that the BALANCE column accepts null values, that there are currently four customers in the CUSTOMER table, and that their respective balances are $100, $200, $300, and null (unknown). When you calculate the average balance, MySQL ignores the null value and obtains a result of $200 (($100 + $200 + $300) / 3). Similarly, if you calculate the total of the balances, MySQL ignores the null value and calculates a total of $600. If you count the number of customers in the table, however, MySQL includes the row containing the null value, and the result is 4. Thus the total of the balances ($600) divided by the number of customers (4) results in an average balance of $150!

Using the DISTINCT Operator

In some situations, the DISTINCT operator is useful when used in conjunction with the COUNT function because it eliminates duplicate values in a query. The **DISTINCT** operator eliminates duplicate values in the results of a query. Before examining such a situation, you need to understand how to use the DISTINCT operator. Examples 18 and 19 illustrate the most common uses of the DISTINCT operator.

EXAMPLE 18

Find the number of each customer that currently has an open order (that is, an order currently in the ORDERS table).

The command seems fairly simple. If a customer currently has an open order, there must be at least one row in the ORDERS table on which that customer's number appears. You could use the query shown in Figure 4-25 to find the customer numbers with open orders.

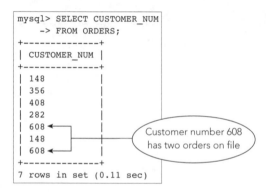

FIGURE 4-25 Numbers of customers with open orders

Notice that customer numbers 148 and 608 each appear more than once in the results; they both currently have more than one open order in the ORDERS table. Suppose you want to list each customer only once, as illustrated in Example 19.

EXAMPLE 19

Find the number of each customer that currently has an open order. List each customer only once.

To ensure uniqueness, you can use the DISTINCT operator, as shown in Figure 4-26.

```
mysql> SELECT DISTINCT(CUSTOMER_NUM)
    -> FROM ORDERS;
+--------------+
| CUSTOMER_NUM |
+--------------+
| 148          |
| 356          |
| 408          |
| 282          |
| 608          |
+--------------+
5 rows in set (0.09 sec)
```

FIGURE 4-26 Numbers of customers with open orders but with duplicates removed

You might wonder about the relationship between COUNT and DISTINCT, because both involve counting rows. Example 20 identifies the differences.

EXAMPLE 20

Count the number of customers that currently have open orders.

The query shown in Figure 4-27 counts the number of customers using the CUSTOMER_NUM column.

```
mysql> SELECT COUNT(CUSTOMER_NUM)
    -> FROM ORDERS;
+---------------------+
| COUNT(CUSTOMER_NUM) |
+---------------------+
|                   7 |
+---------------------+
1 row in set (0.00 sec)
```

FIGURE 4-27 Count that includes duplicate customer numbers

Q & A

Question: What is wrong with the query results shown in Figure 4-27?
Answer: The answer, 7, is the result of counting the customers that have open orders multiple times—once for each separate order currently on file. The result counts each customer number and does not eliminate duplicate customer numbers to provide an accurate count of the number of customers.

MySQL allows you to use the DISTINCT operator to calculate the correct count, as shown in Figure 4-28.

```
mysql> SELECT COUNT(DISTINCT(CUSTOMER_NUM))
    -> FROM ORDERS;
+-------------------------------+
| COUNT(DISTINCT(CUSTOMER_NUM)) |
+-------------------------------+
|                             5 |
+-------------------------------+
1 row in set (0.00 sec)
```

FIGURE 4-28 Count that excludes duplicate customer numbers (using DISTINCT within COUNT)

NESTING QUERIES

Sometimes obtaining the results you need requires two or more steps, as shown in the next two examples.

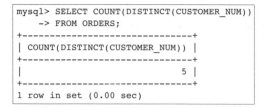

EXAMPLE 21

List the number of each part in class AP.

The command to obtain the answer is shown in Figure 4-29.

```
mysql> SELECT PART_NUM
    -> FROM PART
    -> WHERE CLASS = 'AP';
+----------+
| PART_NUM |
+----------+
| CD52     |
| DR93     |
| DW11     |
| KL62     |
| KT03     |
+----------+
5 rows in set (0.01 sec)
```

FIGURE 4-29 Selecting all parts in class AP

EXAMPLE 22

List the order numbers that contain an order line for a part in class AP.

Example 22 asks you to find the order numbers in the ORDER_LINE table that correspond to the part numbers in the results of the query used in Example 21. After viewing those results (CD52, DR93, DW11, KL62, and KT03), you can use the command shown in Figure 4-30.

```
mysql> SELECT ORDER_NUM
    -> FROM ORDER_LINE
    -> WHERE PART_NUM IN ('CD52','DR93','DW11','KL62','KT03');
+-----------+
| ORDER_NUM |
+-----------+
| 21610     |
| 21610     |
| 21613     |
| 21614     |
| 21617     |
| 21619     |
+-----------+
6 rows in set (0.10 sec)
```

Query results from Figure 4-29

FIGURE 4-30   Query using the results from Figure 4-29

Subqueries

It is possible to place one query inside another. The inner query is called a **subquery**. The subquery is evaluated first. After the subquery has been evaluated, the outer query can use the results of the subquery to find its results, as shown in Example 23.

EXAMPLE 23

Find the answer to Examples 21 and 22 in one step.

You can find the same result as in the previous two examples in a single step by using a subquery. In Figure 4-31, the command shown in parentheses is the subquery. This subquery is evaluated first, producing a temporary table. The temporary table is used only to evaluate the query—it is not available to the user or displayed—and it is deleted after the evaluation of the query is complete. In this example, the temporary table has only a single column (PART_NUM) and five rows (CD52, DR93, DW11, KL62, and KT03). The outer query is evaluated next. In this case, the outer query retrieves the order number on every row in the ORDER_LINE table for which the part number is in the results of the subquery. Because that table contains only the part numbers in class AP, the results display the desired list of order numbers.

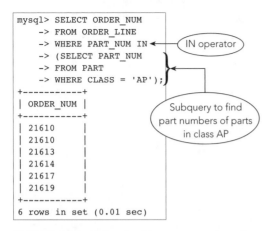

```
mysql> SELECT ORDER_NUM
    -> FROM ORDER_LINE
    -> WHERE PART_NUM IN
    -> (SELECT PART_NUM
    -> FROM PART
    -> WHERE CLASS = 'AP');
+-----------+
| ORDER_NUM |
+-----------+
| 21610     |
| 21610     |
| 21613     |
| 21614     |
| 21617     |
| 21619     |
+-----------+
6 rows in set (0.01 sec)
```

IN operator

Subquery to find part numbers of parts in class AP

FIGURE 4-31   Using the IN operator and a subquery

Figure 4-31 shows duplicate order numbers in the results. To eliminate this duplication, you can use the DISTINCT operator as follows:

```
SELECT DISTINCT(ORDER_NUM)
FROM ORDER_LINE
WHERE PART_NUM IN
(SELECT PART_NUM
FROM PART
WHERE CLASS = 'AP');
```

In this query, each order number appears once.

E X A M P L E   2 4

List the number, name, and balance for each customer whose balance exceeds the average balance of all customers.

In this case, you use a subquery to obtain the average balance. Because this subquery produces a single number, you can compare each customer's balance with this number, as shown in Figure 4-32.

```
mysql> SELECT CUSTOMER_NUM, CUSTOMER_NAME, BALANCE
    -> FROM CUSTOMER
    -> WHERE BALANCE >
    -> (SELECT AVG(BALANCE)
    -> FROM CUSTOMER);
+--------------+---------------------------+----------+
| CUSTOMER_NUM | CUSTOMER_NAME             | BALANCE  |
+--------------+---------------------------+----------+
| 148          | Al's Appliance and Sport  |  6550.00 |
| 356          | Ferguson's                |  5785.00 |
| 408          | The Everything Shop       |  5285.25 |
| 524          | Kline's                   | 12762.00 |
| 842          | All Season                |  8221.00 |
+--------------+---------------------------+----------+
5 rows in set (0.00 sec)
```

FIGURE 4-32   Query using an operator and a subquery

NOTE

You cannot use the condition BALANCE > AVG(BALANCE) in the WHERE clause; you must use a subquery to obtain the average balance. Then you can use the results of the subquery in a condition, as illustrated in Figure 4-32.

GROUPING

Grouping creates groups of rows that share some common characteristic. If you group by credit limit, for example, the first group contains customers with $5,000 credit limits, the second group contains customers with $7,500 credit limits, and so on. If, on the other hand, you group customers by sales rep number, the first group contains those customers represented by sales rep number 20, the second group contains those customers represented by sales rep number 35, and the third group contains those customers represented by sales rep number 65.

When you group rows, any calculations indicated in the SELECT command are performed for the entire group. For example, if you group customers by rep number and the query requests the average balance, the results include the average balance for the group of customers represented by rep number 20, the average balance for the group represented by rep number 35, and the average balance for the group represented by rep number 65. The following examples illustrate this process.

Using the GROUP BY Clause

The **GROUP BY clause** lets you group data on a particular column, such as REP_NUM, and then calculate statistics, if desired, as shown in Example 25.

EXAMPLE 25

For each sales rep, list the rep number and the average balance of the rep's customers.

Because you need to group customers by rep number and then calculate the average balance for all customers in each group, you must use the GROUP BY clause. In this case, GROUP BY REP_NUM puts customers with the same rep number into a separate group. Any statistics indicated in the SELECT command are calculated for each group. It is important to note that the GROUP BY clause does not sort the data in a particular order; you must use the ORDER BY clause to sort data. Assuming that the report should be ordered by rep number, you can use the command shown in Figure 4-33.

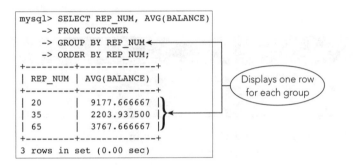

FIGURE 4-33 Grouping records on a column

When rows are grouped, one line of output is produced for each group. The only things that can be displayed are statistics calculated for the group or columns whose values are the same for all rows in a group.

Q & A

Question: Is it appropriate to display the rep number in the query for Example 25?
Answer: Yes, because the rep number in one row in a group must be the same as the rep number in any other row in the group.

Q & A

Question: Would it be appropriate to display a customer number in the query for Example 25?

Answer: No, because the customer number varies on the rows in a group. (The same rep is associated with many customers.) MySQL would not be able to determine which customer number to display for the group. The system displays an error message if you attempt to display a customer number.

Using a HAVING Clause

The HAVING clause is used to restrict the groups that are included, as shown in Example 26.

EXAMPLE 26

Repeat the previous example, but list only those reps who represent fewer than four customers.

The only difference between Examples 25 and 26 is the restriction to display only those reps who represent fewer than four customers. This restriction does not apply to individual rows but rather to *groups*. Because the WHERE clause applies only to rows, you cannot use it to accomplish the kind of selection that is required. Fortunately, the HAVING clause does for groups what the WHERE clause does for rows. The **HAVING clause** limits the groups that are included in the results. In Figure 4-34, the row created for a group is displayed only if the count of the number of rows in the group is less than 4; in addition, all groups are ordered by rep number.

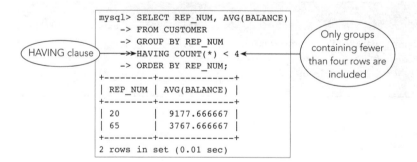

```
mysql> SELECT REP_NUM, AVG(BALANCE)
    -> FROM CUSTOMER
    -> GROUP BY REP_NUM
    ->HAVING COUNT(*) < 4
    -> ORDER BY REP_NUM;
+---------+--------------+
| REP_NUM | AVG(BALANCE) |
+---------+--------------+
| 20      | 9177.666667  |
| 65      | 3767.666667  |
+---------+--------------+
2 rows in set (0.01 sec)
```

HAVING clause

Only groups containing fewer than four rows are included

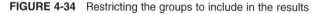

FIGURE 4-34 Restricting the groups to include in the results

HAVING vs. WHERE

Just as you can use the WHERE clause to limit the *rows* that are included in a query's result, you can use the HAVING clause to limit the *groups* that are included. The following examples illustrate the difference between these two clauses.

EXAMPLE 27

List each credit limit and the number of customers having each credit limit.

To count the number of customers that have a given credit limit, you must group the data by credit limit, as shown in Figure 4-35.

```
mysql> SELECT CREDIT_LIMIT, COUNT(*)
    -> FROM CUSTOMER
    -> GROUP BY CREDIT_LIMIT;
+--------------+----------+
| CREDIT_LIMIT | COUNT(*) |
+--------------+----------+
|      5000.00 |        2 |
|      7500.00 |        4 |
|     10000.00 |        3 |
|     15000.00 |        1 |
+--------------+----------+
4 rows in set (0.01 sec)
```

FIGURE 4-35 Counting the number of rows in each group

EXAMPLE 28

Repeat Example 27, but list only those credit limits held by more than one customer.

Because this condition involves a group total, the query includes a HAVING clause, as shown in Figure 4-36.

```
mysql> SELECT CREDIT_LIMIT, COUNT(*)
    -> FROM CUSTOMER
    -> GROUP BY CREDIT_LIMIT
    -> HAVING COUNT(*) > 1;
+--------------+----------+
| CREDIT_LIMIT | COUNT(*) |
+--------------+----------+
|      5000.00 |        2 |
|      7500.00 |        4 |
|     10000.00 |        3 |
+--------------+----------+
3 rows in set (0.00 sec)
```

FIGURE 4-36 Displaying groups that contain more than one row

EXAMPLE 29

List each credit limit and the number of customers of sales rep 20 that have this limit.

The condition involves only rows, so using the WHERE clause is appropriate, as shown in Figure 4-37.

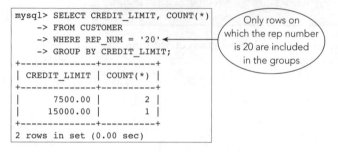

FIGURE 4-37 Restricting the rows to be grouped

EXAMPLE 30

Repeat Example 29, but list only those credit limits held by more than one customer.

Because the conditions involve rows and groups, you must use both a WHERE clause and a HAVING clause, as shown in Figure 4-38.

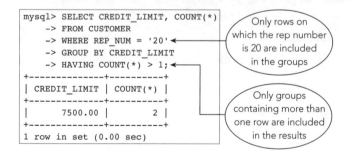

FIGURE 4-38 Restricting the rows and the groups

In Example 30, rows from the original table are considered only if the sales rep number is 20. These rows then are grouped by credit limit and the count is calculated. Only groups for which the calculated count is greater than one are displayed.

NULLS

Sometimes a condition involves a column that can accept null values, as illustrated in Example 31.

EXAMPLE 31

List the number and name of each customer with a null (unknown) street value.

You might expect the condition to be something like STREET = NULL. The correct format actually uses the **IS NULL** operator (STREET IS NULL), as shown in Figure 4-39. (To select a customer whose street is not null, use the **IS NOT NULL** operator (STREET IS NOT NULL).) In the current Premiere Products database, no customer has a null street value; therefore, no rows are retrieved in the query results.

```
mysql> SELECT CUSTOMER_NUM, CUSTOMER_NAME
    -> FROM CUSTOMER
    -> WHERE STREET IS NULL;
Empty set (0.00 sec)
```

FIGURE 4-39   Selecting rows containing null values in the STREET column

SUMMARY OF SQL CLAUSES, FUNCTIONS, AND OPERATORS

In this chapter, you learned how to create queries that retrieve data from a single table by constructing appropriate SELECT commands. In the next chapter, you will learn how to create queries that retrieve data from multiple tables. The queries you created in this chapter used the clauses, functions, and operators shown in Figure 4-40.

Clause, function, or operator	Description
AND operator	Specifies that all simple conditions must be true for the compound condition to be true
AVG function	Calculates the average value in a numeric range
BETWEEN operator	Specifies a range of values in a condition
COUNT function	Counts the number of rows in a table
DESC operator	Sorts the query results in descending order based on the column name
DISTINCT operator	Ensures uniqueness in the condition by eliminating redundant values
FROM clause	Indicates the table from which to retrieve the specified columns
GROUP BY clause	Groups rows based on the specified column
HAVING clause	Limits a condition to the groups that are included
IN clause	Uses the IN operator to find a value in a group of values specified in the condition
IS NOT NULL operator	Finds rows that do not contain a null value in the specified column
IS NULL operator	Finds rows that contain a null value in the specified column
LIKE operator	Indicates a pattern of characters to find in a condition
MAX function	Calculates the maximum value in a numeric range
MIN function	Calculates the minimum value in a numeric range
NOT operator	Reverses the truth or falsity of the original condition
OR operator	Specifies that the compound condition is true whenever any of the simple conditions is true
ORDER BY clause	Lists the query results in the specified order based on the column name
SELECT clause	Specifies the columns to retrieve in the query
SUM function	Totals the values in a numeric range
WHERE clause	Specifies any conditions for the query

FIGURE 4-40 SQL query clauses, functions, and operators

Chapter Summary

The basic form of the SQL SELECT command is SELECT-FROM-WHERE. Specify the columns to be listed after the word SELECT (or type an asterisk (*) to select all columns), and then specify the table name that contains these columns after the word FROM. Optionally, you can include conditions after the word WHERE.

Simple conditions are written in the following form: column name, comparison operator, column name or value. Simple conditions can involve any of the comparison operators: =, >, >=, <, <=, or < > or != (not equal to).

You can form compound conditions by combining simple conditions using the operators AND, OR, and NOT.

Use the BETWEEN operator to indicate a range of values in a condition.

Use computed columns in SQL commands by using arithmetic operators and writing the computation in place of a column name. You can assign a name to the computation by following the computation with the word AS and then the desired name.

To check for a value in a character column that is similar to a particular string of characters, use the LIKE operator. The percent (%) wildcard represents any collection of characters. The underscore (_) wildcard represents any single character.

To determine whether a column contains a value in a set of values, use the IN operator.

Use an ORDER BY clause to sort data. List sort keys in order of importance. To sort in descending order, follow the sort key with the DESC operator.

MySQL processes the aggregate functions COUNT, SUM, AVG, MAX, and MIN. These calculations apply to groups of rows.

To avoid duplicates in a query that uses an aggregate function, precede the column name with the DISTINCT operator.

When one SQL query is placed inside another, it is called a subquery. The inner query (the subquery) is evaluated first.

Use a GROUP BY clause to group data.

Use a HAVING clause to restrict the output to certain groups.

Use the IS NULL operator in a WHERE clause to find rows containing a null value in a particular column. Use the IS NOT NULL operator in a WHERE clause to find rows that do not contain a null value.

Key Terms

aggregate function	DESC
AND	DISTINCT
AVG	FROM clause
BETWEEN	GROUP BY clause
compound condition	grouping
computed column	HAVING clause
COUNT	IN

IN clause

IS NOT NULL

IS NULL

key

LIKE

major sort key

MAX

MIN

minor sort key

NOT

OR

ORDER BY clause

primary sort key

query

secondary sort key

SELECT clause

simple condition

sort key

subquery

SUM

WHERE clause

Review Questions

1. Describe the basic form of the SQL SELECT command.

2. What is the form of a simple condition?

3. How do you form a compound condition?

4. In MySQL, what operator do you use to determine whether a value is between two other values without using an AND condition?

5. How do you use a computed column in MySQL? How do you name the computation?

6. In which clause would you use a wildcard in a condition?

7. What wildcards are available in MySQL, and what do they represent?

8. How do you determine whether a column contains one of a particular set of values without using AND in the condition?

9. How do you sort data?

10. How do you sort data on more than one sort key? What is the more important key called? What is the less important key called?

11. How do you sort data in descending order?

12. What are the SQL aggregate functions?

13. How do you avoid duplicate values in the result of a MySQL query?

14. What is a subquery?

15. How do you group data in a MySQL query?

16. When grouping, how do you restrict the output to only those groups satisfying some condition?

17. How do you find rows in which a particular column contains a null value?

Exercises

Premiere Products

Use MySQL and the Premiere Products database (see Figure 1-2 in Chapter 1) to complete the following exercises. Use the notes at the end of Chapter 3 to print your output if directed to do so by your instructor.

1. List the part number, description, and price for all parts.
2. List all rows and columns for the complete ORDERS table.
3. List the names of customers with credit limits of $7,500 or less.
4. List the order number for each order placed by customer number 148 on 10/20/2007. (*Hint:* If you need help, use the discussion of the DATE data type in Figure 3-11 in Chapter 3.)
5. List the number and name of each customer represented by sales rep 35 or sales rep 65.
6. List the part number and part description of each part that is not in item class SG.
7. List the part number, description, and number of units on hand for each part that has between 10 and 25 units on hand, including both 10 and 25. Do this two ways.
8. List the part number, part description, and on-hand value (units on hand * unit price) of each part in item class AP. (On-hand value is really units on hand * cost, but there is no COST column in the PART table.) Assign the name ON_HAND_VALUE to the computation.
9. List the part number, part description, and on-hand value for each part whose on-hand value is at least $7,500. Assign the name ON_HAND_VALUE to the computation.
10. Use the IN operator to list the part number and part description of each part in item class AP or SG.
11. Find the number and name of each customer whose name begins with the letter "K."
12. List all details about all parts. Order the output by part description.
13. List all details about all parts. Order the output by part number within item class. (That is, order the output by item class and then by part number.)
14. How many customers have balances that are more than their credit limits?
15. Find the total of the balances for all customers represented by sales rep 65 with balances that are less than their credit limits.
16. List the part number, part description, and on-hand value of each part whose number of units on hand is more than the average number of units on hand for all parts. (*Hint:* Use a subquery.)
17. What is the price of the most expensive part in the database?
18. What is the part number, description, and price of the most expensive part in the database? (*Hint:* Use a subquery.)
19. List the sum of the balances of all customers for each sales rep. Order and group the results by sales rep number.
20. List the sum of the balances of all customers for each sales rep, but restrict the output to those sales reps for which the sum is more than $10,000.
21. List the part number of any part with an unknown description.

Single-Table Queries

Henry Books

Use MySQL and the Henry Books database (Figures 1-4 through 1-7 in Chapter 1) to complete the following exercises. Use the notes at the end of Chapter 3 to print your output if directed to do so by your instructor.

1. List the book code and book title of each book.

2. List the complete PUBLISHER table.

3. List the name of each publisher located in Boston.

4. List the name of each publisher not located in Boston.

5. List the name of each branch that has at least nine employees.

6. List the book code and book title of each book that has the type SFI.

7. List the book code and book title of each book that has the type SFI and is in paperback.

8. List the book code and book title of each book that has the type SFI or is published by the publisher with the publisher code SC.

9. List the book code, book title, and price of each book with a price between $20 and $30.

10. List the book code and book title of each book that has the type MYS and a price of less than $20.

11. Customers who are part of a special program get a 10% discount off regular book prices. List the book code, book title, and discounted price of each book. Use DISCOUNTED_PRICE as the name for the computed column, which should calculate 90% of the current price; that is, 100% less a 10% discount.

12. Find the name of each publisher containing the word "and." (*Hint:* Be sure that your query selects only those publishers that contain the word "and" and not those that contain the letters "and" in the middle of a word. For example, your query should select the publisher named "Farrar Straus and Giroux," but should *not* select the publisher named "Random House.")

13. List the book code and book title of each book that has the type SFI, MYS, or ART. Use the IN operator in your command.

14. Repeat Exercise 13, but also list the books in alphabetical order by title.

15. Repeat Exercise 13, but also include the price, and list the books in descending order by price. Within a group of books having the same price, further order the books by title.

16. Display the list of book types in the database. List each book type only once.

17. How many books have the type SFI?

18. For each type of book, list the type and the average price.

19. Repeat Exercise 18, but consider only paperback books.

20. Repeat Exercise 18, but consider only paperback books for those types for which the average price is more than $10.

21. What is the most expensive book in the database?

22. What are the title(s) and price(s) of the least expensive book(s) in the database?

23. How many employees does Henry Books have?

Alexamara Marina Group

Use MySQL and the Alexamara Marina Group database (Figures 1-8 through 1-12 in Chapter 1) to complete the following exercises. Use the notes at the end of Chapter 3 to print your output if directed to do so by your instructor.

1. List the owner number, last name, and first name of every boat owner.
2. List the complete MARINA table (all rows and all columns).
3. List the last name and first name of every owner located in Bowton.
4. List the last name and first name of every owner not located in Bowton.
5. List the marina number and slip number for every slip whose length is equal to or less than 30 feet.
6. List the marina number and slip number for every boat with the type Dolphin 28.
7. List the slip number for every boat with the type Dolphin 28 that is located in marina 1.
8. List the boat name for each boat located in a slip whose length is between 25 and 30 feet.
9. List the slip number for every slip in marina 1 whose rental fee is less than $3,000.
10. Labor is billed at the rate of $60 per hour. List the slip ID, category number, estimated hours, and estimated labor cost for every service request. To obtain the estimated labor cost, multiply the estimated hours by 60. Use the column name ESTIMATED_COST for the estimated labor cost.
11. List the marina number and slip number for all slips containing a boat with the type Sprite 4000, Sprite 3000, or Ray 4025.
12. List the marina number, slip number, and boat name for all boats. Sort the results by boat name within marina number.
13. How many Dolphin 28 boats are stored at both marinas?
14. Calculate the total rental fees Alexamara receives each year based on the length of the slip.

CHAPTER **5**

MULTIPLE-TABLE QUERIES

LEARNING OBJECTIVES

Objectives

- Use joins to retrieve data from more than one table
- Use the IN and EXISTS operators to query multiple tables
- Use a subquery within a subquery
- Use an alias
- Join a table to itself
- Perform set operations (union, intersection, and difference)
- Use the ALL and ANY operators in a query
- Perform special operations (inner join, outer join, and product)

INTRODUCTION

In this chapter, you will learn how to use MySQL to retrieve data from two or more tables using one SQL command. You will join tables together and examine how similar results are obtained using the SQL IN and EXISTS operators. Then you will use aliases to simplify queries and join a table to itself. You also will implement the set operations of union, intersection, and difference using SQL commands. You will examine two related SQL operators: ALL and ANY. Finally, you will perform inner joins, outer joins, and products.

QUERYING MULTIPLE TABLES

In Chapter 4, you learned how to retrieve data from a single table. Many queries require you to retrieve data from two or more tables. To retrieve data from multiple tables, you first must join the tables, and then formulate a query using the same commands that you use for single-table queries.

NOTE

In the following queries, your results might contain the same rows, but they might be listed in a different order. If order is important, you can include an ORDER BY clause in the query to ensure that the results are listed in the desired order.

Joining Two Tables

To retrieve data from more than one table, you must **join** the tables together by finding rows in the two tables that have identical values in matching columns. You can join tables by using a condition in the WHERE clause, as you will see in Example 1.

EXAMPLE 1

List the number and name of each customer, together with the number, last name, and first name of the sales rep who represents the customer.

Because the customer numbers and names are in the CUSTOMER table and the sales rep numbers and names are in the REP table, you need to include both tables in the same SQL command so you can retrieve data from both tables. To join (relate) the tables, you construct the SQL command as follows:

1. In the SELECT clause, list all columns you want to display.
2. In the FROM clause, list all tables involved in the query.
3. In the WHERE clause, list the condition that restricts the data to be retrieved to only those rows from the two tables that match; that is, restrict it to the rows that have common values in matching columns.

As you learned in Chapter 2, it is often necessary to qualify a column to specify the particular column you are referencing. Qualifying column names is especially important when joining tables because you must join tables on *matching* columns that frequently have identical column names. To qualify a column name, precede the name of the column with the name of the table, followed by a period. The matching columns in this example are both named REP_NUM—there is a column in the REP table named REP_NUM and a column in the CUSTOMER table that also is named REP_NUM. The REP_NUM column in the REP table is written as REP.REP_NUM and the REP_NUM column in the CUSTOMER table is written as CUSTOMER.REP_NUM. The query and its results appear in Figure 5-1.

```
mysql> SELECT CUSTOMER_NUM, CUSTOMER_NAME, REP.REP_NUM, LAST_NAME, FIRST_NAME
    -> FROM CUSTOMER, REP
    -> WHERE CUSTOMER.REP_NUM = REP.REP_NUM;
+--------------+--------------------------+---------+-----------+------------+
| CUSTOMER_NUM | CUSTOMER_NAME            | REP_NUM | LAST_NAME | FIRST_NAME |
+--------------+--------------------------+---------+-----------+------------+
| 148          | Al's Appliance and Sport | 20      | Kaiser    | Valerie    |
| 524          | Kline's                  | 20      | Kaiser    | Valerie    |
| 842          | All Season               | 20      | Kaiser    | Valerie    |
| 282          | Brookings Direct         | 35      | Hull      | Richard    |
| 408          | The Everything Shop      | 35      | Hull      | Richard    |
| 687          | Lee's Sport and Appliance | 35     | Hull      | Richard    |
| 725          | Deerfield's Four Seasons | 35      | Hull      | Richard    |
| 356          | Ferguson's               | 65      | Perez     | Juan       |
| 462          | Bargains Galore          | 65      | Perez     | Juan       |
| 608          | Johnson's Department Store | 65    | Perez     | Juan       |
+--------------+--------------------------+---------+-----------+------------+
10 rows in set (0.00 sec)
```

Tables to include

Condition to relate the tables

Columns to include

Results (your order might be different)

FIGURE 5-1 Joining two tables with a single SQL command

When there is potential ambiguity in listing column names, you *must* qualify the columns involved in the query. It is permissible to qualify other columns as well, even if there is no possible confusion. Some people prefer to qualify all column names; in this text, however, you will qualify column names only when it is necessary.

Q & A

Question: In the first row of output in Figure 5-1, the customer number is 148, and the customer name is Al's Appliance and Sport. These values represent the first row of the CUSTOMER table. Why is the sales rep number 20, the last name of the sales rep Kaiser, and the first name Valerie?

Answer: In the CUSTOMER table, the sales rep number for customer number 148 is 20. (This indicates that customer number 148 is *related* to sales rep number 20.) In the REP table, the last name of sales rep number 20 is Kaiser and the first name is Valerie.

EXAMPLE 2

List the number and name of each customer whose credit limit is $7,500, together with the number, last name, and first name of the sales rep who represents the customer.

In Example 1, you used a condition in the WHERE clause only to relate a customer with a sales rep to join the tables. Although relating a customer with a sales rep is essential in this example as well, you also need to restrict the output to only those customers whose credit limits are $7,500. You can restrict the rows by using a compound condition, as shown in Figure 5-2.

```
mysql> SELECT CUSTOMER_NUM, CUSTOMER_NAME, REP.REP_NUM, LAST_NAME, FIRST_NAME
    -> FROM CUSTOMER, REP
    -> WHERE CUSTOMER.REP_NUM = REP.REP_NUM
    -> AND CREDIT_LIMIT = 7500;
+--------------+--------------------------+---------+-----------+------------+
| CUSTOMER_NUM | CUSTOMER_NAME            | REP_NUM | LAST_NAME | FIRST_NAME |
+--------------+--------------------------+---------+-----------+------------+
| 148          | Al's Appliance and Sport | 20      | Kaiser    | Valerie    |
| 842          | All Season               | 20      | Kaiser    | Valerie    |
| 725          | Deerfield's Four Seasons | 35      | Hull      | Richard    |
| 356          | Ferguson's               | 65      | Perez     | Juan       |
+--------------+--------------------------+---------+-----------+------------+
4 rows in set (0.00 sec)
```

Condition to relate the tables

Condition to restrict the rows to customers with credit limits of $7,500

FIGURE 5-2   Restricting the rows in a join

EXAMPLE 3

For every part on order, list the order number, part number, part description, number of units ordered, quoted price, and unit price.

A part is considered "on order" if there is a row in the ORDER_LINE table in which the part appears. You can find the order number, number of units ordered, and quoted price in the ORDER_LINE table. To find the part description and the unit price, however, you need to look in the PART table. Then you need to find rows in the ORDER_LINE table and rows in the PART table that match (rows containing the same part number). The query and its results appear in Figure 5-3.

```
mysql> SELECT ORDER_NUM, ORDER_LINE.PART_NUM, DESCRIPTION, NUM_ORDERED,
    -> QUOTED_PRICE, PRICE
    -> FROM ORDER_LINE, PART
    -> WHERE ORDER_LINE.PART_NUM = PART.PART_NUM;
+-----------+----------+----------------+-------------+--------------+---------+
| ORDER_NUM | PART_NUM | DESCRIPTION    | NUM_ORDERED | QUOTED_PRICE | PRICE   |
+-----------+----------+----------------+-------------+--------------+---------+
| 21608     | AT94     | Iron           | 11          | 21.95        | 24.95   |
| 21610     | DR93     | Gas Range      | 1           | 495.00       | 495.00  |
| 21610     | DW11     | Washer         | 1           | 399.99       | 399.99  |
| 21613     | KL62     | Dryer          | 4           | 329.95       | 349.95  |
| 21614     | KT03     | Dishwasher     | 2           | 595.00       | 595.00  |
| 21617     | BV06     | Home Gym       | 2           | 794.95       | 794.95  |
| 21617     | CD52     | Microwave Oven | 4           | 150.00       | 165.00  |
| 21619     | DR93     | Gas Range      | 1           | 495.00       | 495.00  |
| 21623     | KV29     | Treadmill      | 2           | 1290.00      | 1390.00 |
+-----------+----------+----------------+-------------+--------------+---------+
9 rows in set (0.00 sec)
```

FIGURE 5-3   Joining the ORDER_LINE and PART tables

COMPARING JOIN, IN, AND EXISTS

You join tables in SQL by including a condition in the WHERE clause to ensure that matching columns contain equal values (for example, ORDER_LINE.PART_NUM = PART.PART_NUM). You can obtain similar results by using either the IN operator (described in Chapter 4) or the EXISTS operator with a subquery. The choice is a matter of personal preference, as either approach obtains the same results. The following examples illustrate the use of each operator.

EXAMPLE 4

Find the description of each part included in order number 21610.

Because this query also involves retrieving data from the ORDER_LINE and PART tables as illustrated in Example 3, you could approach it in a similar fashion. There are two basic differences, however, between Examples 3 and 4. First, the query in Example 4 does not require as many columns; second, it involves only order number 21610. Having fewer columns to retrieve means that there will be fewer columns listed in the SELECT clause. You can restrict the query to a single order by adding the condition ORDER_NUM = '21610' to the WHERE clause. The query and its results appear in Figure 5-4.

```
mysql> SELECT DESCRIPTION
    -> FROM ORDER_LINE, PART
    -> WHERE ORDER_LINE.PART_NUM = PART.PART_NUM
    -> AND ORDER_NUM = '21610';
+-------------+
| DESCRIPTION |
+-------------+
| Gas Range   |
| Washer      |
+-------------+
2 rows in set (0.00 sec)
```

FIGURE 5-4   Restricting the rows when joining the ORDER_LINE and PART tables

Notice that the ORDER_LINE table is listed in the FROM clause, even though you do not need to display any columns from the ORDER_LINE table. The WHERE clause contains columns from the ORDER_LINE table, so it is necessary to include the table in the FROM clause.

Using the IN Operator

Another way to retrieve data from multiple tables in a query is to use the IN operator with a subquery. In Example 4 on the previous page, you first could use a subquery to find all part numbers in the ORDER_LINE table that appear in any row on which the order number is 21610. Then you could find the part description for any part whose part number is in this list. The query and its results appear in Figure 5-5.

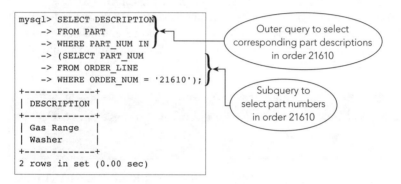

FIGURE 5-5   Using the IN operator instead of a join to query two tables

In Figure 5-5, evaluating the subquery produces a temporary table consisting of those part numbers (DR93 and DW11) that are present in order number 21610. Executing the remaining portion of the query produces part descriptions for each part whose number is in this temporary table; in this case, Gas Range (DR93) and Washer (DW11).

Using the EXISTS Operator

You also can use the EXISTS operator to retrieve data from more than one table, as shown in Example 5. The **EXISTS** operator checks for the existence of rows that satisfy some criterion.

EXAMPLE 5

Find the order number and order date for each order that contains part number DR93.

This query is similar to the one in Example 4, but this time the query involves the ORDERS table and not the PART table. In this case, you can write the query in either of the ways previously demonstrated. For example, you could use the IN operator with a subquery, as shown in Figure 5-6.

```
mysql> SELECT ORDER_NUM, ORDER_DATE
    -> FROM ORDERS
    -> WHERE ORDER_NUM IN
    -> (SELECT ORDER_NUM
    -> FROM ORDER_LINE
    -> WHERE PART_NUM = 'DR93');
+-----------+------------+
| ORDER_NUM | ORDER_DATE |
+-----------+------------+
| 21610     | 2007-10-20 |
| 21619     | 2007-10-23 |
+-----------+------------+
2 rows in set (0.00 sec)
```

FIGURE 5-6   Using the IN operator to select order information

Using the EXISTS operator provides another approach to solving Example 5, as shown in Figure 5-7.

```
mysql> SELECT ORDER_NUM, ORDER_DATE
    -> FROM ORDERS
    -> WHERE EXISTS
    -> (SELECT *
    -> FROM ORDER_LINE
    -> WHERE ORDERS.ORDER_NUM = ORDER_LINE.ORDER_NUM
    -> AND PART_NUM = 'DR93');
+-----------+------------+
| ORDER_NUM | ORDER_DATE |
+-----------+------------+
| 21610     | 2007-10-20 |
| 21619     | 2007-10-23 |
+-----------+------------+
2 rows in set (0.01 sec)
```

FIGURE 5-7   Using the EXISTS operator to select order information

The subquery in Figure 5-7 is the first one you have seen that involves a table listed in the outer query. This type of subquery is called a **correlated subquery**. In this case, the ORDERS table, which is listed in the FROM clause of the outer query, is used in the subquery. For this reason, you need to qualify the ORDER_NUM column in the subquery (ORDERS.ORDER_NUM). You did not need to qualify the columns in the previous queries involving the IN operator.

The query shown in Figure 5-7 works as follows. For each row in the ORDERS table, the subquery is executed using the value of ORDERS.ORDER_NUM that occurs in that row. The inner query produces a list of all rows in the ORDER_LINE table in which ORDER_LINE.ORDER_NUM matches this value and in which PART_NUM is equal to DR93. You can precede a subquery with the EXISTS operator to create a condition that is true if one or more rows are obtained when the subquery is executed; otherwise, the condition is false.

To illustrate the process, consider order numbers 21610 and 21613 in the ORDERS table. Order number 21610 is included because a row exists in the ORDER_LINE table with this order number and part number DR93. When the subquery is executed, there will be at least one row in the results, which in turn makes the EXISTS condition true. Order number 21613, however, will not be included because no row exists in the ORDER_LINE table with this order number and part number DR93. There will be no rows contained in the results of the subquery, which in turn makes the EXISTS condition false.

Using a Subquery Within a Subquery

You can use MySQL to create a **nested subquery** (a subquery within a subquery), as illustrated in Example 6.

EXAMPLE 6

Find the order number and order date for each order that includes a part located in warehouse 3.

One way to approach this problem is first to determine the list of part numbers in the PART table for each part located in warehouse 3. Then you obtain a list of order numbers in the ORDER_LINE table with a corresponding part number in the part number list. Finally, you retrieve those order numbers and order dates in the ORDERS table for which the order number is in the list of order numbers obtained during the second step. The query and its results appear in Figure 5-8.

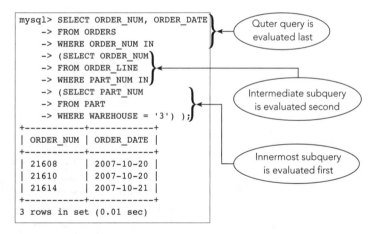

FIGURE 5-8   Nested subqueries (a subquery within a subquery)

As you might expect, MySQL evaluates the queries from the innermost query to the outermost query. The query in this example is evaluated in three steps:

1. The innermost subquery is evaluated first, producing a temporary table of part numbers for those parts located in warehouse 3.
2. The next (intermediate) subquery is evaluated, producing a second temporary table with a list of order numbers. Each order number in this collection

has a row in the ORDER_LINE table for which the part number is in the temporary table produced in Step 1.

3. The outer query is evaluated last, producing the desired list of order numbers and order dates. Only those orders whose numbers are in the temporary table produced in Step 2 are included in the results.

Another approach to solving Example 6 involves joining the ORDERS, ORDER_LINE, and PART tables. The query and its results appear in Figure 5-9.

```
mysql> SELECT ORDERS.ORDER_NUM, ORDER_DATE
    -> FROM ORDER_LINE, ORDERS, PART
    -> WHERE ORDER_LINE.ORDER_NUM = ORDERS.ORDER_NUM
    -> AND ORDER_LINE.PART_NUM = PART.PART_NUM
    -> AND WAREHOUSE = '3';
+-----------+------------+
| ORDER_NUM | ORDER_DATE |
+-----------+------------+
| 21608     | 2007-10-20 |
| 21610     | 2007-10-20 |
| 21614     | 2007-10-21 |
+-----------+------------+
3 rows in set (0.00 sec)
```

FIGURE 5-9   Joining three tables

In this query, the following conditions join the tables:

```
ORDER_LINE.ORDER_NUM = ORDERS.ORDER_NUM
ORDER_LINE.PART_NUM = PART.PART_NUM
```

The condition WAREHOUSE = '3' restricts the output to only those parts located in warehouse 3.

The query results are correct regardless of which formulation you use. You can use whichever approach you prefer.

You might wonder whether one approach is more efficient than the other. MySQL performs many built-in optimizations that analyze queries to determine the best way to satisfy them. Given a good optimizer, it should not make any difference how you formulate the query. If you are using a DBMS without an optimizer, however, the formulation of a query *can* make a difference in the speed with which the query is executed. If you are working with a very large database and efficiency is a prime concern, consult the DBMS's manual or try some timings yourself. Try running the same query both ways to see whether you notice a difference in the speed of execution. In small databases, there should not be a significant time difference between the two approaches.

NOTE

You can use the IN and EXISTS operators with subqueries in MySQL versions 4.1 and higher. It is not possible to create subqueries in earlier versions of MySQL.

A Comprehensive Example

The query used in Example 7 involves several of the features already presented. The query illustrates all the major clauses that you can use in a SELECT command. It also illustrates the order in which these clauses must appear.

EXAMPLE 7

List the customer number, order number, order date, and order total for each order with a total that exceeds $1,000. Rename the order total as ORDER_TOTAL.

The query and its results appear in Figure 5-10.

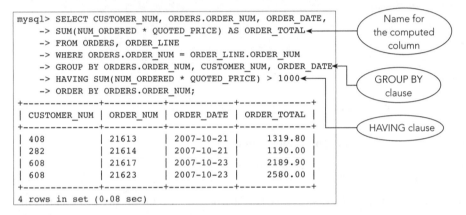

FIGURE 5-10   Comprehensive example

In this query, the ORDERS and ORDER_LINE tables are joined by listing both tables in the FROM clause and relating them in the WHERE clause. Selected data is sorted by order number using the ORDER BY clause. The GROUP BY clause indicates that the data is to be grouped by order number, customer number, and order date. For each group, the SELECT clause displays the customer number, order number, order date, and order total (SUM(NUM_ORDERED * QUOTED_PRICE)). In addition, the total was renamed ORDER_TOTAL. Not all groups will be displayed, however. The HAVING clause displays only those groups whose SUM(NUM_ORDERED * QUOTED_PRICE) is greater than $1,000.

The order number, customer number, and order date are unique for each order. Thus, it would seem that merely grouping by order number would be sufficient. MySQL requires that both the customer number and the order date be listed in the GROUP BY clause. Recall that a SELECT clause can include statistics calculated for only the groups or columns whose values are identical for each row in a group. By stating that the data is to be grouped by order number, customer number, and order date, you tell MySQL that the values in these columns must be the same for each row in a group.

Using an Alias

When tables are listed in the FROM clause, you can give each table an **alias**, or an alternate name, that you can use in the rest of the statement. You create an alias by typing the name of the table, pressing the Spacebar, and then typing the name of the alias. No commas or periods are necessary to separate the two names.

One reason for using an alias is simplicity. In Example 8, you assign the REP table the alias R and the CUSTOMER table the alias C. By doing this, you can type R instead of REP and C instead of CUSTOMER in the remainder of the query. The query in this example is simple, so you might not see the full benefit of this feature. If a query is complex and requires you to qualify the names, using aliases can simplify the process.

EXAMPLE 8

List the number, last name, and first name for each sales rep together with the number and name for each customer the sales rep represents.

The query and its results using aliases appear in Figure 5-11.

```
mysql> SELECT R.REP_NUM, LAST_NAME, FIRST_NAME, C.CUSTOMER_NUM, CUSTOMER_NAME
    -> FROM REP R, CUSTOMER C                    Alias
    -> WHERE R.REP_NUM = C.REP_NUM;
+---------+-----------+------------+--------------+-----------------------------+
| REP_NUM | LAST_NAME | FIRST_NAME | CUSTOMER_NUM | CUSTOMER_NAME               |
+---------+-----------+------------+--------------+-----------------------------+
| 20      | Kaiser    | Valerie    | 148          | Al's Appliance and Sport    |
| 35      | Hull      | Richard    | 282          | Brookings Direct            |
| 65      | Perez     | Juan       | 356          | Ferguson's                  |
| 35      | Hull      | Richard    | 408          | The Everything Shop         |
| 65      | Perez     | Juan       | 462          | Bargains Galore             |
| 20      | Kaiser    | Valerie    | 524          | Kline's                     |
| 65      | Perez     | Juan       | 608          | Johnson's Department Store  |
| 35      | Hull      | Richard    | 687          | Lee's Sport and Appliance   |
| 35      | Hull      | Richard    | 725          | Deerfield's Four Seasons    |
| 20      | Kaiser    | Valerie    | 842          | All Season                  |
+---------+-----------+------------+--------------+-----------------------------+
10 rows in set (0.01 sec)
```

FIGURE 5-11   Using aliases in a query

NOTE

Technically, it is unnecessary to qualify CUSTOMER_NUM because it is included only in the CUSTOMER table. It is qualified in Figure 5-11 for illustration purposes only.

Joining a Table to Itself

A second situation for using an alias is to join a table to itself, called a **self-join**, as illustrated in Example 9.

EXAMPLE 9

For each pair of customers located in the same city, display the customer number, customer name, and city.

If you had two separate tables for customers and the query requested customers in the first table having the same city as customers in the second table, you could use a normal join operation to find the answer. In this case, however, there is only *one* table (CUSTOMER) that stores all the customer information. You can treat the CUSTOMER table as if it were two tables in the query by creating an alias, as illustrated in Example 8 on the previous page. In this case, you use the following FROM clause:

```
FROM CUSTOMER F, CUSTOMER S
```

MySQL treats this clause as a query of two tables: one that has the alias F (first), and another that has the alias S (second). The fact that both tables are really the same CUSTOMER table is not a problem. The query and its results appear in Figure 5-12.

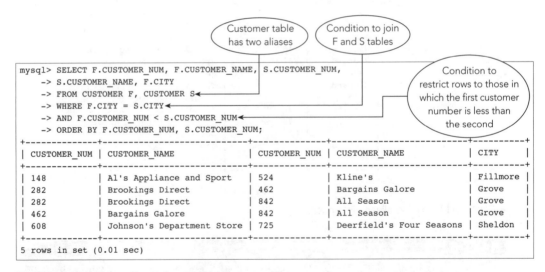

FIGURE 5-12   Using aliases for a self-join

You are requesting a customer number and name from the F table, followed by a customer number and name from the S table, and then the city. (Because the city in the first table must match the city in the second table, you can select the city from either table.) The WHERE clause contains two conditions: the cities must match, and the customer number from the first table must be less than the customer number from the second table. In addition, the ORDER BY clause ensures that the data is sorted by the first customer number. For those rows with the same first customer number, the data is further sorted by the second customer number.

Q & A

Question: Why is the condition F.CUSTOMER_NUM < S.CUSTOMER_NUM important in the query formulation?

Answer: If you did not include this condition, you would get the query results shown in Figure 5-13. The first row is included because it is true that customer number 148 (Al's Appliance and Sport) in the F table has the same city as customer number 148 (Al's Appliance and Sport) in the S table. The second row indicates that customer number 148 (Al's Appliance and Sport) has the same city as customer number 524 (Kline's). The eleventh row, however, repeats the same information because customer number 524 (Kline's) has the same city as customer number 148 (Al's Appliance and Sport). Of these three rows, the only row that should be included in the query results is the second row. The second row also is the only one of the three rows in which the first customer number (148) is less than the second customer number (524). This is why the query requires the condition F.CUSTOMER_NUM < S.CUSTOMER_NUM.

```
mysql> SELECT F.CUSTOMER_NUM, F.CUSTOMER_NAME, S.CUSTOMER_NUM,
    -> S.CUSTOMER_NAME, F.CITY
    -> FROM CUSTOMER F, CUSTOMER S
    -> WHERE F.CITY = S.CITY
    -> ORDER BY F.CUSTOMER_NUM, S.CUSTOMER_NUM;
```

CUSTOMER_NUM	CUSTOMER_NAME	CUSTOMER_NUM	CUSTOMER_NAME	CITY
148	Al's Appliance and Sport	148	Al's Appliance and Sport	Fillmore
148	Al's Appliance and Sport	524	Kline's	Fillmore
282	Brookings Direct	282	Brookings Direct	Grove
282	Brookings Direct	462	Bargains Galore	Grove
282	Brookings Direct	842	All Season	Grove
356	Ferguson's	356	Ferguson's	Northfield
408	The Everything Shop	408	The Everything Shop	Crystal
462	Bargains Galore	282	Brookings Direct	Grove
462	Bargains Galore	462	Bargains Galore	Grove
462	Bargains Galore	842	All Season	Grove
524	Kline's	148	Al's Appliance and Sport	Fillmore
524	Kline's	524	Kline's	Fillmore
608	Johnson's Department Store	608	Johnson's Department Store	Sheldon
608	Johnson's Department Store	725	Deerfield's Four Seasons	Sheldon
687	Lee's Sport and Appliance	687	Lee's Sport and Appliance	Altonville
725	Deerfield's Four Seasons	608	Johnson's Department Store	Sheldon
725	Deerfield's Four Seasons	725	Deerfield's Four Seasons	Sheldon
842	All Season	282	Brookings Direct	Grove
842	All Season	462	Bargains Galore	Grove
842	All Season	842	All Season	Grove

```
20 rows in set (0.00 sec)
```

FIGURE 5-13   Incorrect joining of a table to itself

Using a Self-Join on a Primary Key

Figure 5-14 shows some fields from an EMPLOYEE table whose primary key is EMPLOYEE_NUM. Another field in the table is MGR_EMPLOYEE_NUM, which represents the number of the employee's manager, who also is an employee. If you look at the row for employee 206 (Joan Dykstra), you will see she is managed by employee 198 (Mona Canzler). By looking at the row for employee 198 (Mona Canzler), you see that her manager is employee 108 (Martin Holden). In the row for employee 108 (Martin Holden), the manager number is null, indicating that he has no manager.

```
mysql> SELECT EMPLOYEE_NUM, LAST_NAME, FIRST_NAME, MGR_EMPLOYEE_NUM
    -> FROM EMPLOYEE
    -> ORDER BY EMPLOYEE_NUM;
+--------------+-----------+------------+-------------------+
| EMPLOYEE_NUM | LAST_NAME | FIRST_NAME | MGR_EMPLOYEE_NUM |
+--------------+-----------+------------+-------------------+
|    108       | Holden    | Martin     | NULL              |
|    198       | Canzler   | Mona       | 108               |
|    206       | Dykstra   | Joan       | 198               |
|    255       | Murray    | Steven     | 301               |
|    301       | Galvez    | Benito     | 108               |
|    366       | Peterman  | Beth       | 198               |
|    391       | Traynor   | Matt       | 301               |
|    402       | Brent     | Ashton     | 301               |
|    466       | Scholten  | Alyssa     | 108               |
|    551       | Wiltzer   | Morgan     | 198               |
+--------------+-----------+------------+-------------------+
10 rows in set (0.01 sec)
```

Employee numbers

Employee 108 has no manager

Employee 198 manages employee 206

Number of employee's manager

FIGURE 5-14   Employee and manager data

Suppose you need to list the employee number, employee last name, and employee first name along with the number, last name, and first name of each employee's manager. Just as in the previous self-join, you would list the EMPLOYEE table twice in the FROM clause with aliases.

The command shown in Figure 5-15 uses the letter E as an alias for the employee and M as an alias for the manager. Thus E.EMPLOYEE_NUM is the employee's number and M.EMPLOYEE_NUM is the number for the employee's manager. In the SQL command, M.EMPLOYEE_NUM is renamed as MGR_NUM, M.LAST_NAME is renamed as MGR_LAST, and M.FIRST_NAME is renamed as MGR_FIRST. The condition in the WHERE clause ensures that E.MGR_EMPLOYEE_NUM (the number of the employee's manager) matches M.EMPLOYEE_NUM (the employee number on the manager's row in the table).

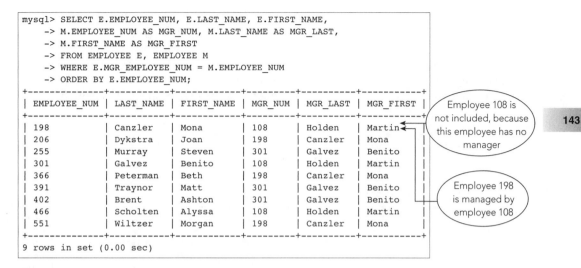

```
mysql> SELECT E.EMPLOYEE_NUM, E.LAST_NAME, E.FIRST_NAME,
    -> M.EMPLOYEE_NUM AS MGR_NUM, M.LAST_NAME AS MGR_LAST,
    -> M.FIRST_NAME AS MGR_FIRST
    -> FROM EMPLOYEE E, EMPLOYEE M
    -> WHERE E.MGR_EMPLOYEE_NUM = M.EMPLOYEE_NUM
    -> ORDER BY E.EMPLOYEE_NUM;
+--------------+-----------+------------+---------+----------+-----------+
| EMPLOYEE_NUM | LAST_NAME | FIRST_NAME | MGR_NUM | MGR_LAST | MGR_FIRST |
+--------------+-----------+------------+---------+----------+-----------+
| 198          | Canzler   | Mona       | 108     | Holden   | Martin    |
| 206          | Dykstra   | Joan       | 198     | Canzler  | Mona      |
| 255          | Murray    | Steven     | 301     | Galvez   | Benito    |
| 301          | Galvez    | Benito     | 108     | Holden   | Martin    |
| 366          | Peterman  | Beth       | 198     | Canzler  | Mona      |
| 391          | Traynor   | Matt       | 301     | Galvez   | Benito    |
| 402          | Brent     | Ashton     | 301     | Galvez   | Benito    |
| 466          | Scholten  | Alyssa     | 108     | Holden   | Martin    |
| 551          | Wiltzer   | Morgan     | 198     | Canzler  | Mona      |
+--------------+-----------+------------+---------+----------+-----------+
9 rows in set (0.00 sec)
```

Employee 108 is not included, because this employee has no manager

143

Employee 198 is managed by employee 108

FIGURE 5-15   Employees and their managers' names

Joining Several Tables

It is possible to join several tables, as illustrated in Example 10. For each pair of tables you join, you must include a condition indicating how the columns are related.

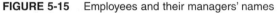

EXAMPLE 10

For each part on order, list the part number, number ordered, order number, order date, customer number, and customer name, along with the last name of the sales rep who represents each customer.

A part is on order if it occurs on any row in the ORDER_LINE table. The part number, number ordered, and order number appear in the ORDER_LINE table. If these requirements represent the entire query, you would write the query as follows:

```
SELECT PART_NUM, NUM_ORDERED, ORDER_NUM
FROM ORDER_LINE;
```

This formulation is not sufficient, however. You also need the order date, which is in the ORDERS table; the customer number and name, which are in the CUSTOMER table; and the rep last name, which is in the REP table. Thus, you need to join *four* tables: ORDER_LINE, ORDERS, CUSTOMER, and REP. The procedure for joining more than two tables is essentially the same as the one for joining two tables. The difference is that the condition in the WHERE clause will be a compound condition. In this case, you would write the WHERE clause as follows:

```
WHERE ORDERS.ORDER_NUM = ORDER_LINE.ORDER_NUM
AND CUSTOMER.CUSTOMER_NUM = ORDERS.CUSTOMER_NUM
AND REP.REP_NUM = CUSTOMER.REP_NUM
```

The first condition relates an order to an order line with a matching order number. The second condition relates the customer to the order with a matching customer number. The final condition relates the rep to a customer with a matching sales rep number.

For the complete query, you list all the desired columns in the SELECT clause and qualify any columns that appear in more than one table. In the FROM clause, you list the tables that are involved in the query. The query and its results appear in Figure 5-16.

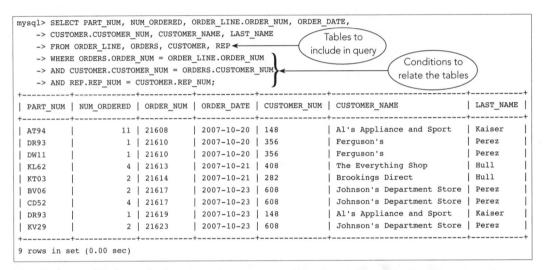

```
mysql> SELECT PART_NUM, NUM_ORDERED, ORDER_LINE.ORDER_NUM, ORDER_DATE,
    -> CUSTOMER.CUSTOMER_NUM, CUSTOMER_NAME, LAST_NAME
    -> FROM ORDER_LINE, ORDERS, CUSTOMER, REP
    -> WHERE ORDERS.ORDER_NUM = ORDER_LINE.ORDER_NUM
    -> AND CUSTOMER.CUSTOMER_NUM = ORDERS.CUSTOMER_NUM
    -> AND REP.REP_NUM = CUSTOMER.REP_NUM;
```

Tables to include in query

Conditions to relate the tables

PART_NUM	NUM_ORDERED	ORDER_NUM	ORDER_DATE	CUSTOMER_NUM	CUSTOMER_NAME	LAST_NAME
AT94	11	21608	2007-10-20	148	Al's Appliance and Sport	Kaiser
DR93	1	21610	2007-10-20	356	Ferguson's	Perez
DW11	1	21610	2007-10-20	356	Ferguson's	Perez
KL62	4	21613	2007-10-21	408	The Everything Shop	Hull
KT03	2	21614	2007-10-21	282	Brookings Direct	Hull
BV06	2	21617	2007-10-23	608	Johnson's Department Store	Perez
CD52	4	21617	2007-10-23	608	Johnson's Department Store	Perez
DR93	1	21619	2007-10-23	148	Al's Appliance and Sport	Kaiser
KV29	2	21623	2007-10-23	608	Johnson's Department Store	Perez

9 rows in set (0.00 sec)

FIGURE 5-16   Joining four tables in a query

Q & A

Question: Why is the PART_NUM column, which appears in the PART and ORDER_LINE tables, not qualified in the SELECT clause?
Answer: Among the tables listed in the query, only one table contains a column named PART_NUM, so it is not necessary to qualify the table. If the PART table also appeared in the FROM clause, you would need to qualify PART_NUM to avoid confusion between the PART_NUM columns in the PART and ORDER_LINE tables.

The query shown in Figure 5-16 is more complex than many of the previous ones you have examined. You might think that SQL is not such an easy language to use after all. If you take it one step at a time, however, the query in Example 10 really is not that difficult. To construct a detailed query in a step-by-step fashion, do the following:

1. List in the SELECT clause all the columns that you want to display. If the name of a column appears in more than one table, precede the column name with the table name (that is, qualify the column name).
2. List in the FROM clause all the tables involved in the query. Usually you include the tables that contain the columns listed in the SELECT clause. Occasionally, however, there might be a table that does not contain any columns used

in the SELECT clause but that does contain columns used in the WHERE clause. In this case, you also must list the table in the FROM clause. For example, if you do not need to list a customer number or name, but you do need to list the rep name, you would not include any columns from the CUSTOMER table in the SELECT clause. The CUSTOMER table still is required, however, because you must include a column from it in the WHERE clause.

3. Take one pair of related tables at a time and indicate in the WHERE clause the condition that relates the tables. Join these conditions with the AND operator. If there are any other conditions, include them in the WHERE clause and connect them to the other conditions with the AND operator. For example, if you want to view parts present on orders placed by only those customers with $10,000 credit limits, you would add one more condition to the WHERE clause, as shown in Figure 5-17.

```
mysql> SELECT PART_NUM, NUM_ORDERED, ORDER_LINE.ORDER_NUM, ORDER_DATE,
    -> CUSTOMER.CUSTOMER_NUM, CUSTOMER_NAME, LAST_NAME
    -> FROM ORDER_LINE, ORDERS, CUSTOMER, REP
    -> WHERE ORDERS.ORDER_NUM = ORDER_LINE.ORDER_NUM
    -> AND CUSTOMER.CUSTOMER_NUM = ORDERS.CUSTOMER_NUM
    -> AND REP.REP_NUM = CUSTOMER.REP_NUM
    -> AND CREDIT_LIMIT = 10000;
+----------+-------------+-----------+------------+--------------+---------------------------+-----------+
| PART_NUM | NUM_ORDERED | ORDER_NUM | ORDER_DATE | CUSTOMER_NUM | CUSTOMER_NAME             | LAST_NAME |
+----------+-------------+-----------+------------+--------------+---------------------------+-----------+
| KT03     |           2 | 21614     | 2007-10-21 | 282          | Brookings Direct          | Hull      |
| BV06     |           2 | 21617     | 2007-10-23 | 608          | Johnson's Department Store | Perez     |
| CD52     |           4 | 21617     | 2007-10-23 | 608          | Johnson's Department Store | Perez     |
| KV29     |           2 | 21623     | 2007-10-23 | 608          | Johnson's Department Store | Perez     |
+----------+-------------+-----------+------------+--------------+---------------------------+-----------+
4 rows in set (0.01 sec)
```

FIGURE 5-17 Restricting the rows when joining four tables

SET OPERATIONS

In MySQL, you can use the set operations for taking the union, intersection, and difference of two tables. The **union** of two tables uses the **UNION** operator to create a temporary table containing every row that is in either the first table, the second table, or both tables. The **intersection** of two tables uses the **INTERSECT** operator to create a temporary table containing all rows that are in both tables. The **difference** of two tables uses the **MINUS** operator to create a temporary table containing the set of all rows that are in the first table but that are not in the second table.

For example, suppose that TEMP1 is a table containing the number and name of each customer represented by sales rep 65. Further suppose that TEMP2 is a table containing the number and name of those customers that currently have orders on file, as shown in Figure 5-18.

TEMP1

CUSTOMER_NUM	CUSTOMER_NAME
356	Ferguson's
462	Bargains Galore
608	Johnson's Department Store

TEMP2

CUSTOMER_NUM	CUSTOMER_NAME
148	Al's Appliance and Sport
282	Brookings Direct
356	Ferguson's
408	The Everything Shop
608	Johnson's Department Store

FIGURE 5-18   Customers of rep 65 and customers with open orders

The union of TEMP1 and TEMP2 (TEMP1 UNION TEMP2) consists of the number and name of those customers that are represented by sales rep 65 *or* that currently have orders on file, *or* both. The intersection of these two tables (TEMP1 INTERSECT TEMP2) contains those customers that are represented by sales rep 65 *and* that have orders on file. The difference of these two tables (TEMP1 MINUS TEMP2) contains those customers that are represented by sales rep 65 but that *do not* have orders on file. The results of these set operations are shown in Figure 5-19.

TEMP1 UNION TEMP2

CUSTOMER_NUM	CUSTOMER_NAME
148	Al's Appliance and Sport
282	Brookings Direct
356	Ferguson's
408	The Everything Shop
462	Bargains Galore
608	Johnson's Department Store

TEMP1 INTERSECT TEMP2

CUSTOMER_NUM	CUSTOMER_NAME
356	Ferguson's
608	Johnson's Department Store

TEMP1 MINUS TEMP2

CUSTOMER_NUM	CUSTOMER_NAME
462	Bargains Galore

FIGURE 5-19   Union, intersection, and difference of the TEMP1 and TEMP2 tables

There is a restriction on set operations. It does not make sense, for example, to talk about the union of the CUSTOMER table and the ORDERS table because these tables do not contain the same columns. What might rows in this union look like? The two tables in the union *must* have the same structure for a union to be appropriate; the formal term is "union compatible." Two tables are **union compatible** if they have the same number of columns and their corresponding columns have identical data types and lengths.

Note that the definition of union compatible does not state that the columns of the two tables must be identical but rather that the columns must be of the same type. Thus, if one column is CHAR(20), the matching column also must be CHAR(20).

EXAMPLE 11

List the number and name of each customer that either is represented by sales rep 65 or that currently has orders on file, or both.

You can create a temporary table containing the number and name of each customer that is represented by sales rep 65 by selecting the customer numbers and names from the CUSTOMER table for which the sales rep number is 65. Then you can create another temporary table containing the number and name of each customer that currently has orders on file by joining the CUSTOMER and ORDERS tables. The two temporary tables created by this process have the same structure; that is, they both contain the CUSTOMER_NUM and CUSTOMER_NAME columns. Because the temporary tables are union compatible, it is possible to take the union of these two tables. The query and its results appear in Figure 5-20.

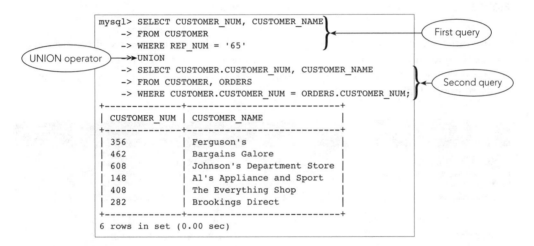

```
mysql> SELECT CUSTOMER_NUM, CUSTOMER_NAME
    -> FROM CUSTOMER
    -> WHERE REP_NUM = '65'                                      First query
    -> UNION
    -> SELECT CUSTOMER.CUSTOMER_NUM, CUSTOMER_NAME
    -> FROM CUSTOMER, ORDERS
    -> WHERE CUSTOMER.CUSTOMER_NUM = ORDERS.CUSTOMER_NUM;        Second query
+--------------+----------------------------+
| CUSTOMER_NUM | CUSTOMER_NAME              |
+--------------+----------------------------+
| 356          | Ferguson's                |
| 462          | Bargains Galore           |
| 608          | Johnson's Department Store |
| 148          | Al's Appliance and Sport  |
| 408          | The Everything Shop       |
| 282          | Brookings Direct          |
+--------------+----------------------------+
6 rows in set (0.00 sec)
```

UNION operator

FIGURE 5-20   Using the UNION operator

If you want to sort the results in a specific order, such as by customer number, you can use an ORDER BY clause as shown in Figure 5-21. Notice that you do not need to qualify CUSTOMER_NUM when using the ORDER BY clause with the UNION operator because the ORDER BY clause refers to the single temporary table produced by the UNION operation.

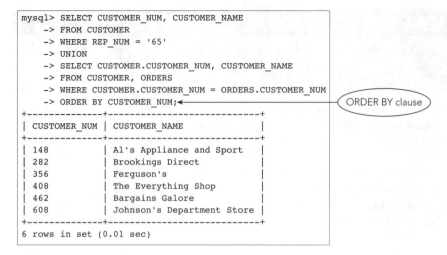

```
mysql> SELECT CUSTOMER_NUM, CUSTOMER_NAME
    -> FROM CUSTOMER
    -> WHERE REP_NUM = '65'
    -> UNION
    -> SELECT CUSTOMER.CUSTOMER_NUM, CUSTOMER_NAME
    -> FROM CUSTOMER, ORDERS
    -> WHERE CUSTOMER.CUSTOMER_NUM = ORDERS.CUSTOMER_NUM
    -> ORDER BY CUSTOMER_NUM;
+--------------+----------------------------+
| CUSTOMER_NUM | CUSTOMER_NAME              |
+--------------+----------------------------+
| 148          | Al's Appliance and Sport  |
| 282          | Brookings Direct          |
| 356          | Ferguson's                |
| 408          | The Everything Shop       |
| 462          | Bargains Galore           |
| 608          | Johnson's Department Store|
+--------------+----------------------------+
6 rows in set (0.01 sec)
```

ORDER BY clause

FIGURE 5-21   Ordering rows when using the UNION operator

If your SQL implementation truly supports the union operation, it will remove any duplicate rows automatically. For example, any customer that is represented by sales rep 65 *and* that currently has orders on file will appear only once in the results. MySQL correctly removes duplicates.

EXAMPLE 12

List the number and name of each customer that is represented by sales rep 65 and that currently has orders on file.

The only difference between this query and the one in Example 11 is that here, the appropriate operator is INTERSECT. The query formulation is as follows:

```
SELECT CUSTOMER_NUM, CUSTOMER_NAME
FROM CUSTOMER
WHERE REP_NUM = '65'
INTERSECT
SELECT CUSTOMER.CUSTOMER_NUM, CUSTOMER_NAME
FROM CUSTOMER, ORDERS
WHERE CUSTOMER.CUSTOMER_NUM = ORDERS.CUSTOMER_NUM;
```

Many SQL implementations, including MySQL, do not support the INTERSECT operator, so you need to take a different approach. The command shown in Figure 5-22 produces the same results as the INTERSECT operator by using the IN operator and a subquery. The command selects the number and name of each customer that is represented by sales rep 65 and whose customer number also appears in the collection of customer numbers in the ORDERS table.

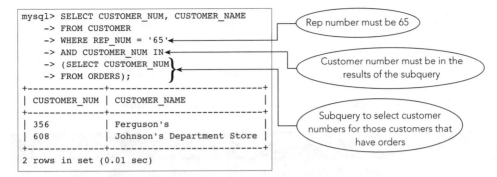

```
mysql> SELECT CUSTOMER_NUM, CUSTOMER_NAME
    -> FROM CUSTOMER
    -> WHERE REP_NUM = '65'
    -> AND CUSTOMER_NUM IN
    -> (SELECT CUSTOMER_NUM
    -> FROM ORDERS);
+--------------+----------------------------+
| CUSTOMER_NUM | CUSTOMER_NAME              |
+--------------+----------------------------+
| 356          | Ferguson's                |
| 608          | Johnson's Department Store |
+--------------+----------------------------+
2 rows in set (0.01 sec)
```

Rep number must be 65

Customer number must be in the results of the subquery

Subquery to select customer numbers for those customers that have orders

FIGURE 5-22   Performing an intersection without using the INTERSECT operator

EXAMPLE 13

List the number and name of each customer that is represented by sales rep 65 but that does not have orders currently on file.

The query uses the MINUS operator as follows:

```
SELECT CUSTOMER_NUM, CUSTOMER_NAME
FROM CUSTOMER
WHERE REP_NUM = '65'
MINUS
SELECT CUSTOMER.CUSTOMER_NUM, CUSTOMER_NAME
FROM CUSTOMER, ORDERS
WHERE CUSTOMER.CUSTOMER_NUM = ORDERS.CUSTOMER_NUM;
```

Just as with the INTERSECT operator, many SQL implementations, including MySQL, do not support the MINUS operator. In such cases, you need to take a different approach, such as the one shown in Figure 5-23. This command produces the same results by selecting the number and name of each customer that is represented by sales rep 65 and whose customer number does *not* appear in the collection of customer numbers in the ORDERS table.

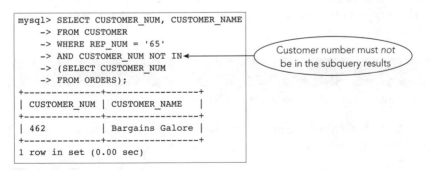

```
mysql> SELECT CUSTOMER_NUM, CUSTOMER_NAME
    -> FROM CUSTOMER
    -> WHERE REP_NUM = '65'
    -> AND CUSTOMER_NUM NOT IN
    -> (SELECT CUSTOMER_NUM
    -> FROM ORDERS);
+--------------+-----------------+
| CUSTOMER_NUM | CUSTOMER_NAME   |
+--------------+-----------------+
| 462          | Bargains Galore |
+--------------+-----------------+
1 row in set (0.00 sec)
```

Customer number must *not* be in the subquery results

FIGURE 5-23   Performing a difference without using the MINUS operator

ALL AND ANY

You can use the ALL and ANY operators with subqueries to produce a single column of numbers. If you precede the subquery by the **ALL** operator, the condition is true only if it satisfies *all* values produced by the subquery. If you precede the subquery by the **ANY** operator, the condition is true only if it satisfies *any* value (one or more) produced by the subquery. The following examples illustrate the use of these operators.

EXAMPLE 14

Find the customer number, name, current balance, and rep number of each customer whose balance exceeds the maximum balance of all customers represented by sales rep 65.

You can satisfy this query by finding the maximum balance of the customers represented by sales rep 65 in a subquery and then finding all customers whose balances are greater than this number. There is an alternative formulation that is simpler, however. You can use the ALL operator, as shown in Figure 5-24.

```
mysql> SELECT CUSTOMER_NUM, CUSTOMER_NAME, BALANCE, REP_NUM
    -> FROM CUSTOMER
    -> WHERE BALANCE > ALL ◄─────────────────────────────  ( ALL operator )
    -> (SELECT BALANCE
    -> FROM CUSTOMER
    -> WHERE REP_NUM = '65');
+--------------+-------------------------+----------+---------+
| CUSTOMER_NUM | CUSTOMER_NAME           | BALANCE  | REP_NUM |
+--------------+-------------------------+----------+---------+
| 148          | Al's Appliance and Sport|  6550.00 | 20      |
| 524          | Kline's                 | 12762.00 | 20      |
| 842          | All Season              |  8221.00 | 20      |
+--------------+-------------------------+----------+---------+
3 rows in set (0.00 sec)
```

FIGURE 5-24 SELECT command that uses the ALL operator

To some users, this formulation might seem more natural than finding the maximum balance in the subquery. For other users, the opposite might be true. You can use whichever approach you prefer.

Q & A

Question: How would you get the same result for Example 14 without using the ALL operator?
Answer: You could select each customer whose balance is greater than the maximum balance of any customer of sales rep 65, as shown in Figure 5-25.

```
mysql> SELECT CUSTOMER_NUM, CUSTOMER_NAME, BALANCE, REP_NUM
    -> FROM CUSTOMER
    -> WHERE BALANCE >
    -> (SELECT MAX(BALANCE)
    -> FROM CUSTOMER
    -> WHERE REP_NUM = '65');
+--------------+--------------------------+----------+---------+
| CUSTOMER_NUM | CUSTOMER_NAME            | BALANCE  | REP_NUM |
+--------------+--------------------------+----------+---------+
| 148          | Al's Appliance and Sport |  6550.00 | 20      |
| 524          | Kline's                  | 12762.00 | 20      |
| 842          | All Season               |  8221.00 | 20      |
+--------------+--------------------------+----------+---------+
3 rows in set (0.00 sec)
```

FIGURE 5-25   Alternative to using the ALL operator

EXAMPLE 15

Find the customer number, name, current balance, and rep number of each customer whose balance is greater than the balance of at least one customer of sales rep 65.

You can satisfy this query by finding the minimum balance of the customers represented by sales rep 65 in a subquery and then finding all customers whose balance is greater than this number. To simplify the process, you can use the ANY operator, as shown in Figure 5-26.

```
mysql> SELECT CUSTOMER_NUM, CUSTOMER_NAME, BALANCE, REP_NUM
    -> FROM CUSTOMER
    -> WHERE BALANCE > ANY  ◄─────────────────────────  ( ANY operator )
    -> (SELECT BALANCE
    -> FROM CUSTOMER
    -> WHERE REP_NUM = '65');
+--------------+--------------------------+----------+---------+
| CUSTOMER_NUM | CUSTOMER_NAME            | BALANCE  | REP_NUM |
+--------------+--------------------------+----------+---------+
| 148          | Al's Appliance and Sport |  6550.00 | 20      |
| 356          | Ferguson's               |  5785.00 | 65      |
| 408          | The Everything Shop      |  5285.25 | 35      |
| 462          | Bargains Galore          |  3412.00 | 65      |
| 524          | Kline's                  | 12762.00 | 20      |
| 687          | Lee's Sport and Appliance |  2851.00 | 35      |
| 842          | All Season               |  8221.00 | 20      |
+--------------+--------------------------+----------+---------+
7 rows in set (0.00 sec)
```

FIGURE 5-26   SELECT command with an ANY operator

```
mysql> SELECT CUSTOMER_NUM, CUSTOMER_NAME, BALANCE, REP_NUM
    -> FROM CUSTOMER
    -> WHERE BALANCE >
    -> (SELECT MIN(BALANCE)
    -> FROM CUSTOMER
    -> WHERE REP_NUM = '65');
+--------------+--------------------------+----------+---------+
| CUSTOMER_NUM | CUSTOMER_NAME            | BALANCE  | REP_NUM |
+--------------+--------------------------+----------+---------+
| 148          | Al's Appliance and Sport |  6550.00 | 20      |
| 356          | Ferguson's               |  5785.00 | 65      |
| 408          | The Everything Shop      |  5285.25 | 35      |
| 462          | Bargains Galore          |  3412.00 | 65      |
| 524          | Kline's                  | 12762.00 | 20      |
| 687          | Lee's Sport and Appliance |  2851.00 | 35      |
| 842          | All Season               |  8221.00 | 20      |
+--------------+--------------------------+----------+---------+
7 rows in set (0.00 sec)
```

FIGURE 5-27 Alternative to using the ANY operator

SPECIAL OPERATIONS

You can perform special operations within SQL, such as the self-join that you already used. Three other special operations are the inner join, the outer join, and the product.

Inner Join

A join that compares the tables in a FROM clause and lists only those rows that satisfy the condition in the WHERE clause is called an **inner join**. The joins that you have performed so far in this text have been inner joins. Example 16 illustrates the inner join.

EXAMPLE 16

Display the customer number, customer name, order number, and order date for each order. Sort the results by customer number.

This example requires the same type of join that you have been using. The command is:

```
SELECT CUSTOMER.CUSTOMER_NUM, CUSTOMER_NAME, ORDER_NUM, ORDER_DATE
FROM CUSTOMER, ORDERS
WHERE CUSTOMER.CUSTOMER_NUM = ORDERS.CUSTOMER_NUM
ORDER BY CUSTOMER.CUSTOMER_NUM;
```

The previous approach should work in any SQL implementation. An update to the SQL standard approved in 1992, called SQL-92, provides an alternative way of performing an inner join, as demonstrated in Figure 5-28. MySQL supports inner join and outer join commands.

FIGURE 5-28   Query that uses an INNER JOIN clause

In the FROM clause, list the first table, then include an INNER JOIN clause that includes the name of the second table. Instead of a WHERE clause, use an ON clause containing the same condition that you would have included in the WHERE clause.

Outer Join

Sometimes you need to list all the rows from one of the tables in a join, regardless of whether they match any rows in a second table. For example, you can perform the join of the CUSTOMER and ORDERS tables in the query for Example 16, but display all customers—even the ones without orders. This type of join is called an **outer join**.

There are actually three types of outer joins. In a **left outer join**, all rows from the table on the left (the table listed first in the query) are included regardless of whether they match rows from the table on the right (the table listed second in the query). Rows from the table on the right are included only if they match. In a **right outer join**, all rows from the table on the right are included regardless of whether they match rows from the table on the left. Rows from the table on the left are included only if they match. In a **full outer join**, all rows from both tables are included regardless of whether they match rows from the other table. (The full outer join is rarely used.)

Example 17 illustrates the use of a left outer join.

EXAMPLE 17

Display the customer number, customer name, order number, and order date for all orders. Include all customers in the results. For customers that do not have orders, omit the order number and order date.

To include all customers, you must perform an outer join. Assuming the CUSTOMER table is listed first, the join should be a left outer join. In MySQL, you use the LEFT JOIN clause to perform a left outer join as shown in Figure 5-29. (You would use a RIGHT JOIN clause to perform a right outer join.)

```
mysql> SELECT CUSTOMER.CUSTOMER_NUM, CUSTOMER_NAME, ORDER_NUM, ORDER_DATE
    -> FROM CUSTOMER
    -> LEFT JOIN ORDERS                          Clause to perform
    -> ON CUSTOMER.CUSTOMER_NUM = ORDERS.CUSTOMER_NUM    a left outer join
    -> ORDER BY CUSTOMER.CUSTOMER_NUM;
+--------------+---------------------------+-----------+------------+
| CUSTOMER_NUM | CUSTOMER_NAME             | ORDER_NUM | ORDER_DATE |
+--------------+---------------------------+-----------+------------+
| 148          | Al's Appliance and Sport  | 21608     | 2007-10-20 |
| 148          | Al's Appliance and Sport  | 21619     | 2007-10-23 |
| 282          | Brookings Direct          | 21614     | 2007-10-21 |
| 356          | Ferguson's                | 21610     | 2007-10-20 |
| 408          | The Everything Shop       | 21613     | 2007-10-21 |
| 462          | Bargains Galore           | NULL      | NULL       |  Customers without
| 524          | Kline's                   | NULL      | NULL       |  matching orders
| 608          | Johnson's Department Store| 21623     | 2007-10-23 |  also are included
| 608          | Johnson's Department Store| 21617     | 2007-10-23 |
| 687          | Lee's Sport and Appliance | NULL      | NULL       |
| 725          | Deerfield's Four Seasons  | NULL      | NULL       |
| 842          | All Season                | NULL      | NULL       |
+--------------+---------------------------+-----------+------------+
12 rows in set (0.01 sec)
```

FIGURE 5-29   Query that uses a LEFT JOIN clause

All customers are included in the results. For customers without orders, the order number and date are blank. Technically, these blank values are null.

Product

The **product** (formally called the **Cartesian product**) of two tables is the combination of all rows in the first table and all rows in the second table.

NOTE

The product operation is not common. You need to be aware of it, however, because it is easy to create a product inadvertently by omitting the WHERE clause when you are attempting to join tables.

EXAMPLE 18

Form the product of the CUSTOMER and ORDERS tables. Display the customer number and name from the CUSTOMER table, along with the order number and order date from the ORDERS table.

Forming a product is actually very easy. You simply omit the WHERE clause, as shown in Figure 5-30.

```
mysql> SELECT CUSTOMER.CUSTOMER_NUM, CUSTOMER_NAME, ORDER_NUM, ORDER_DATE
    -> FROM CUSTOMER, ORDERS;
+--------------+-------------------------+-----------+------------+
| CUSTOMER_NUM | CUSTOMER_NAME           | ORDER_NUM | ORDER_DATE |
+--------------+-------------------------+-----------+------------+
| 148          | Al's Appliance and Sport| 21608     | 2007-10-20 |
| 282          | Brookings Direct        | 21608     | 2007-10-20 |
| 356          | Ferguson's              | 21608     | 2007-10-20 |
| 408          | The Everything Shop     | 21608     | 2007-10-20 |
| 462          | Bargains Galore         | 21608     | 2007-10-20 |
| 524          | Kline's                 | 21608     | 2007-10-20 |
| 608          | Johnson's Department Store | 21608  | 2007-10-20 |
| 687          | Lee's Sport and Appliance | 21608   | 2007-10-20 |
| 725          | Deerfield's Four Seasons| 21608     | 2007-10-20 |
| 842          | All Season              | 21608     | 2007-10-20 |
| 148          | Al's Appliance and Sport| 21610     | 2007-10-20 |
| 282          | Brookings Direct        | 21610     | 2007-10-20 |
| 356          | Ferguson's              | 21610     | 2007-10-20 |
| 408          | The Everything Shop     | 21610     | 2007-10-20 |
| 462          | Bargains Galore         | 21610     | 2007-10-20 |
| 524          | Kline's                 | 21610     | 2007-10-20 |
| 608          | Johnson's Department Store | 21610  | 2007-10-20 |
| 687          | Lee's Sport and Appliance | 21610   | 2007-10-20 |
| 725          | Deerfield's Four Seasons| 21610     | 2007-10-20 |
| 842          | All Season              | 21610     | 2007-10-20 |
| .            | .                       | .         | .          |
| .            | .                       | .         | .          |
| .            | .                       | .         | .          |
```

No condition is used to relate the tables in the FROM clause

FIGURE 5-30   Query that produces a product of two tables

Q & A

Question: Figure 5-30 does not show all the rows in the result. How many rows are actually included?
Answer: The CUSTOMER table has 10 rows and the ORDERS table has 7 rows. Because each of the 10 customer rows is matched with each of the 7 order rows, there are 70 (10 times 7) rows in the result.

Chapter Summary

To join tables, indicate in the SELECT clause all columns to display, list in the FROM clause all tables to join, and then include in the WHERE clause any conditions requiring values in matching columns to be equal.

When referring to matching columns in different tables, you must qualify the column names to avoid confusion. You qualify column names using the following format: table name.column name.

Use the IN or EXISTS operators with an appropriate subquery as an alternate way of performing a join.

A subquery can contain another subquery. The innermost subquery is executed first.

The name of a table in a FROM clause can be followed by an alias, which is an alternate name for a table. The alias can be used in place of the table name throughout the SQL command. By using two different aliases for the same table in a single SQL command, you can join a table to itself.

The UNION operator creates a union of two tables (the collection of rows that are in either or both tables). The INTERSECT operator creates the intersection of two tables (the collection of rows that are in both tables). The MINUS operator creates the difference of two tables (the collection of rows that are in the first table but not in the second table). To perform any of these operations, the tables involved must be union compatible. Two tables are union compatible if they have the same number of columns and their corresponding columns have identical data types and lengths.

If the ALL operator precedes a subquery, the condition is true only if it is satisfied by *all* values produced by the subquery.

If the ANY operator precedes a subquery, the condition is true only if it is satisfied by *any* value (one or more) produced by the subquery.

In an inner join, only matching rows from both tables are included. You can use the INNER JOIN clause to perform an inner join.

In a left outer join, all rows from the table on the left (the table listed first in the query) are included regardless of whether they match rows from the table on the right (the table listed second in the query). Rows from the table on the right are included only if they match. You can use the LEFT JOIN clause to perform a left outer join. In a right outer join, all rows from the table on the right are included regardless of whether they match rows from the table on the left. Rows from the table on the left are included only if they match. You can use the RIGHT JOIN clause to perform a right outer join.

The product (Cartesian product) of two tables is the combination of all rows in the first table and all rows in the second table. To form a product of two tables, include both tables in the FROM clause and omit the WHERE clause.

Key Terms

alias	Cartesian product
ALL	correlated subquery
ANY	difference

EXISTS	nested subquery
full outer join	outer join
inner join	product
INTERSECT	right outer join
intersection	self-join
join	union
left outer join	UNION
MINUS	union compatible

Review Questions

1. How do you join tables in MySQL?

2. When must you qualify names in MySQL commands? How do you do so?

3. List two operators that you can use with subqueries as an alternate way of performing joins.

4. What is a nested subquery? In which order does MySQL evaluate nested subqueries?

5. What is an alias? How do you specify one in MySQL? How do you use an alias?

6. How do you join a table to itself in MySQL?

7. How do you take the union of two tables in MySQL? How do you take the intersection of two tables in MySQL? How do you take the difference of two tables in MySQL? Are there any restrictions on the tables when performing any of these operations?

8. What does it mean for two tables to be union compatible?

9. How do you use the ALL operator with a subquery?

10. How do you use the ANY operator with a subquery?

11. Which rows are included in an inner join? What clause can you use to perform an inner join in MySQL?

12. Which rows are included in a left outer join? What clause can you use to perform a left outer join in MySQL?

13. Which rows are included in a right outer join? What clause can you use to perform a right outer join in MySQL?

14. What is the formal name for the product of two tables? How do you form a product in MySQL?

Exercises

Premiere Products

Use MySQL and the Premiere Products database (see Figure 1-2 in Chapter 1) to complete the following exercises. Use the notes at the end of Chapter 3 to print your output if directed to do so by your instructor.

1. For each order, list the order number and order date along with the number and name of the customer that placed the order.

2. For each order placed on October 21, 2007, list the order number along with the number and name of the customer that placed the order.

3. For each order, list the order number, order date, part number, number of units ordered, and quoted price for each order line that makes up the order.

4. Use the IN operator to find the number and name of each customer that placed an order on October 21, 2007.

5. Repeat Exercise 4, but this time use the EXISTS operator in your answer.

6. Find the number and name of each customer that did not place an order on October 21, 2007.

7. For each order, list the order number, order date, part number, part description, and item class for each part that makes up the order.

8. Repeat Exercise 7, but this time order the rows by item class and then by order number.

9. Use a subquery to find the rep number, last name, and first name of each sales rep who represents at least one customer with a credit limit of $5,000. List each sales rep only once in the results.

10. Repeat Exercise 9, but this time do not use a subquery.

11. Find the number and name of each customer that currently has an order on file for a Gas Range.

12. List the part number, part description, and item class for each pair of parts that are in the same item class. (For example, one such pair would be part AT94 and part FD21, because the item class for both parts is HW.)

13. List the order number and order date for each order placed by the customer named Johnson's Department Store. (*Hint*: To enter an apostrophe (single quotation mark) within a string of characters, type two single quotation marks.)

14. List the order number and order date for each order that contains an order line for an Iron.

15. List the order number and order date for each order that either was placed by Johnson's Department Store or that contains an order line for a Gas Range.

16. List the order number and order date for each order that was placed by Johnson's Department Store and that contains an order line for a Gas Range.

17. List the order number and order date for each order that was placed by Johnson's Department Store but that does not contain an order line for a Gas Range.

18. List the part number, part description, unit price, and item class for each part that has a unit price greater than the unit price of every part in item class AP. Use either the ALL or ANY operator in your query. (*Hint*: Make sure you select the correct operator.)

19. If you used ALL in Exercise 18, repeat the exercise using ANY. If you used ANY, repeat the exercise using ALL, and then run the new command. What question does this command answer?

20. For each part, list the part number, description, units on hand, order number, and number of units ordered. All parts should be included in the results. For those parts that are currently not on order, the order number and number of units ordered should be left blank. Order the results by part number.

Henry Books

Use MySQL and the Henry Books database (Figures 1-4 through 1-7 in Chapter 1) to complete the following exercises. Use the notes at the end of Chapter 3 to print your output if directed to do so by your instructor.

1. For each book, list the book code, book title, publisher code, and publisher name. Order the results by publisher name.

2. For each book published by Plume, list the book code, book title, and price.

3. List the book title, book code, and price of each book published by Plume that has a book price of at least $14.

4. List the book code, book title, and units on hand for each book in branch number 4.

5. List the book title for each book that has the type PSY and that is published by Jove Publications.

6. Find the book title for each book written by author number 18. Use the IN operator in your formulation.

7. Repeat Exercise 6, but this time use the EXISTS operator in your formulation.

8. Find the book code and book title for each book located in branch number 2 and written by author 20.

9. List the book codes for each pair of books that have the same price. (For example, one such pair would be book 0200 and book 7559, because the price of both books is $8.00.) The first book code listed should be the major sort key, and the second book code should be the minor sort key.

10. Find the book title, author last name, and units on hand for each book in branch number 4.

11. Repeat Exercise 10, but this time list only paperback books.

12. Find the book code and book title for each book whose price is more than $10 or that was published in Boston.

13. Find the book code and book title for each book whose price is more than $10 and that was published in Boston.

14. Find the book code and book title for each book whose price is more than $10 but that was not published in Boston.

15. Find the book code and book title for each book whose price is greater than the book price of every book that has the type HOR.

16. Find the book code and book title for each book whose price is greater than the price of at least one book that has the type HOR.

17. List the book code, book title, and units on hand for each book in branch number 2. Be sure each book is included, regardless of whether there are any copies of the book currently on hand in branch 2. Order the output by book code.

Alexamara Marina Group

Use MySQL and the Alexamara Marina Group database (Figures 1-8 through 1-12 in Chapter 1) to complete the following exercises. Use the notes at the end of Chapter 3 to print your output if directed to do so by your instructor.

1. For every boat, list the marina number, slip number, boat name, owner number, owner's first name, and owner's last name.

2. For every completed or open service request for routine engine maintenance, list the slip ID, description, and status.

3. For every service request for routine engine maintenance, list the slip ID, marina number, slip number, estimated hours, spent hours, owner number, and owner's last name.

4. List the first and last names of all owners who have a boat in a 40-foot slip. Use the IN operator in your formulation.

5. Repeat Exercise 4, but this time use the EXISTS operator in your formulation.

6. List the names of any pair of boats that have the same type. For example, one pair would be *Anderson II* and *Escape*, because the boat type for both boats is Sprite 4000. The first name listed should be the major sort key and the second name should be the minor sort key.

7. List the boat name, owner number, owner last name, and owner first name for each boat in marina 1.

8. Repeat Exercise 7, but this time only list boats in 30-foot slips.

9. List the marina number, slip number, and boat name for boats whose owners live in Glander Bay or whose type is Sprite 4000.

10. List the marina number, slip number, and boat name for boats whose owners live in Glander Bay and whose type is Sprite 4000.

11. List the marina number, slip number, and boat name for boats whose owners live in Glander Bay but whose type is not Sprite 4000.

12. Find the service ID and slip ID for each service request whose estimated hours is greater than the number of estimated hours of at least one service request on which the category number is 3.

13. Find the service ID and slip ID for each service request whose estimated hours is greater than the number of estimated hours on every service request on which the category number is 3.

14. List the slip ID, boat name, owner number, service ID, number of estimated hours, and number of spent hours for each service request on which the category number is 2.

15. Repeat Exercise 14, but this time be sure each slip is included regardless of whether the boat in the slip currently has any service requests for category 2.

CHAPTER **6**

UPDATING DATA

LEARNING OBJECTIVES

Objectives

- Create a new table from an existing table
- Change data using the UPDATE command
- Add new data using the INSERT command
- Delete data using the DELETE command
- Use nulls in UPDATE commands
- Change the structure of an existing table
- Use the COMMIT and ROLLBACK commands to make permanent data updates or to reverse updates
- Understand transactions and the role of COMMIT and ROLLBACK in supporting transactions
- Drop a table

INTRODUCTION

In this chapter, you will learn how to create a new table from an existing table and make changes to the data in a table. You will use the UPDATE command to change data in one or more rows in a table, and use the INSERT command to add new rows. You will use the DELETE command to delete rows. You also will use nulls in update operations. You will learn how to change the structure of a table in a variety of ways and drop existing tables. Finally, you will use the COMMIT command to make changes permanent and use the ROLLBACK command to undo changes.

CREATING A NEW TABLE FROM AN EXISTING TABLE

It is possible to create a new table using data in an existing table, as illustrated in the following examples.

EXAMPLE 1

Create a new table named LEVEL1_CUSTOMER containing the following columns from the CUSTOMER table: CUSTOMER_NUM, CUSTOMER_NAME, BALANCE, CREDIT_LIMIT, and REP_NUM. The columns in the new LEVEL1_CUSTOMER table should have the same characteristics as the corresponding columns in the CUSTOMER table.

You describe the new table named LEVEL1_CUSTOMER by using the CREATE TABLE command shown in Figure 6-1.

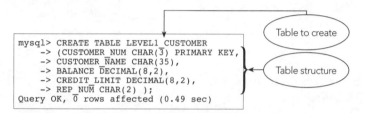

FIGURE 6-1   Creating the LEVEL1_CUSTOMER table

NOTE

If you are creating a new table that is exactly like an existing table, you can use a shortcut. You can type CREATE TABLE, followed by the name of the table you want to create, the word LIKE, and the name of the existing table. For example, you can create the LEVEL1_CUSTOMER table by typing the following command:

```
CREATE TABLE LEVEL1_CUSTOMER LIKE CUSTOMER;
```

After executing this command, the LEVEL1_CUSTOMER table has precisely the same fields, data types, and sizes as the CUSTOMER table, but the new table does not contain any rows. You add rows to the new table as illustrated in the following example.

EXAMPLE 2

Insert into the LEVEL1_CUSTOMER table the customer number, customer name, balance, credit limit, and rep number for customers with credit limits of $7,500.

You can create a SELECT command to select the desired data from the CUSTOMER table, just as you did in Chapter 4. By placing this SELECT command in an INSERT command, you can add the query results to a table. The INSERT command appears in Figure 6-2; this command inserts four rows into the LEVEL1_CUSTOMER table.

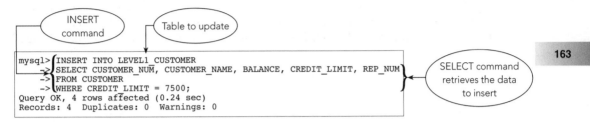

FIGURE 6-2   Inserting data into the LEVEL1_CUSTOMER table

The SELECT command shown in Figure 6-3 displays the data in the LEVEL1_CUSTOMER table. Notice that the data comes from the new table you just created (LEVEL1_CUSTOMER), and not from the CUSTOMER table.

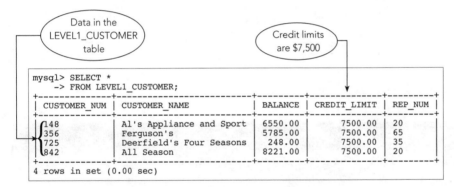

FIGURE 6-3   LEVEL1_CUSTOMER data

CHANGING EXISTING DATA IN A TABLE

The data stored in your tables is subject to constant change; prices, addresses, commission amounts, and other data in a database change on a regular basis. To keep data current, you must be able to make these changes to the data in your tables. You can use the **UPDATE** command to change rows for which a specific condition is true.

EXAMPLE 3

Change the name of customer 842 in the LEVEL1_CUSTOMER table to All Season Sport.

The format for the UPDATE command is the word UPDATE, followed by the name of the table to be updated. The next portion of the command consists of the word SET, followed by the name of the column to be updated, an equals sign, and the new value. When necessary, include a WHERE clause to indicate the row(s) on which the change is to occur. The command shown in Figure 6-4 changes the name of customer 842 to All Season Sport. The SELECT command shown in Figure 6-4 shows the data in the table after the change has been made. (This SELECT command is not part of the update.) It is a good idea to use a SELECT command to display the data you changed to verify that the correct change was made.

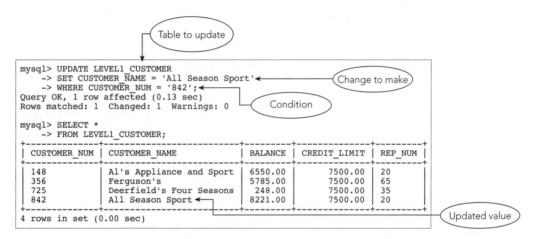

FIGURE 6-4   Updating a row in a table

E X A M P L E   4

For each customer that is represented by sales rep 20 in the LEVEL1_CUSTOMER table and that also has a balance that does not exceed the credit limit, increase the customer's credit limit to $8,000.

The only difference between Examples 3 and 4 is that Example 4 uses a compound condition to identify the row(s) to be changed. The UPDATE command and the SELECT command that shows its results appear in Figure 6-5.

```
mysql> UPDATE LEVEL1_CUSTOMER
    -> SET CREDIT_LIMIT = 8000
    -> WHERE REP_NUM = '20'
    -> AND BALANCE < CREDIT_LIMIT;      }  Compound
Query OK, 1 row affected (0.12 sec)          condition
Rows matched: 1  Changed: 1  Warnings: 0

mysql> SELECT *
    -> FROM LEVEL1_CUSTOMER;
+--------------+-------------------------+---------+--------------+---------+
| CUSTOMER_NUM | CUSTOMER_NAME           | BALANCE | CREDIT_LIMIT | REP_NUM |
+--------------+-------------------------+---------+--------------+---------+
|     148      | Al's Appliance and Sport| 6550.00 |      8000.00 |   20    |
|     356      | Ferguson's              | 5785.00 |      7500.00 |   65    |
|     725      | Deerfield's Four Seasons|  248.00 |      7500.00 |   35    |
|     842      | All Season Sport        | 8221.00 |      7500.00 |   20    |   Updated value
+--------------+-------------------------+---------+--------------+---------+
4 rows in set (0.00 sec)
```

FIGURE 6-5   Using a compound condition to update a row

You also can use the existing value in a column to update the value using a calculation. For example, if you need to increase the credit limit by 10% instead of changing it to a specific value, you can multiply the existing credit limit by 1.10. The following SET clause makes this change:

```
SET CREDIT_LIMIT = CREDIT_LIMIT * 1.10
```

ADDING NEW ROWS TO AN EXISTING TABLE

In Chapter 3, you used the INSERT command to add the initial rows to the tables in the database. You also can use the INSERT command to add additional rows to tables.

EXAMPLE 5

Add customer number 895 to the LEVEL1_CUSTOMER table. The name is Peter and Margaret's, the balance is 0, the credit limit is $8,000, and the rep number is 20.

The appropriate INSERT command is shown in Figure 6-6. The SELECT command shown in the figure verifies that the row was successfully added.

```
                                    ┌──────────────────┐
                                    │  Table to update │
                                    └──────────────────┘
                                             │
                                             ▼
mysql> INSERT INTO LEVEL1_CUSTOMER
    -> VALUES
    -> ('895','Peter and Margaret''s',0,8000,'20');◄─    ┌──────────────┐
Query OK, 1 row affected (0.13 sec)                      │  Values for  │
                                                         │ the new row  │
mysql> SELECT *                                          └──────────────┘
    -> FROM LEVEL1_CUSTOMER;
+--------------+-------------------------+---------+--------------+---------+
| CUSTOMER_NUM | CUSTOMER_NAME           | BALANCE | CREDIT_LIMIT | REP_NUM |
+--------------+-------------------------+---------+--------------+---------+
|     148      | Al's Appliance and Sport| 6550.00 |     8000.00  |   20    |
|     356      | Ferguson's              | 5785.00 |     7500.00  |   65    |
|     725      | Deerfield's Four Seasons|  248.00 |     7500.00  |   35    |
|     842      | All Season Sport        | 8221.00 |     7500.00  |   20    |
|     895      | Peter and Margaret's    |    0.00 |     8000.00  |   20 ◄──   ┌──────────────────┐
+--------------+-------------------------+---------+--------------+---------+   │ New row added    │
5 rows in set (0.00 sec)                                                       │    to table      │
                                                                               └──────────────────┘
```

FIGURE 6-6   Inserting a row

NOTE

Your output might be sorted in a different order from what is shown in Figure 6-6. If you need to sort the rows in a specific order, use an ORDER BY clause with the desired sort key(s).

NOTE

Because the name Peter and Margaret's contains an apostrophe, you type two single quotation marks to create the apostrophe, as shown in Figure 6-6.

DELETING EXISTING ROWS FROM A TABLE

To delete rows from a table, use the DELETE command as illustrated in Example 6.

EXAMPLE 6

In the LEVEL1_CUSTOMER table, delete customer 895.

To delete data from the database, use the DELETE command. The format for the **DELETE** command is the word DELETE followed by the name of the table from which the row(s) is to be deleted. Next, use a WHERE clause with a condition to select the row(s) to delete. All rows satisfying the condition will be deleted.

The commands shown in Figure 6-7 delete customer 895, and then display the data in the table, verifying the deletion.

```
mysql> DELETE FROM LEVEL1_CUSTOMER
    -> WHERE CUSTOMER_NUM = '895';
Query OK, 1 row affected (0.12 sec)

mysql> SELECT *
    -> FROM LEVEL1_CUSTOMER;
+--------------+------------------------+----------+--------------+---------+
| CUSTOMER_NUM | CUSTOMER_NAME          | BALANCE  | CREDIT_LIMIT | REP_NUM |
+--------------+------------------------+----------+--------------+---------+
| 148          | Al's Appliance and Sport | 6550.00 |      8000.00 | 20      |
| 356          | Ferguson's             | 5785.00  |      7500.00 | 65      |
| 725          | Deerfield's Four Seasons | 248.00  |      7500.00 | 35      |
| 842          | All Season Sport       | 8221.00  |      7500.00 | 20      |
+--------------+------------------------+----------+--------------+---------+
4 rows in set (0.00 sec)
```

Condition to determine the row(s) to be deleted

One row was deleted

FIGURE 6-7 Deleting a row

Q & A

Question: What happens if you run a DELETE command that does not contain a WHERE clause?
Answer: Without a condition to specify which row(s) to delete, all rows will be deleted from the table.

CHANGING A VALUE IN A COLUMN TO NULL

There are some special issues involved when dealing with nulls. You already have seen how to add a row in which some of the values are null and how to select rows in which a given column is null. You also must be able to change the value in a column in an existing row to null, as shown in Example 7. Remember that to make this type of change, the affected column must accept nulls. If you specified NOT NULL for the column when you created the table, then changing a value in a column to null is prohibited.

EXAMPLE 7

Change the balance of customer 725 in the LEVEL1_CUSTOMER table to null.

The command for changing a value to null is exactly what it would be for changing any other value. You simply use the value NULL as the replacement value, as shown in Figure 6-8. Notice that value NULL is *not* enclosed in single quotation marks. If it were, the command would change the balance to the word NULL.

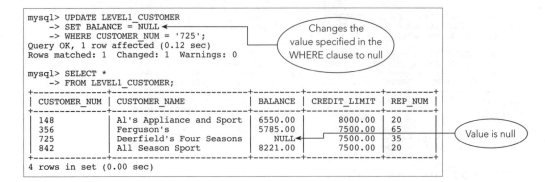

FIGURE 6-8   Changing a value in a column to null

CHANGING A TABLE'S STRUCTURE

One of the nicest features of a relational DBMS, such as MySQL, is the ease with which you can change table structures. You can add new tables, delete tables that are no longer required, add new columns to a table, and change the physical characteristics of existing columns. Next, you will see how to accomplish these changes.

You can change a table's structure in MySQL by using the **ALTER TABLE** command, as illustrated in the following examples.

EXAMPLE 8

Premiere Products decides to maintain a customer type for each customer in the database. These types are R for regular customers, D for distributors, and S for special customers. Add this information in a new column named CUSTOMER_TYPE in the LEVEL1_CUSTOMER table.

To add a new column, use the **ADD clause** of the ALTER TABLE command. The format for the ALTER TABLE command is the words ALTER TABLE followed by the name of the table to be altered, followed by an appropriate clause. The ADD clause consists of the word ADD followed by the name of the column to be added, followed by the characteristics of the column. Figure 6-9 shows the appropriate ALTER TABLE command for this example.

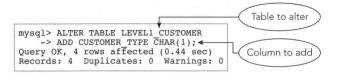

FIGURE 6-9   Adding a column to an existing table

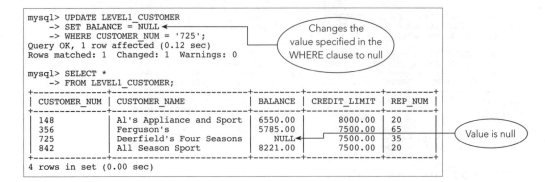

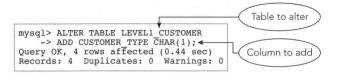

The LEVEL1_CUSTOMER table now contains a column named CUSTOMER_TYPE, a CHAR column with a length of 1. Any new rows added to the table must include values for the new column. Effective immediately, all existing rows also contain this new column. The data in any existing row will contain the new column the next time the row is updated. Any time a row is selected for any reason, however, the system treats the row as though the column is actually present. Thus, to the user, it seems as though the structure was changed immediately.

For existing rows, some value of CUSTOMER_TYPE must be assigned. The simplest approach (from the point of view of the DBMS, not the user) is to assign the value NULL as a CUSTOMER_TYPE in all existing rows. This process requires the CUSTOMER_TYPE column to accept null values, and some systems actually insist on this. The default for MySQL is to accept null values.

To change the values for a column that has been added, follow the ALTER TABLE command with an UPDATE command like the one shown in Figure 6-10. The SELECT command in the figure verifies that the value in the CUSTOMER_TYPE column for all rows is R.

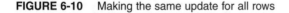

```
                Command to
         change CUSTOMER_TYPE
              values to R

mysql> UPDATE LEVEL1_CUSTOMER
    -> SET CUSTOMER_TYPE = 'R';              Omitting the
Query OK, 4 rows affected (0.12 sec)       WHERE clause updates          All rows have
Rows matched: 4  Changed: 4  Warnings: 0        all rows                customer type R

mysql> SELECT *
    -> FROM LEVEL1_CUSTOMER;
+--------------+------------------------+---------+--------------+---------+---------------+
| CUSTOMER_NUM | CUSTOMER_NAME          | BALANCE | CREDIT_LIMIT | REP_NUM | CUSTOMER_TYPE |
+--------------+------------------------+---------+--------------+---------+---------------+
|     148      | Al's Appliance and Sport| 6550.00|      8000.00 |   20    |      R        |
|     356      | Ferguson's             | 5785.00 |      7500.00 |   65    |      R        |
|     725      | Deerfield's Four Seasons|   NULL |      7500.00 |   35    |      R        |
|     842      | All Season Sport       | 8221.00 |      7500.00 |   20    |      R        |
+--------------+------------------------+---------+--------------+---------+---------------+
4 rows in set (0.00 sec)
```

FIGURE 6-10   Making the same update for all rows

EXAMPLE 9

Two customers in the LEVEL1_CUSTOMER table have a type other than R. Change the types for customers 842 and 148 to S and D, respectively.

The previous example assigned type R to every customer. To change individual types to something other than type R, use the UPDATE command. The appropriate UPDATE commands to make these changes appear in Figure 6-11.

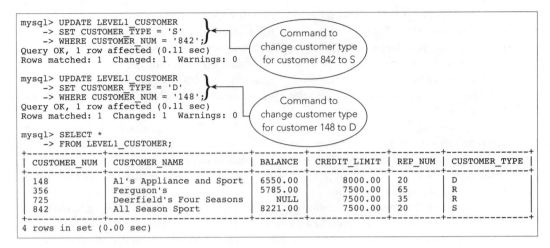

```
mysql> UPDATE LEVEL1_CUSTOMER
    -> SET CUSTOMER_TYPE = 'S'
    -> WHERE CUSTOMER_NUM = '842';
Query OK, 1 row affected (0.11 sec)
Rows matched: 1  Changed: 1  Warnings: 0
```

Command to change customer type for customer 842 to S

```
mysql> UPDATE LEVEL1_CUSTOMER
    -> SET CUSTOMER_TYPE = 'D'
    -> WHERE CUSTOMER_NUM = '148';
Query OK, 1 row affected (0.11 sec)
Rows matched: 1  Changed: 1  Warnings: 0
```

Command to change customer type for customer 148 to D

```
mysql> SELECT *
    -> FROM LEVEL1_CUSTOMER;
+--------------+-------------------------+---------+--------------+---------+---------------+
| CUSTOMER_NUM | CUSTOMER_NAME           | BALANCE | CREDIT_LIMIT | REP_NUM | CUSTOMER_TYPE |
+--------------+-------------------------+---------+--------------+---------+---------------+
| 148          | Al's Appliance and Sport| 6550.00 |      8000.00 | 20      | D             |
| 356          | Ferguson's              | 5785.00 |      7500.00 | 65      | R             |
| 725          | Deerfield's Four Seasons|    NULL |      7500.00 | 35      | R             |
| 842          | All Season Sport        | 8221.00 |      7500.00 | 20      | S             |
+--------------+-------------------------+---------+--------------+---------+---------------+
4 rows in set (0.00 sec)
```

FIGURE 6-11   Updating individual rows

The SELECT command in the figure shows the results of these UPDATE commands. The customer type for customer 842 is S and the type for customer 148 is D. The type for all other customers is R.

Figure 6-12 uses the SHOW COLUMNS command to display the structure of the LEVEL1_CUSTOMER table, which now includes the CUSTOMER_TYPE column.

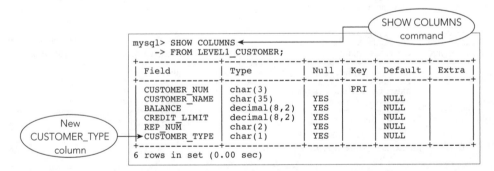

SHOW COLUMNS command

```
mysql> SHOW COLUMNS
    -> FROM LEVEL1_CUSTOMER;
+---------------+--------------+------+-----+---------+-------+
| Field         | Type         | Null | Key | Default | Extra |
+---------------+--------------+------+-----+---------+-------+
| CUSTOMER_NUM  | char(3)      |      | PRI |         |       |
| CUSTOMER_NAME | char(35)     | YES  |     | NULL    |       |
| BALANCE       | decimal(8,2) | YES  |     | NULL    |       |
| CREDIT_LIMIT  | decimal(8,2) | YES  |     | NULL    |       |
| REP_NUM       | char(2)      | YES  |     | NULL    |       |
| CUSTOMER_TYPE | char(1)      | YES  |     | NULL    |       |
+---------------+--------------+------+-----+---------+-------+
6 rows in set (0.00 sec)
```

New CUSTOMER_TYPE column

FIGURE 6-12   Structure of the LEVEL1_CUSTOMER table

EXAMPLE 10

The length of the CUSTOMER_NAME column in the LEVEL1_CUSTOMER table is too short. Increase its length to 50 characters. In addition, change the CREDIT_LIMIT column so it cannot accept nulls.

You can change the characteristics of existing columns by using the **MODIFY clause** of the ALTER TABLE command. Figure 6-13 shows the ALTER TABLE command that changes the length of the CUSTOMER_NAME column from 35 to 50 characters. The figure also shows the ALTER TABLE command to change the CREDIT_LIMIT column so it does not accept null values.

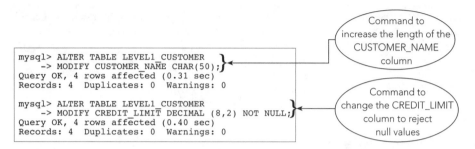

FIGURE 6-13 Changing the structure of the LEVEL1_CUSTOMER table

NOTE

You also can decrease the size of columns, but you might lose some data currently in the column. For example, if you decrease the size of the CUSTOMER_NAME column from 35 to 20 characters, only the first 20 characters of the current customer names will be included. Any characters from position 21 on will be lost. Thus, you should only decrease column sizes when you are positive that you will not lose any data stored in the column.

NOTE

You can change the size of DECIMAL columns in the same manner that you change the size of CHAR columns.

The SHOW COLUMNS command shown in Figure 6-14 shows the revised structure of the LEVEL1_CUSTOMER table. The length of the CUSTOMER_NAME column is 50 characters. The missing value of "YES" in the Null column for the CREDIT_LIMIT column indicates that the CREDIT_LIMIT column no longer accepts null values.

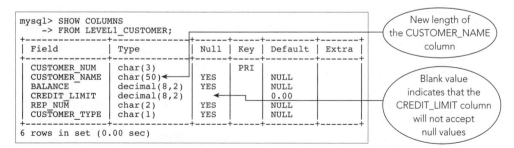

FIGURE 6-14 Revised structure of the LEVEL1_CUSTOMER table

Making Complex Changes

In some cases, you might need to change a table's structure in ways that are either beyond the capabilities of MySQL or that are so complex that it would take longer to make the changes than to re-create the table. Perhaps you need to eliminate multiple columns, rearrange the order of several columns, or combine data from two tables into one. For example, if you try to change a column with a data type of VARCHAR to CHAR, MySQL still uses VARCHAR if the table contains other variable-length columns. In these situations, you can use a CREATE TABLE command to describe the new table (which must use a different name than the existing table), and then insert values from the existing table into it using the INSERT command combined with an appropriate SELECT command.

COMMIT AND ROLLBACK

In some cases, when you update the data in a table, your updates are only temporary and you can reverse (cancel) them at any time during your current work session. Updates become permanent automatically when you exit from MySQL. During your current work session, however, you can **commit** (save) your changes immediately by executing the **COMMIT** command.

If you decide that you do not want to save the changes you have made during your current work session, you can **roll back** (reverse) the changes by executing the **ROLLBACK** command. Any updates made since you ran the most recent COMMIT command are reversed when you run the ROLLBACK command. If you have not run the COMMIT command, executing the ROLLBACK command reverses all updates made during the current work session. You should note that the ROLLBACK command only reverses changes made to the data; it does not reverse changes made to a table's structure. For example, if you change the length of a character column, you cannot use the ROLLBACK command to return the column length to its original state. (To do so, you would need to run an UPDATE command with the appropriate clause.)

If you determine that a data update was made incorrectly, you can use the ROLLBACK command to return the data to its original state. If, on the other hand, you have verified that the update you made is correct, you can use the COMMIT command to make the update permanent. You do this by typing COMMIT and a semicolon after running the update. You should note that the COMMIT command is permanent, however; running the ROLLBACK command cannot reverse the update.

173

To illustrate the use of the ROLLBACK command, Figure 6-15 shows the changes you could have made to the LEVEL1_CUSTOMER table. The first command changes the name of a customer, and the second command deletes a customer.

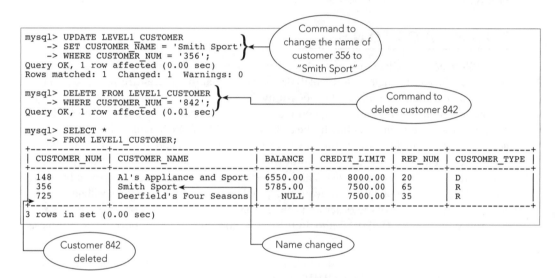

FIGURE 6-15 Updating a row and deleting a row from LEVEL1_CUSTOMER

Figure 6-16 shows the ROLLBACK command, which reverses the changes made in Figure 6-15, and a SELECT command, which lists the current data in the LEVEL1_CUSTOMER table. Notice that the name of customer 356 is Ferguson's and the row for customer 842 is present. All updates made prior to the previous commit still are reflected in the data.

```
mysql> ROLLBACK;
Query OK, 0 rows affected (0.08 sec)        ROLLBACK command

mysql> SELECT *
    -> FROM LEVEL1_CUSTOMER;
+--------------+-------------------------+---------+--------------+---------+---------------+
| CUSTOMER_NUM | CUSTOMER_NAME           | BALANCE | CREDIT_LIMIT | REP_NUM | CUSTOMER_TYPE |
+--------------+-------------------------+---------+--------------+---------+---------------+
|      148     | Al's Appliance and Sport| 6550.00 |      8000.00 |   20    | D             |
|      356     | Ferguson's              | 5785.00 |      7500.00 |   65    | R             |
|      725     | Deerfield's Four Seasons|    NULL |      7500.00 |   35    | R             |
|      842     | All Season Sport        | 8221.00 |      7500.00 |   20    | S             |
+--------------+-------------------------+---------+--------------+---------+---------------+
4 rows in set (0.00 sec)
```

Customer 842 is not deleted

Original name

FIGURE 6-16   Performing a rollback

TRANSACTIONS

A **transaction** is a logical unit of work. A transaction can be viewed as a sequence of steps that accomplishes a single task. In a DBMS, it is essential that the entire sequence related to each transaction is completed successfully.

For example, to enter an order, you must add the corresponding order to the ORDERS table, and then add each order line in the order to the ORDER_LINE table. These multiple steps accomplish the "single" task of entering an order. Suppose you added the order and the first order line, but find you are unable to enter the second order line for some reason; perhaps the part in the order line does not exist. This problem would leave the order in a partially entered state, which is unacceptable. To prevent this problem, you would execute a rollback, thus reversing the insertion of the order and the first order line.

You can use the COMMIT and ROLLBACK commands to support transactions as follows:

- Before beginning the updates for a transaction, commit any previous updates by executing the COMMIT command.
- Complete the updates for the transaction. If any update cannot be completed, execute the ROLLBACK command and discontinue the updates for the current transaction.
- If you can complete all updates successfully, execute the COMMIT command after completing the final update.

DROPPING A TABLE

As you learned in Chapter 3, you can delete a table that is no longer needed by using the DROP TABLE command.

EXAMPLE 11

Delete the LEVEL1_CUSTOMER table because it is no longer needed in the Premiere Products database.

The command to delete the table is shown in Figure 6-17.

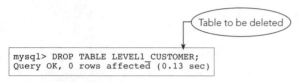

Table to be deleted

```
mysql> DROP TABLE LEVEL1_CUSTOMER;
Query OK, 0 rows affected (0.13 sec)
```

FIGURE 6-17   Dropping a table

When this command is executed, the LEVEL1_CUSTOMER table and all its data are permanently removed from the database.

Chapter Summary

To create a new table from an existing table, first create the new table by using the CREATE TABLE command. Then use an INSERT command containing a SELECT command to select the desired data to be included from the existing table.

Use the UPDATE command to change existing data in a table.

Use the INSERT command to add new rows to a table.

Use the DELETE command to delete existing rows from a table.

To change all values in a column to null, use the SET clause followed by the column name, an equals sign, and the word NULL. To change a specific value in a column to null, use a condition to select the row.

To add a column to a table, use the ALTER TABLE command with an ADD clause.

To change the characteristics of a column, use the ALTER TABLE command with a MODIFY clause.

Use the COMMIT command to make updates permanent; use the ROLLBACK command to reverse any updates that have not been committed.

Use the DROP TABLE command to delete a table and all its data.

Key Terms

ADD clause	MODIFY clause
ALTER TABLE	roll back
commit	ROLLBACK
COMMIT	transaction
DELETE	UPDATE

Review Questions

1. Which command creates a new table?
2. Which command and clause adds an individual row to a table?
3. How do you add the results of a query to a table?
4. Which command changes data in a table?
5. Which command makes updates permanent?
6. Which command reverses updates? Which updates are reversed?
7. Which command removes rows from a table?
8. What is the format of the SET clause that changes the value of a column to null in an UPDATE command?
9. Which command and clause adds a column to an existing table?
10. Which command and clause changes the characteristics of an existing column in a table?
11. How do you use the COMMIT and ROLLBACK commands to support transactions?
12. Which command deletes a table and all its data?

Exercises

Premiere Products

Use MySQL to make the following changes to the Premiere Products database (see Figure 1-2 in Chapter 1). After each change, execute an appropriate query to show that the change was made correctly. Use the notes at the end of Chapter 3 to print your output if directed to do so by your instructor.

1. Create a NONAPPLIANCE table with the structure shown in Figure 6-18.

NONAPPLIANCE

Column	Type	Length	Decimal Places	Nulls Allowed?	Description
PART_NUM	CHAR	4		No	Part number (primary key)
DESCRIPTION	CHAR	15			Part description
ON_HAND	DECIMAL	4	0		Number of units on hand
CLASS	CHAR	2			Item class
PRICE	DECIMAL	6	2		Unit price

FIGURE 6-18   NONAPPLIANCE table layout

2. Insert into the NONAPPLIANCE table the part number, part description, number of units on hand, item class, and unit price from the PART table for each part that is *not* in item class AP.

3. In the NONAPPLIANCE table, change the description of part number AT94 to "Deluxe Iron."

4. In the NONAPPLIANCE table, increase the price of each item in item class SG by 2%. (*Hint*: Multiply each price by 1.02.)

5. Add the following part to the NONAPPLIANCE table: part number: TL92; description: Trimmer; number of units on hand: 11; class: HW; and price: 29.95.

6. Delete every part in the NONAPPLIANCE table for which the class is SG.

7. In the NONAPPLIANCE table, change the class for part FD21 to null.

8. Add a column named ON_HAND_VALUE to the NON_APPLIANCE table. The on-hand value is a seven-digit number with two decimal places that represents the product of the number of units on hand and the price. Then set all values of ON_HAND_VALUE to ON_HAND * PRICE.

9. In the NONAPPLIANCE table, increase the length of the DESCRIPTION column to 30 characters.

10. Remove the NONAPPLIANCE table from the Premiere Products database.

Henry Books

Use MySQL to make the following changes to the Henry Books database (Figures 1-4 through 1-7 in Chapter 1). After each change, execute an appropriate query to show that the change was made correctly. Use the notes at the end of Chapter 3 to print your output if directed to do so by your instructor.

1. Create a MYSTERY table with structure shown in Figure 6-19.

MYSTERY

Column	Type	Length	Decimal Places	Nulls Allowed?	Description
BOOK_CODE	CHAR	4		No	Book code (primary key)
TITLE	CHAR	40			Book title
PUBLISHER_CODE	CHAR	3			Publisher code
PRICE	DECIMAL	4	2		Book price

FIGURE 6-19   MYSTERY table layout

2. Insert into the MYSTERY table the book code, book title, publisher code, and price from the BOOK table for only those books having type MYS.

3. The publisher with code JP has decreased the price of its mystery books by 4%. Update the prices in the MYSTERY table accordingly.

4. Insert a new book into the MYSTERY table. The book code is 9946, the title is *Like Me*, the publisher is MP, and the price is 11.95.

5. Delete the book in the MYSTERY table having the book code 9882.

6. The price of the book entitled *The Edge* has been increased to an unknown amount. Change the value in the MYSTERY table to reflect this change.

7. Add to the MYSTERY table a new character column named BEST_SELLER that is one character in length. Then set the default value for all columns to N.

8. Change the BEST_SELLER column in the MYSTERY table to Y for the book entitled *Second Wind*.

9. Change the length of the TITLE column in the MYSTERY table to 50 characters.

10. Change the BEST_SELLER column in the MYSTERY table to reject nulls.

11. Delete the MYSTERY table from the database.

Alexamara Marina Group

Use MySQL to make the following changes to the Alexamara Marina Group database (Figures 1-8 through 1-12 in Chapter 1). After each change, execute an appropriate query to show that the change was made correctly. Use the notes at the end of Chapter 3 to print your output if directed to do so by your instructor.

1. Create a LARGE_SLIP table with the structure shown in Figure 6-20. (*Hint*: If you have trouble creating the primary key, see Figure 3-25 in Chapter 3.)

LARGE_SLIP

Column	Type	Length	Decimal Places	Nulls Allowed?	Description
MARINA_NUM	CHAR	4		No	Marina number (primary key)
SLIP_NUM	CHAR	4		No	Slip number in the marina (primary key)
RENTAL_FEE	DECIMAL	8	2		Annual rental fee for the slip
BOAT_NAME	CHAR	50			Name of boat currently in the slip
OWNER_NUM	CHAR	4			Number of boat owner renting the slip

FIGURE 6-20   LARGE_SLIP table layout

2. Insert into the LARGE_SLIP table the marina number, slip number, rental fee, boat name, and owner number for those slips whose length is 40 feet.

3. Alexamara has increased the rental fee of each large slip by $100. Update the rental fees in the LARGE_SLIP table accordingly.

4. After increasing the rental fee of each large slip by $100 (Exercise 3), Alexamara decides to decrease the rental fee of any slip whose fee is more than $4,000 by 1%. Update the rental fees in the LARGE_SLIP table accordingly.

5. Insert a new slip into the LARGE_SLIP table. The marina number is 1, the slip number is A4, the rental fee is $3,900.00, the boat name is *Bilsan*, and the owner number is FE82.

6. Delete all slips in the LARGE_SLIP table for which the owner number is TR72.

7. The name of the boat in marina 1 and slip A1 is in the process of being changed to an unknown name. Change the name of this boat in the LARGE_SLIP table to null.

8. Add to the LARGE_SLIP table a new character column named CHARTER that is one character in length. (This column will indicate whether the boat is available to be chartered.) Set the value for the CHARTER column on all rows to N.

9. Change the CHARTER column in the LARGE_SLIP table to Y for the slip containing the boat named *Our Toy*.

10. Change the length of the BOAT_NAME column in the LARGE_SLIP table to 60 characters.

11. Change the RENTAL_FEE column in the LARGE_SLIP table to reject nulls.

12. Delete the LARGE_SLIP table from the database.

CHAPTER **7**

DATABASE ADMINISTRATION

LEARNING OBJECTIVES

Objectives

- Understand, define, and drop views
- Recognize the benefits of using views
- Use a view to update data
- Grant and revoke users' database privileges
- Understand the purpose, advantages, and disadvantages of using an index
- Create, use, and drop an index
- Understand and obtain information from the system catalog
- Use integrity constraints to control data entry

INTRODUCTION

There are some special issues involved in managing a database. This process, often called **database administration**, is especially important when more than one person uses the database. In a business organization, a person or an entire group known as the **database administrator** is charged with managing the database.

In Chapter 6, you learned about one function of the database administrator: changing the structure of a database. In this chapter, you will see how the database administrator can give each user his or her own view of the database. You will use the GRANT and REVOKE commands to assign different database privileges to different users. You will use indexes to improve database performance. You'll learn how

MySQL stores information about the database structure in a special object called the system catalog and how to access that information. Finally, you will learn how to specify integrity constraints that establish rules for the data in the database.

DEFINING AND USING VIEWS

Most database management systems support the creation of views. A **view** is an application program's or an individual user's picture of the database. The existing, permanent tables in a relational database are called **base tables**. A view is a derived table because the data in it comes from one or more base tables. To the user, a view appears to be an actual table, but it is not. In many cases, a user can examine table data using a view. Because a view usually includes less information than the full database, its use can represent a great simplification. Views also provide a measure of security, because omitting sensitive tables or columns from a view renders them unavailable to anyone accessing the database through the view.

To help you understand the concept of a view, suppose that Juan is interested in the part number, part description, units on hand, and unit price of parts in item class HW. He is not interested in any other columns in the PART table, nor is he interested in any rows that correspond to parts in other item classes. Viewing this data would be simpler for Juan if the other rows and columns were not even present. Although you cannot change the structure of the PART table and omit some of its rows just for Juan, you can do the next best thing. You can provide him with a view that consists of only the rows and columns that he needs to access.

NOTE

MySQL version 4.1 does not currently support views. Support for views is planned for MySQL version 5.0. If you are using MySQL 4.1, you cannot complete the steps in this section, but it is very important that you read this material so you understand this important concept. The steps in this section show how to perform these tasks in MySQL 5.0.

A view is defined by creating a **defining query**, which indicates the rows and columns to include in the view. The SQL command (or the defining query) to create the view for Juan is illustrated in Example 1.

EXAMPLE 1

Define a view named HOUSEWARES that consists of the part number, part description, units on hand, and unit price of each part in item class HW.

To define a view, use the **CREATE VIEW** command, which includes the words CREATE VIEW, followed by the name of the view, the word AS, and then a query. The CREATE VIEW command shown in Figure 7-1 creates a view of the PART table that contains only the specified columns.

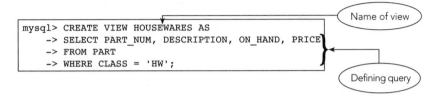

```
mysql> CREATE VIEW HOUSEWARES AS
    -> SELECT PART_NUM, DESCRIPTION, ON_HAND, PRICE
    -> FROM PART
    -> WHERE CLASS = 'HW';
```

Name of view

Defining query

FIGURE 7-1 Creating the HOUSEWARES view

Given the current data in the Premiere Products database, the HOUSEWARES view contains the data shown in Figure 7-2.

HOUSEWARES

PART_NUM	DESCRIPTION	ON_HAND	PRICE
AT94	Iron	50	$24.95
DL71	Cordless Drill	21	$129.95
FD21	Stand Mixer	22	$159.95

FIGURE 7-2 HOUSEWARES view

The data does not actually exist in this form, nor will it *ever* exist in this form. It is tempting to think that when this view is used, the query is executed and produces some sort of temporary table, named HOUSEWARES, that Juan then can access, but this is *not* what actually happens. Instead, the query acts as a sort of "window" into the database, as shown in Figure 7-3. As far as Juan is concerned, the entire database is just the darker shaded portion of the PART table. Juan can see any change that affects the darker portion of the PART table, but he is totally unaware of any other changes that are made in the database.

PART

PART_NUM	DESCRIPTION	ON_HAND	CLASS	WAREHOUSE	PRICE
AT94	Iron	50	HW	3	$24.95
BV06	Home Gym	45	SG	2	$794.95
CD52	Microwave Oven	32	AP	1	$165.00
DL71	Cordless Drill	21	HW	3	$129.95
DR93	Gas Range	8	AP	2	$495.00
DW11	Washer	12	AP	3	$399.99
FD21	Stand Mixer	22	HW	3	$159.95
KL62	Dryer	12	AP	1	$349.95
KT03	Dishwasher	8	AP	3	$595.00
KV29	Treadmill	9	SG	2	$1,390.00

FIGURE 7-3   Juan's view of the PART table

When you create a query that involves a view, SQL changes the query to one that selects data from the table(s) in the database that created the view. For example, suppose Juan creates the query shown in Figure 7-4.

```
mysql> SELECT *
    -> FROM HOUSEWARES          Data selected from the
    -> WHERE ON_HAND > 10;      HOUSEWARES view


+----------+----------------+---------+--------+
| PART_NUM | DESCRIPTION    | ON_HAND | PRICE  |
+----------+----------------+---------+--------+
| AT94     | Iron           |      50 |  24.95 |
| DL71     | Cordless Drill |      21 | 129.95 |
| FD21     | Stand Mixer    |      22 | 159.95 |
+----------+----------------+---------+--------+
```

FIGURE 7-4   Using the HOUSEWARES view

The DBMS does not execute the query in this form. Instead, it merges the query Juan entered with the query that defines the view to form the query that is actually executed. When the DBMS merges the query that creates the view with Juan's query to select rows for which the ON_HAND value is more than 10, the query that the DBMS actually executes is:

```
SELECT PART_NUM, DESCRIPTION, ON_HAND, PRICE
FROM PART
WHERE CLASS = 'HW'
AND ON_HAND > 10;
```

In the query that the DBMS executes, the FROM clause lists the PART table rather than the HOUSEWARES view, the SELECT clause lists columns from the PART table instead of * to select all columns from the HOUSEWARES view, and the WHERE clause contains a compound condition to select only those parts in the HW class (as Juan sees in the HOUSEWARES view) and only those parts with ON_HAND values of more than 10. This new query is the one that the DBMS actually executes.

Juan, however, is unaware that this kind of activity is taking place. To Juan, it seems that he is really using a table named HOUSEWARES. One advantage of this approach is that because the HOUSEWARES view never exists in its own right, any update to the PART table is *immediately* available in the HOUSEWARES view. If the HOUSEWARES view were really a table, this immediate update would not be possible.

You also can assign column names that are different from those in the base table, as illustrated in the next example.

EXAMPLE 2

Define a view named HSEWRES that consists of the part number, part description, units on hand, and unit price of all parts in item class HW. In this view, change the names of the PART_NUM, DESCRIPTION, ON_HAND, and PRICE columns to NUM, DSC, OH, and PRCE, respectively.

When renaming columns, you include the new column names in parentheses following the name of the view, as shown in Figure 7-5. In this case, anyone accessing the HSEWRES view will refer to PART_NUM as NUM, to DESCRIPTION as DSC, to ON_HAND as OH, and to PRICE as PRCE. If you select all columns from the HSEWRES view, the output displays the new column names, as shown in Figure 7-5.

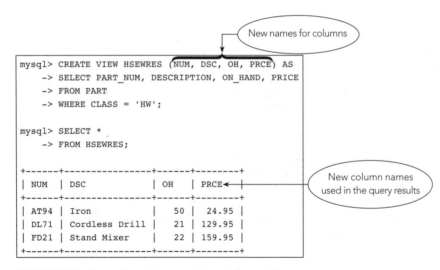

```
mysql> CREATE VIEW HSEWRES (NUM, DSC, OH, PRCE) AS
    -> SELECT PART_NUM, DESCRIPTION, ON_HAND, PRICE
    -> FROM PART
    -> WHERE CLASS = 'HW';

mysql> SELECT *
    -> FROM HSEWRES;

+------+---------------+------+--------+
| NUM  | DSC           | OH   | PRCE   |
+------+---------------+------+--------+
| AT94 | Iron          |   50 |  24.95 |
| DL71 | Cordless Drill|   21 | 129.95 |
| FD21 | Stand Mixer   |   22 | 159.95 |
+------+---------------+------+--------+
```

New names for columns

New column names used in the query results

FIGURE 7-5 Renaming columns when creating a view

The HSEWRES view is an example of a **row-and-column subset view** because it consists of a subset of the rows and columns in some base table—in this case, in the PART table. Because the defining query can be any valid SQL query, a view also can join two or more tables or involve statistics. The next example illustrates a view that joins two tables.

EXAMPLE 3

Define a view named REP_CUST consisting of the sales rep number (named RNUM), sales rep last name (named RLAST), sales rep first name (named RFIRST), customer number (named CNUM), and customer name (named CNAME) for all sales reps and matching customers in the REP and CUSTOMER tables.

The command to create this view appears in Figure 7-6.

```
mysql> CREATE VIEW REP_CUST (RNUM, RLAST, RFIRST, CNUM, CNAME) AS
    -> SELECT REP.REP_NUM, LAST_NAME, FIRST_NAME, CUSTOMER_NUM, CUSTOMER_NAME
    -> FROM REP, CUSTOMER
    -> WHERE REP.REP_NUM = CUSTOMER.REP_NUM;
```

View joins two tables

FIGURE 7-6 Creating the REP_CUST view

Given the current data in the Premiere Products database, the REP_CUST view contains the data shown in Figure 7-7.

```
mysql> SELECT *
    -> FROM REP_CUST;

+------+--------+---------+------+----------------------------+
| RNUM | RLAST  | RFIRST  | CNUM | CNAME                      |
+------+--------+---------+------+----------------------------+
| 20   | Kaiser | Valerie | 148  | Al's Appliance and Sport   |
| 35   | Hull   | Richard | 282  | Brookings Direct           |
| 65   | Perez  | Juan    | 356  | Ferguson's                 |
| 35   | Hull   | Richard | 408  | The Everything Shop        |
| 65   | Perez  | Juan    | 462  | Bargains Galore            |
| 20   | Kaiser | Valerie | 524  | Kline's                    |
| 65   | Perez  | Juan    | 608  | Johnson's Department Store |
| 35   | Hull   | Richard | 687  | Lee's Sport and Appliance  |
| 35   | Hull   | Richard | 725  | Deerfield's Four Seasons   |
| 20   | Kaiser | Valerie | 842  | All Season                 |
+------+--------+---------+------+----------------------------+
```

FIGURE 7-7 Using the REP_CUST view

A view also can involve statistics, as illustrated in Example 4.

EXAMPLE 4

Define a view named CRED_CUST that consists of each credit limit (CREDIT_LIMIT) and the number of customers having this credit limit (NUM_CUSTOMERS). Sort the credit limits in ascending order.

The command shown in Figure 7-8 creates this view; the SELECT command displays the current data in the Premiere Products database for this view.

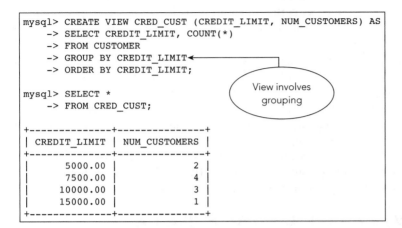

```
mysql> CREATE VIEW CRED_CUST (CREDIT_LIMIT, NUM_CUSTOMERS) AS
    -> SELECT CREDIT_LIMIT, COUNT(*)
    -> FROM CUSTOMER
    -> GROUP BY CREDIT_LIMIT
    -> ORDER BY CREDIT_LIMIT;

mysql> SELECT *
    -> FROM CRED_CUST;

+--------------+---------------+
| CREDIT_LIMIT | NUM_CUSTOMERS |
+--------------+---------------+
|      5000.00 |             2 |
|      7500.00 |             4 |
|     10000.00 |             3 |
|     15000.00 |             1 |
+--------------+---------------+
```

View involves grouping

FIGURE 7-8   Creating and using the CRED_CUST view

The use of views provides several benefits. First, views provide data independence. If the database structure changes (by adding columns or changing the way objects are related, for example) in such a way that the view still can be derived from existing data, the user still can access and use the same view. If adding extra columns to tables in the database is the only change, and these columns are not required by the view's user, the defining query might not even need to be changed for the user to continue using the view. If table relationships are changed, the defining query might be different, but because users are not aware of the defining query, they are unaware of this difference. Users continue accessing the database through the same view, as though nothing has changed. For example, suppose that customers are assigned to territories, that each territory is assigned to a single sales rep, that a sales rep can have more than one territory, and that a customer is represented by the sales rep who covers the customer's assigned territory. To implement these changes, you might choose to restructure the database as follows:

```
REP(REP_NUM, LAST_NAME, FIRST_NAME, STREET, CITY,
      STATE, ZIP, COMMISSION, RATE)
TERRITORY(TERRITORY_NUM, DESCRIPTION, REP_NUM)
CUSTOMER(CUSTOMER_NUM, CUSTOMER_NAME, STREET, CITY,
      STATE, ZIP, BALANCE, CREDIT_LIMIT, TERRITORY_NUM)
```

Assuming that the REP_CUST view shown earlier still is required, the defining query could be changed as follows:

```
CREATE VIEW REP_CUST (RNUM, RLAST, RFIRST,
      CNUM, CNAME) AS
SELECT REP.REP_NUM, REP.LAST_NAME, REP.FIRST_NAME,
      CUSTOMER_NUM, CUSTOMER_NAME
FROM REP, TERRITORY, CUSTOMER
WHERE REP.REP_NUM = TERRITORY.REP_NUM
AND TERRITORY.TERRITORY_NUM = CUSTOMER.TERRITORY_NUM;
```

The user of this view still can retrieve the number and name of a sales rep together with the number and name of each customer the sales rep represents. The user is unaware, however, of the new structure in the database.

The second benefit of using views is that different users can view the same data in different ways through their own views. In other words, the display of data can be customized to meet each user's needs.

The final benefit of using views is that a view can contain only those columns required by a given user. This practice has two advantages. First, because the view usually contains fewer columns than the overall database and is conceptually a single table, rather than a collection of tables, a view greatly simplifies the user's perception of the database. Second, views provide a measure of security. Columns that are not included in the view are not accessible to the view's user. For example, omitting the BALANCE column from a view ensures that the view's user cannot access any customer's balance. Likewise, rows that are not included in the view are not accessible. A user of the HOUSEWARES view, for example, cannot obtain any information about parts in the AP or SG classes.

USING A VIEW TO UPDATE DATA

The benefits of using views hold true only when views are used for retrieval purposes. When updating the database, the issues involved in updating data through a view depend on the type of view, as you will see next.

Updating Row-and-Column Subset Views

Consider the row-and-column subset view for the HOUSEWARES view. There are columns in the underlying base table (PART) that are not present in the view. Thus, if you attempt to add a row with the data ('BB99','PAN',50,14.95), the DBMS must determine how to enter the data in those columns from the PART table that are not included in the HOUSEWARES view (CLASS and WAREHOUSE). In this case, it is clear what data to enter in the CLASS column. According to the view definition, all rows are item class HW, but it is not clear what data to enter in the WAREHOUSE column. The only possibility would be NULL. Thus, provided that every column not included in a view can accept nulls, you can add new rows using the INSERT command. There is another problem, however. Suppose the user attempts to add a row to the HOUSEWARES view containing the data ('BV06','Waffle Maker',5,29.95). Because part number BV06 already exists in the PART table, the system *must* reject this attempt. Because this part is not in item class HW (and therefore is not in the HOUSEWARES view), this rejection certainly will seem strange to the user, because there is no such part in the user's view.

On the other hand, updates or deletions cause no particular problem in this view. If the description of part number FD21 changes from Stand Mixer to Pan, this change is made in the PART table. If part number DL71 is deleted, this deletion occurs in the PART table. One surprising change could take place, however. Suppose that the CLASS column is included in the HOUSEWARES view and a user changes the class of part number AT94 from HW to AP. Because this item would no longer satisfy the criterion for being included in the HOUSEWARES view, part number AT94 would disappear from the user's view!

Although there are problems to overcome when updating row-and-column subset views, it seems possible to update the database through the HOUSEWARES view. This does not imply that *any* row-and-column subset view is updatable, however. Consider the REP_CRED view and data shown in Figure 7-9. (The DISTINCT operator is used to omit duplicate rows from the view.)

```
mysql> CREATE VIEW REP_CRED AS
    -> SELECT DISTINCT CREDIT_LIMIT, REP_NUM
    -> FROM CUSTOMER;

mysql> SELECT *
    -> FROM REP_CRED;

+--------------+---------+
| CREDIT_LIMIT | REP_NUM |
+--------------+---------+
|      7500.00 |      20 |
|     10000.00 |      35 |
|      7500.00 |      65 |
|      5000.00 |      35 |
|     10000.00 |      65 |
|     15000.00 |      20 |
|      7500.00 |      35 |
+--------------+---------+
```

FIGURE 7-9   Creating and using the REP_CRED view

How would you add the row 15000,'35' to this view? In the underlying base table (CUSTOMER), at least one customer must be added whose credit limit is $15,000 and whose sales rep number is 35, but which customer is it? You cannot leave the other columns null in this case, because one of them is CUSTOMER_NUM, which is the base table's primary key. What would it mean to change the row 5000,'35' to 15000,'35'? Would it mean changing the credit limit to $15,000 for each customer represented by sales rep number 35 that currently has a credit limit of $5,000? Would it mean changing the credit limit of one of these customers and deleting the rest? What would it mean to delete the row 5000,'35'? Would it mean deleting all customers with credit limits of $5,000 and represented by sales rep number 35, or would it mean assigning these customers a different sales rep or a different credit limit?

Why does the REP_CRED view involve a number of serious problems that are not present in the HOUSEWARES view? The basic reason is that the HOUSEWARES view includes, as one of its columns, the primary key of the underlying base table, but the REP_CRED view does not. A row-and-column subset view that contains the primary key of the underlying base table is updatable (subject, of course, to some of the concerns already discussed).

Updating Views Involving Joins

In general, views that involve joins of base tables can cause problems when updating data. Consider the relatively simple REP_CUST view, for example, described earlier (see Figures 7-6 and 7-7). The fact that some columns in the underlying base tables are not included in this view presents some of the same problems discussed earlier. Assuming that you can overcome these problems by using nulls, there are more serious problems when attempting to update the database through this view. On the surface, changing the row ('35','Hull','Richard','282','Brookings Direct') to ('35','Baldwin','Sara','282','Brookings Direct'), might not appear to pose any problems other than some inconsistency in the data. (In the new version of the row, the name of sales rep 35 is Sara Baldwin; whereas in the fourth row in the table, the name of sales rep 35, *the same sales rep*, is Richard Hull.)

The problem is actually more serious than that—making this change is not possible. The name of a sales rep is stored only once in the underlying REP table. Changing the name of sales rep 35 from Richard Hull to Sara Baldwin in this one row of the view causes the change to be made to the single row for sales rep 35 in the REP table. Because the view simply displays data from the base tables, for each row in which the sales rep number is 35, the sales rep name is now Sara Baldwin. In other words, it appears that the same change has been made in the other rows. In this case, this change ensures consistency in the data. In general, however, the unexpected changes caused by an update are not desirable.

Before concluding the topic of views that involve joins, you should note that all joins do not create the preceding problem. If two base tables have the same primary key and the primary key is used as the join column, updating the database using the view is not a problem. For example, suppose that the actual database contains two tables (REP_DEMO and REP_FIN) instead of one table (REP). Figure 7-10 shows the data in these hypothetical tables.

REP_DEMO

REP_NUM	LAST_NAME	FIRST_NAME	STREET	CITY	STATE	ZIP
20	Kaiser	Valerie	624 Randall	Grove	FL	33321
35	Hull	Richard	532 Jackson	Sheldon	FL	33553
65	Perez	Juan	1626 Taylor	Fillmore	FL	33336

REP_FIN

REP_NUM	COMMISSION	RATE
20	$20,542.50	0.05
35	$39,216.00	0.07
65	$23,487.00	0.05

FIGURE 7-10 REP_DEMO and REP_FIN tables

In this case, what was a single table in the original Premiere Products design has been divided into two separate tables. Users who need to see the rep data in a single table can use a view that joins these two tables using the REP_NUM column. The view definition appears in Figure 7-11.

```
mysql> CREATE VIEW SALES_REP AS                    Name of view
    -> SELECT REP_DEMO.REP_NUM, LAST_NAME, FIRST_NAME, STREET, CITY, STATE,
    -> ZIP, COMMISSION, RATE
    -> FROM REP_DEMO, REP_FIN                   View joins the REP_DEMO
    -> WHERE REP_DEMO.REP_NUM = REP_FIN.REP_NUM;    and REP_FIN tables
```

FIGURE 7-11 Creating the SALES_REP view

The data in the SALES_REP view appears in Figure 7-12.

```
mysql> SELECT *
    -> FROM SALES_REP;
```

REP_NUM	LAST_NAME	FIRST_NAME	STREET	CITY	STATE	ZIP	COMMISSION	RATE
20	Kaiser	Valerie	624 Randall	Grove	FL	33321	20542.50	0.05
35	Hull	Richard	532 Jackson	Sheldon	FL	33553	39216.00	0.07
65	Perez	Juan	1626 Taylor	Fillmore	FL	33336	23487.00	0.05

FIGURE 7-12 Using the SALES_REP view

It is easy to update the SALES_REP view. To add a row, simply add a row to each underlying base table. To update data in a row, make the change in the appropriate base table. To delete a row from the view, delete the corresponding rows from both underlying base tables.

Q & A

Question: How would you add the row ('10','Peters','Jean','14 Brink','Holt','FL','46223', 107.50,0.05) to the SALES_REP view?
Answer: Use an INSERT command to add the row ('10','Peters','Jean','14 Brink','Holt','FL','46223') to the REP_DEMO table, and then use another INSERT command to add the row ('10',107.50,0.05) to the REP_FIN table.

Q & A

Question: How would you change the name of sales rep 20 to Valerie Lewis?
Answer: Use an UPDATE command to change the name in the REP_DEMO table.

Updates (additions, changes, or deletions) to the SALES_REP view do not cause any problems. The main reason that the SALES_REP view is updatable—and that other views involving joins are not—is that this view is derived from joining two base tables *on the primary key of each table*. In contrast, the REP_CUST view is derived by joining two tables by matching the primary key of one table with a column that is *not* the primary key in the other table. Even more severe problems are encountered if neither of the join columns is a primary key column.

Updating Views Involving Statistics

A view that involves statistics calculated from one or more base tables is the most troublesome view when attempting to update data. Consider the CRED_CUST view, for example (see Figure 7-8). How would you add the row 9000,3 to indicate that there are three customers that have credit limits of $9,000 each? Likewise, changing the row 5000,2 to 5000,5 means you are adding 3 new customers with credit limits of $5,000 each, for a total of 5 customers. Clearly these are impossible tasks; you cannot add rows to a view that includes calculations.

DROPPING A VIEW

When a view is no longer needed, you can remove it using the DROP VIEW command.

The following **DROP VIEW** command deletes the HSEWRES view. The DROP VIEW command removes only a view definition; the tables and data on which the view is based still exist:

```
DROP VIEW HSEWRES;
```

SECURITY

Security is the prevention of unauthorized access to a database. Within an organization, the database administrator determines the types of access various users can have to the database. Some users might be able to retrieve and update anything in the database. Other users might be able to retrieve any data from the database but not make any changes to it. Still other users might be able to access only a portion of the database. For example, Bill might be able to retrieve and update customer data, but is prevented from accessing data about sales reps, orders, order lines, or parts. Valerie might be able to retrieve part data and nothing else. Sam might be able to retrieve and update data on parts in the HW class, but cannot retrieve data in any other classes.

After the database administrator has determined the access different users of the database should have, these access rules are enforced by whatever security mechanism the DBMS provides. In MySQL, there are two security mechanisms. You already have seen that views furnish a certain amount of security; if users are accessing the database through a view, they cannot access any data that is not included in the view. The main mechanism for providing access to a database, however, is the **GRANT** command.

The basic idea of the GRANT command is that the database administrator can grant different types of privileges to users and then revoke them later, if necessary. These privileges include the right to select, insert, update, and delete table data. You can grant and revoke user privileges using the GRANT and REVOKE commands. The following examples illustrate various uses of the GRANT command when the named users already exist in the database.

NOTE

You should not attempt to execute the commands in this section unless your instructor specifically directs you to do so.

EXAMPLE 6

User Johnson must be able to retrieve data from the REP table.

The following GRANT command permits a user named Johnson to execute SELECT commands for the REP table:

```
GRANT SELECT ON REP TO JOHNSON;
```

EXAMPLE 7

Users Smith and Brown must be able to add new parts to the PART table.

The following GRANT command permits two users named Smith and Brown to execute INSERT commands for the PART table. Notice that a comma separates the user names:

```
GRANT INSERT ON PART TO SMITH, BROWN;
```

EXAMPLE 8

User Anderson must be able to change the name and street address of customers.

The following GRANT command permits a user named Anderson to execute UPDATE commands involving the CUSTOMER_NAME and STREET columns in the CUSTOMER table. Notice that the SQL command includes the column names in parentheses before the ON clause:

```
GRANT UPDATE (CUSTOMER_NAME, STREET) ON CUSTOMER TO ANDERSON;
```

EXAMPLE 9

User Thompson must be able to delete order lines.

The following GRANT command permits a user named Thompson to execute DELETE commands for the ORDER_LINE table:

```
GRANT DELETE ON ORDER_LINE TO THOMPSON;
```

EXAMPLE 10

Every user must be able to retrieve part numbers, part descriptions, and item classes.

The GRANT command to indicate that all users can retrieve data using a SELECT command includes the word PUBLIC, as follows:

```
GRANT SELECT (PART_NUM, DESCRIPTION, CLASS) ON PART TO PUBLIC;
```

EXAMPLE 11

User Roberts must be able to create an index on the REP table.

You will learn about indexes and their uses in the next section. The following GRANT command permits a user named Roberts to create an index on the REP table:

```
GRANT INDEX ON REP TO ROBERTS;
```

EXAMPLE 12

User Thomas must be able to change the structure of the CUSTOMER table.

The following GRANT command permits a user named Thomas to execute ALTER commands for the CUSTOMER table to change the table's structure:

```
GRANT ALTER ON CUSTOMER TO THOMAS;
```

EXAMPLE 13

User Wilson must have all privileges for the REP table.

The GRANT command to indicate that a user has all privileges includes the ALL privilege, as follows:

```
GRANT ALL ON REP TO WILSON;
```

The privileges that can be granted are SELECT to retrieve data, UPDATE to change data, DELETE to delete data, INSERT to add new data, INDEX to create an index, and ALTER to change the table structure. The database administrator usually assigns privileges. Normally, when the database administrator grants a particular privilege to a user, the user cannot pass that privilege along to other users. If the user needs to be able to pass the privilege to other users, the GRANT command must include the **WITH GRANT OPTION** clause. This clause grants the indicated privilege to the user and also permits the user to grant the same privileges (or a subset of them) to other users.

The database administrator uses the **REVOKE** command to revoke privileges from users. The format of the REVOKE command is essentially the same as that of the GRANT command, but with two differences: the word GRANT is replaced by the word REVOKE, and the word TO is replaced by the word FROM. In addition, the clause WITH GRANT OPTION obviously is not meaningful as part of a REVOKE command. Incidentally, the revoke cascades, so if Johnson is granted privileges WITH GRANT OPTION and then Johnson grants these same privileges to Smith, revoking the privileges from Johnson revokes Smith's privileges at the same time. Example 14 illustrates the use of the REVOKE command.

EXAMPLE 14

User Johnson is no longer allowed to retrieve data from the REP table.

The following REVOKE command revokes the SELECT privilege for the REP table from the user named Johnson:

```
REVOKE SELECT ON REP FROM JOHNSON;
```

The GRANT and REVOKE commands also can be applied to views so that access is restricted to only certain rows within tables.

INDEXES

When you query a database, you are usually searching for a row (or collection of rows) that satisfies some condition. Examining every row in a table to find the ones you need often takes too much time to be practical, especially in tables with thousands of rows. Fortunately, you can create and use an index to speed up the searching process significantly. An index in MySQL is similar to an index in a book. If you want to find a discussion of a given topic in a book, you could scan the entire book from start to finish, looking for references to the topic you need. More than likely, however, you would not have to resort to this technique. If the book has a good index, you could use it to identify the pages on which your topic is discussed.

Within relational model systems on both mainframes and personal computers, the main mechanism for increasing the efficiency with which data is retrieved from the database is the **index**. Conceptually, these indexes are very much like the index in a book. Consider Figure 7-13, for example, which shows the CUSTOMER table for Premiere Products together with one extra column named ROW_NUMBER. This extra column gives the location of the row in the table (customer 148 is the first row in the table and is on row 1, customer 282 is on row 2, and so on). These row numbers are assigned automatically and used by the DBMS, not by the users, and that is why you do not see them.

CUSTOMER

ROW_ NUMBER	CUSTOMER_ NUM	CUSTOMER_ NAME	STREET	CITY	STATE	ZIP	BALANCE	CREDIT_ LIMIT	REP_ NUM
1	148	Al's Appliance and Sport	2837 Greenway	Fillmore	FL	33336	$6,550.00	$7,500.00	20
2	282	Brookings Direct	3827 Devon	Grove	FL	33321	$431.50	$10,000.00	35
3	356	Ferguson's	382 Wildwood	Northfield	FL	33146	$5,785.00	$7,500.00	65
4	408	The Everything Shop	1828 Raven	Crystal	FL	33503	$5,285.25	$5,000.00	35
5	462	Bargains Galore	3829 Central	Grove	FL	33321	$3,412.00	$10,000.00	65
6	524	Kline's	838 Ridgeland	Fillmore	FL	33336	$12,762.00	$15,000.00	20
7	608	Johnson's Department Store	372 Oxford	Sheldon	FL	33553	$2,106.00	$10,000.00	65
8	687	Lee's Sport and Appliance	282 Evergreen	Altonville	FL	32543	$2,851.00	$5,000.00	35
9	725	Deerfield's Four Seasons	282 Columbia	Sheldon	FL	33553	$248.00	$7,500.00	35
10	842	All Season	28 Lakeview	Grove	FL	33321	$8,221.00	$7,500.00	20

FIGURE 7-13 CUSTOMER table with row numbers

To access a customer's row using its customer number, you might create and use an index, as shown in Figure 7-14. The index has two columns: the first column contains a customer number, and the second column contains the number of the row on which the customer number is found. To find a customer, you look up the customer's number in the first column in the index. The value in the second column indicates which row to retrieve from the CUSTOMER table, then the row for the desired customer is retrieved.

CUSTOMER_NUM Index

CUSTOMER_NUM	ROW_NUMBER
148	1
282	2
356	3
408	4
462	5
524	6
608	7
687	8
725	9
842	10

FIGURE 7-14 Index for the CUSTOMER table on the CUSTOMER_NUM column

Because customer numbers are unique, there is only a single row number in this index. This is not always the case, however. Suppose that you wanted to access all customers with a specific credit limit or all customers that are represented by a specific sales rep. You might choose to create and use an index on the CREDIT_LIMIT column and an index on the REP_NUM column, as shown in Figure 7-15. In the CREDIT_LIMIT index, the first column contains a credit limit and the second column contains the numbers of *all* rows on which that credit limit is found. The REP_NUM index is similar, except that the first column contains a sales rep number.

CREDIT_LIMIT Index

CREDIT_LIMIT	ROW_NUMBER
$5,000.00	4, 8
$7,500.00	1, 3, 9, 10
$10,000.00	2, 5, 7
$15,000.00	6

REP_NUM Index

REP_NUM	ROW_NUMBER
20	1, 6, 10
35	2, 4, 8, 9
65	3, 5, 7

FIGURE 7-15 Indexes for the CUSTOMER table on the CREDIT_LIMIT and REP_NUM columns

Q & A

Question: How would you use the index shown in Figure 7-15 to find every customer with a $10,000 credit limit?
Answer: Look up $10,000 in the CREDIT_LIMIT index to find a collection of row numbers (2, 5, and 7). Use these row numbers to find the corresponding rows in the CUSTOMER table (Brookings Direct, Bargains Galore, and Johnson's Department Store).

Q & A

Question: How would you use the index shown in Figure 7-15 to find every customer represented by sales rep 35?
Answer: Look up 35 in the REP_NUM index to find a collection of row numbers (2, 4, 8, and 9). Use these row numbers to find the corresponding rows in the CUSTOMER table (Brookings Direct, The Everything Shop, Lee's Sport and Appliance, and Deerfield's Four Seasons).

The actual structure of an index is more complicated than what is shown in the figures. Fortunately, you do not have to be concerned with the details of manipulating and using indexes because MySQL manages them for you—your only job is to determine the columns on which to build the indexes. Typically, you can create and maintain an index for any column or combination of columns in any table. After creating an index, MySQL uses it to speed up data retrieval.

As you would expect, the use of any index has advantages and disadvantages. An important advantage was already mentioned: an index makes certain types of retrieval more efficient.

There are two disadvantages. First, an index occupies disk space. Using this space for an index, however, is technically unnecessary because any retrieval that you can make using an index also can be made without the index; the index just speeds up the retrieval. The second disadvantage is that MySQL must update the index whenever corresponding data in the database is updated. Without the index, MySQL would not need to make these updates. The main question that you must ask when considering whether to create a given index is this: do the benefits derived during retrieval outweigh the additional storage required and the extra processing involved in update operations? In a very large database, you might find that indexes are essential to decrease the time required to retrieve records. In a small database, however, an index might not provide any significant benefits.

You can add and drop indexes as necessary. You can create an index after the database is built; it does not need to be created at the same time as the database. Likewise, if it appears that an existing index is unnecessary, you can drop it.

Creating an Index

Suppose that some users at Premiere Products need to display customer records ordered by balance. Other users need to access a customer's name using the customer's number. In addition, some users need to produce a report in which customer records are listed by credit limit in descending order. Within the group of customers having the same credit limit, the customer records must be ordered by name.

Each of the previous requirements is carried out more efficiently when you create the appropriate index. The command used to create an index is **CREATE INDEX**, as illustrated in Example 15.

EXAMPLE 15

Create an index named BALIND on the BALANCE column in the CUSTOMER table. Create an index named REPNAME on the combination of the LAST_NAME and FIRST_NAME columns in the REP table. Create an index named CREDNAME on the combination of the CREDIT_LIMIT and CUSTOMER_NAME columns in the CUSTOMER table, with the credit limits listed in descending order.

The appropriate CREATE INDEX commands to create these indexes appear in Figure 7-16. Each command lists the name of the index and the table name on which the index is to be created. The column name(s) are listed in parentheses. If any column is to be included in descending order, the column name is followed by the DESC operator.

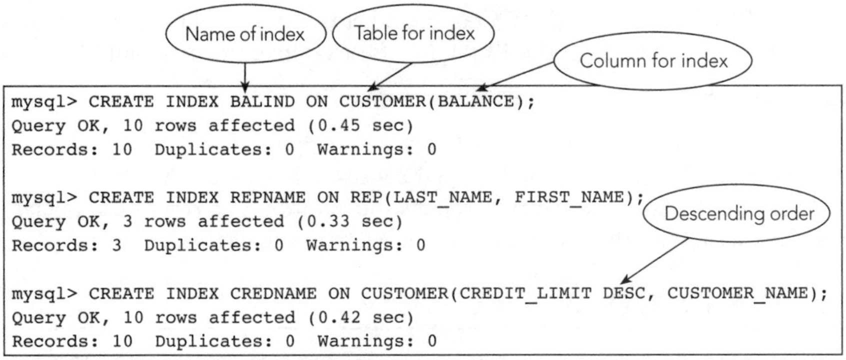

```
mysql> CREATE INDEX BALIND ON CUSTOMER(BALANCE);
Query OK, 10 rows affected (0.45 sec)
Records: 10  Duplicates: 0  Warnings: 0

mysql> CREATE INDEX REPNAME ON REP(LAST_NAME, FIRST_NAME);
Query OK, 3 rows affected (0.33 sec)
Records: 3  Duplicates: 0  Warnings: 0

mysql> CREATE INDEX CREDNAME ON CUSTOMER(CREDIT_LIMIT DESC, CUSTOMER_NAME);
Query OK, 10 rows affected (0.42 sec)
Records: 10  Duplicates: 0  Warnings: 0
```

FIGURE 7-16 Creating indexes

If customers are listed using the CREDNAME index, the records appear in order by descending credit limit. Within any credit limit, the customers are listed alphabetically by name.

Dropping an Index

The command used to drop (delete) an index is **DROP INDEX**, which consists of the words DROP INDEX followed by the name of the index to drop, the word ON, and then the table on which the index was created. To delete the CREDNAME index on the CUSTOMER table, for example, the command is:

```
DROP INDEX CREDNAME ON CUSTOMER;
```

The DROP INDEX command permanently deletes the index. CREDNAME was the index MySQL used when listing customer records in descending credit limit order and then by customer name within credit limit. MySQL still can list customers in this order; however, it cannot do so as efficiently without the index.

Creating Unique Indexes

When you specify a table's primary key, MySQL automatically ensures that the values entered in the primary key column(s) are unique. For example, MySQL rejects an attempt to add a second customer whose number is 148 in the CUSTOMER table because customer 148 already exists. Thus, you do not need to take any special action to make sure that values in the primary key column are unique; MySQL does it for you.

Occasionally, a nonprimary key column might store unique values. For example, in the REP table, the primary key is REP_NUM. If the REP table also contains a column for Social Security numbers, the values in this column also must be unique. Because the Social Security number column is not the table's primary key, however, you need to take special action in order for MySQL to ensure that there are no duplicate values in this column.

To ensure the uniqueness of values in a nonprimary key column, you can create a **unique index** by using the **CREATE UNIQUE INDEX** command. To create a unique index named SSN on the SOC_SEC_NUM column of the REP table, for example, the command is:

```
CREATE UNIQUE INDEX SSN ON REP(SOC_SEC_NUM);
```

This unique index has all the properties of indexes already discussed, along with one additional property: MySQL rejects any update that causes a duplicate value in the SOC_SEC_NUM column. In this case, MySQL rejects the addition of a rep whose Social Security number is the same as that of another rep already in the database.

SYSTEM CATALOG

Information about the tables in the database is kept in the **system catalog** (**catalog**) or the **data dictionary**. This section describes the types of items kept in the catalog and the way in which you can query it to access information about the database structure.

NOTE

Most users need privileges to view system catalog data, so you might not be able to execute these commands.

In MySQL, use the **SHOW TABLES** command to list all the tables in the database. Use the **SHOW COLUMNS** command to list all the columns in a given table. To list all the columns in the CUSTOMER table, for example, the command is:

```
SHOW COLUMNS FROM CUSTOMER;
```

EXAMPLE 16

List the name of each table in the PREMIERE database.

The command to list the table names is shown in Figure 7-17. Notice that the command does not specify the PREMIERE database. Rather, the command simply lists all tables in the default database. If the default database were named HENRY, the SHOW TABLES command would identify the tables in the HENRY database.

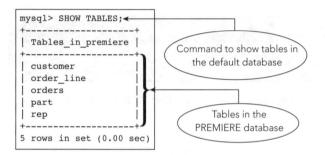

FIGURE 7-17 Tables in the default database

EXAMPLE 17

List the columns in the CUSTOMER table. For each column, list the name of the column and the data type.

The MySQL command to accomplish this task is the SHOW COLUMNS command, as illustrated in Figure 7-18.

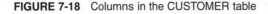

```
mysql> SHOW COLUMNS
    -> FROM CUSTOMER;
+---------------+--------------+------+-----+---------+-------+
| Field         | Type         | Null | Key | Default | Extra |
+---------------+--------------+------+-----+---------+-------+
| CUSTOMER_NUM  | char(3)      |      | PRI |         |       |
| CUSTOMER_NAME | char(35)     |      |     |         |       |
| STREET        | char(15)     | YES  |     | NULL    |       |
| CITY          | char(15)     | YES  |     | NULL    |       |
| STATE         | char(2)      | YES  |     | NULL    |       |
| ZIP           | char(5)      | YES  |     | NULL    |       |
| BALANCE       | decimal(8,2) | YES  | MUL | NULL    |       |
| CREDIT_LIMIT  | decimal(8,2) | YES  |     | NULL    |       |
| REP_NUM       | char(2)      | YES  |     | NULL    |       |
+---------------+--------------+------+-----+---------+-------+
9 rows in set (0.07 sec)
```

Command to show details about the columns in the CUSTOMER table

FIGURE 7-18 Columns in the CUSTOMER table

EXAMPLE 18

List all indexes associated with the CUSTOMER table.

The MySQL command to accomplish this task is the **SHOW INDEX** command, as illustrated in Figure 7-19.

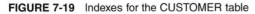

Command to show details about indexes associated with the CUSTOMER table

```
mysql> SHOW INDEX
    -> FROM CUSTOMER;
+----------+------------+----------+--------------+-------------+
| Table    | Non_unique | Key_name | Seq_in_index | Column_name |
+----------+------------+----------+--------------+-------------+
| CUSTOMER |          0 | PRIMARY  |            1 | CUSTOMER_NUM |
| CUSTOMER |          1 | BALIND   |            1 | BALANCE     |
+----------+------------+----------+--------------+-------------+
2 rows in set (0.00 sec)
```

Additional columns in the results are omitted

FIGURE 7-19 Indexes for the CUSTOMER table

N O T E

The command shown in Figure 7-19 includes additional columns that were omitted because they do not fit within the margins of this book.

EXAMPLE 19

List all privileges that have been granted to user Wilson.

The MySQL command to accomplish this task is the **SHOW GRANTS** command, as illustrated in Figure 7-20. Notice that you use the word FOR (FOR WILSON) rather than the word FROM as in the previous examples. The @% characters at the end of the user's name in the results indicate that the user can connect to the database from any location.

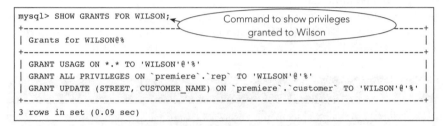

```
mysql> SHOW GRANTS FOR WILSON;                Command to show privileges
+---------------------------------             granted to Wilson          ------+
| Grants for WILSON@%                                                            |
+-------------------------------------------------------------------------------+
| GRANT USAGE ON *.* TO 'WILSON'@'%'                                            |
| GRANT ALL PRIVILEGES ON `premiere`.`rep` TO 'WILSON'@'%'                      |
| GRANT UPDATE (STREET, CUSTOMER_NAME) ON `premiere`.`customer` TO 'WILSON'@'%' |
+-------------------------------------------------------------------------------+
3 rows in set (0.09 sec)
```

FIGURE 7-20   Privileges granted to user Wilson

INTEGRITY CONSTRAINTS IN SQL

An **integrity constraint** is a rule for the data in the database. Examples of integrity constraints in the Premiere Products database are as follows:

- A sales rep's number must be unique.
- The sales rep number for a customer must match the number of a sales rep currently in the database. For example, because there is no sales rep number 11, a customer cannot be assigned to sales rep 11.
- Item classes for parts must be AP, HW, or SG because these are the only item classes used.

If a user enters data in the database that violates any of these integrity constraints, the database develops serious problems. For example, two sales reps with the same number, a customer with a nonexistent sales rep, or a part in a nonexistent item class would compromise the integrity of data in the database. To manage these types of problems, MySQL provides **integrity support**, the process of specifying and enforcing integrity constraints for a database. MySQL has clauses to support three types of integrity constraints that you can specify within a CREATE TABLE or an ALTER TABLE command. The only difference between these two commands is that an ALTER TABLE command is followed by the word ADD to indicate that you are adding the constraint to the list of existing constraints. To change an integrity constraint after it has been created, just enter the new constraint, which immediately takes the place of the original.

The types of constraints supported in MySQL are primary keys, foreign keys, and legal values. In most cases, you specify a table's primary key when you create the table. To add a primary key after creating a table, you can use the **ADD PRIMARY KEY** clause of the ALTER TABLE command. For example, to indicate that REP_NUM is the primary key for the REP table, the ALTER TABLE command is:

```
ALTER TABLE REP
ADD PRIMARY KEY (REP_NUM);
```

The PRIMARY KEY clause is PRIMARY KEY followed by the column name that makes up the primary key in parentheses. If the primary key contains more than one column, use commas to separate the column names.

A **foreign key** is a column in one table whose values match the primary key in another table. (One example is the CUSTOMER_NUM column in the ORDERS table. Values in this column are required to match those of the primary key in the CUSTOMER table.)

E X A M P L E 2 0

Specify the CUSTOMER_NUM column in the ORDERS table as a foreign key that must match the CUSTOMER table.

When a table contains a foreign key, you identify it using the **ADD FOREIGN KEY** clause of the ALTER TABLE command. In this clause, you specify *both* the column that is a foreign key *and* the table it matches. The general form for assigning a foreign key is FOREIGN KEY, the column name(s) of the foreign key, the REFERENCES clause, and then the table name that the foreign key must match, as shown in Figure 7-21.

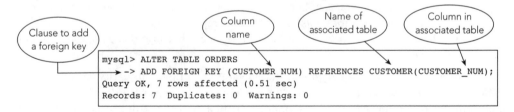

FIGURE 7-21 Adding a foreign key to an existing table

After creating a foreign key, MySQL rejects any update that violates the foreign key constraint. For example, MySQL rejects the INSERT command shown in Figure 7-22 because it attempts to add an order for which the customer number (850) does not match any customer in the CUSTOMER table. MySQL also rejects the DELETE command in Figure 7-22 because it attempts to delete customer number 148; rows in the ORDERS table for which the customer number is 148 would no longer match any row in the CUSTOMER table.

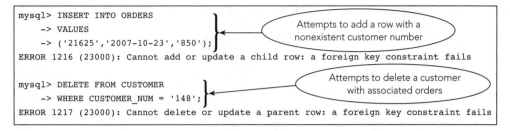

```
mysql> INSERT INTO ORDERS
    -> VALUES
    -> ('21625','2007-10-23','850');
ERROR 1216 (23000): Cannot add or update a child row: a foreign key constraint fails

mysql> DELETE FROM CUSTOMER
    -> WHERE CUSTOMER_NUM = '148';
ERROR 1217 (23000): Cannot delete or update a parent row: a foreign key constraint fails
```

Attempts to add a row with a nonexistent customer number

Attempts to delete a customer with associated orders

FIGURE 7-22   Updates that violate foreign key constraints

Note that the error messages shown in Figure 7-22 include the words "parent" and "child." When you specify a foreign key, the table containing the foreign key is the **child**, and the table referenced by the foreign key is the **parent**. For example, the CUSTOMER_NUM column in the ORDERS table is a foreign key that references the CUSTOMER table. For this foreign key, the CUSTOMER table is the parent, and the ORDERS table is the child. The first error message indicates that there is no parent for the order (there is no customer number 850). The second error message indicates that there are child records (rows) for customer 148 (customer 148 has orders). MySQL rejects both updates because they violate referential integrity.

Chapter Summary

A view contains data that is derived from existing base tables when users attempt to access the view.

To define a view, use the CREATE VIEW command, which includes a defining query that describes the portion of the database included in the view. When a user retrieves data from the view, MySQL merges the query entered by the user with the defining query and produces the query that MySQL actually executes.

Views provide data independence, allow database access control, and simplify the database structure for users. You cannot update views that involve statistics and views with joins of nonprimary key columns. Updates for these types of views must be made in the base table.

Use the DROP VIEW command to delete a view.

Use the GRANT command to give users access privileges to data in the database.

Use the REVOKE command to terminate previously granted privileges.

You can create and use an index to make data retrieval more efficient. Use the CREATE INDEX command to create an index. Use the CREATE UNIQUE INDEX command to enforce a rule so only unique values are allowed in a nonprimary key column.

Use the DROP INDEX command to delete an index.

The DBMS, not the user, chooses which index to use to accomplish a given task.

Information about the tables in the database is kept in the system catalog (catalog) or the data dictionary. Use the SHOW TABLES command to list all the tables in the default database. Use the SHOW COLUMNS command to list all the columns in a given table. Use the SHOW INDEX command to list the indexes associated with a table. Use the SHOW GRANTS command to list the privileges granted to a user.

You usually specify primary key constraints when you create a table, but you can specify them later using the ADD PRIMARY KEY clause.

To specify a foreign key, use the ADD FOREIGN KEY clause.

Key Terms

ADD FOREIGN KEY	DROP INDEX
ADD PRIMARY KEY	DROP VIEW
base table	foreign key
catalog	GRANT
child	index
CREATE INDEX	integrity constraint
CREATE UNIQUE INDEX	integrity support
CREATE VIEW	parent
data dictionary	REVOKE
database administration	row-and-column subset view
database administrator	security
defining query	SHOW COLUMNS

SHOW GRANTS   unique index

SHOW INDEX   view

SHOW TABLES   WITH GRANT OPTION

system catalog

Review Questions

1. What is a view?

2. Which command defines a view?

3. What is a defining query?

4. What happens when a user retrieves data from a view?

5. What are three advantages of using views?

6. Which types of views cannot be updated?

7. Which command deletes a view?

8. Which command gives users access privileges to various portions of the database?

9. Which command terminates previously granted privileges?

10. What is the purpose of an index?

11. How do you create an index? How do you create a unique index? What is the difference between an index and a unique index?

12. Which command deletes an index?

13. Does the DBMS or the user make the choice of which index to use to accomplish a given task?

14. How do you obtain a list of tables in the default database? How do you obtain a list of columns in a given table?

15. How do you obtain a list of indexes associated with a given table?

16. How do you obtain a list of privileges granted to a given user?

17. What are integrity constraints?

18. When are primary key constraints usually specified? Can you specify them after creating a table? How?

19. How do you specify a foreign key?

Exercises

Premiere Products

Use MySQL to make the following changes to the Premiere Products database (see Figure 1-2 in Chapter 1). Use the notes at the end of Chapter 3 to print your output if directed to do so by your instructor. For any exercises that use commands not supported by your version of MySQL, write the command to accomplish the task.

1. Define a view named MAJOR_CUSTOMER. It consists of the customer number, name, balance, credit limit, and rep number for every customer whose credit limit is $10,000 or less.

   a. Write and execute the CREATE VIEW command to create the MAJOR_CUSTOMER view.

   b. Write and execute the command to retrieve the customer number and name of each customer in the MAJOR_CUSTOMER view with a balance that exceeds the credit limit.

   c. Write and execute the query that the DBMS actually executes.

   d. Does updating the database through this view create any problems? If so, what are they? If not, why not?

2. Define a view named PART_ORDER. It consists of the part number, description, price, order number, order date, number ordered, and quoted price for all order lines currently on file.

   a. Write and execute the CREATE VIEW command to create the PART_ORDER view.

   b. Write and execute the command to retrieve the part number, description, order number, and quoted price for all orders in the PART_ORDER view for parts with quoted prices that exceed $100.

   c. Write and execute the query that the DBMS actually executes.

   d. Does updating the database through this view create any problems? If so, what are they? If not, why not?

3. Define a view named ORDER_TOTAL. It consists of the order number and order total for each order currently on file. (The order total is the sum of the number of units ordered times the quoted price on each order line for each order.) Sort the rows by order number. Use TOTAL_AMOUNT as the name for the order total.

   a. Write and execute the CREATE VIEW command to create the ORDER_TOTAL view.

   b. Write and execute the command to retrieve the order number and order total for only those orders totaling more than $1,000.

   c. Write and execute the query that the DBMS actually executes.

   d. Does updating the database through this view create any problems? If so, what are they? If not, why not?

4. Write, but do not execute, the commands to grant the following privileges:

   a. User Ashton must be able to retrieve data from the PART table.

   b. Users Kelly and Morgan must be able to add new orders and order lines.

   c. User James must be able to change the price for all parts.

   d. User Danielson must be able to delete customers.

   e. All users must be able to retrieve each customer's number, name, street, city, state, and zip code.

   f. User Perez must be able to create an index on the ORDERS table.

   g. User Washington must be able to change the structure of the PART table.

   h. User Grinstead must have all privileges on the ORDERS table.

5. Write, but do not execute, the command to revoke all privileges from user Ashton.

Chapter 7

6. Perform the following tasks:

   a. Create an index named PART_INDEX1 on the PART_NUM column in the ORDER_LINE table.

   b. Create an index named PART_INDEX2 on the CLASS column in the PART table.

   c. Create an index named PART_INDEX3 on the CLASS and WAREHOUSE columns in the PART table.

   d. Create an index named PART_INDEX4 on the CLASS and WAREHOUSE columns in the PART table. List item classes in descending order.

7. Delete the index named PART_INDEX3.

8. Write the commands to obtain the following information from the system catalog. Do not execute these commands unless your instructor asks you to do so.

   a. List every table that you own.

   b. List every column in the PART table and its associated data type.

   c. List the indexes associated with the PART table.

   d. List the privileges assigned to user Ashton.

9. Add ORDER_NUM as a foreign key in the ORDER_LINE table.

Henry Books

Use MySQL to make the following changes to the Henry Books database (see Figures 1-4 through 1-7 in Chapter 1). Use the notes at the end of Chapter 3 to print your output if directed to do so by your instructor. For any exercises that use commands not supported by your version of MySQL, write the command to accomplish the task.

1. Define a view named SCRIBNER. It consists of the book code, title, type, and price for every book published by the publisher whose code is SC.

   a. Write and execute the CREATE VIEW command to create the SCRIBNER view.

   b. Write and execute the command to retrieve the book code, title, and price for every book with a price of less than $15.

   c. Write and execute the query that the DBMS actually executes.

   d. Does updating the database through this view create any problems? If so, what are they? If not, why not?

2. Define a view named NONPAPERBACK. It consists of the book code, title, publisher name, and price for every book that is not available in paperback.

   a. Write and execute the CREATE VIEW command to create the NONPAPERBACK view.

   b. Write and execute the command to retrieve the book title, publisher name, and price for every book in the NONPAPERBACK view with a price of less than $20.

   c. Write and execute the query that the DBMS actually executes.

   d. Does updating the database through this view create any problems? If so, what are they? If not, why not?

209

3. Define a view named BOOK_INVENTORY. It consists of the branch number and the total number of books on hand for each branch. Use UNITS as the name for the count of books on hand. Group and order the rows by branch number.

    a. Write and execute the CREATE VIEW command to create the BOOK_INVENTORY view.

    b. Write and execute the command to retrieve the branch number and units for each branch having more than 25 books on hand.

    c. Write and execute the query that the DBMS actually executes.

    d. Does updating the database through this view create any problems? If so, what are they? If not, why not?

4. Write, but do not execute, the commands to grant the following privileges:

    a. User Rodriquez must be able to retrieve data from the BOOK table.

    b. Users Gomez and Liston must be able to add new books and publishers to the database.

    c. Users Andrews and Zimmer must be able to change the price of any book.

    d. All users must be able to retrieve the book title, book code, and book price for every book.

    e. User Golden must be able to add and delete publishers.

    f. User Andrews must be able to create an index for the BOOK table.

    g. Users Andrews and Golden must be able to change the structure of the AUTHOR table.

    h. User Golden must have all privileges on the BRANCH table.

5. Write, but do not execute, the command to revoke all privileges from user Andrews.

6. Create the following indexes:

    a. Create an index named BOOK_INDEX1 on the TITLE column in the BOOK table.

    b. Create an index named BOOK_INDEX2 on the TYPE column in the BOOK table.

    c. Create an index named BOOK_INDEX3 on the CITY and PUBLISHER_NAME columns in the PUBLISHER table.

7. Delete the index named BOOK_INDEX3.

8. Write the commands to obtain the following information from the system catalog. Do not execute these commands unless your instructor asks you to do so.

    a. List every table that you own.

    b. List every column in the PUBLISHER table and its associated data type.

    c. List the indexes associated with the PUBLISHER table.

    d. List the privileges assigned to user Golden.

9. Add PUBLISHER_CODE as a foreign key in the BOOK table.

Alexamara Marina Group

Use MySQL to make the following changes to the Alexamara Marina Group database (Figures 1-8 through 1-12 in Chapter 1). Use the notes at the end of Chapter 3 to print your output if directed to do so by your instructor. For any exercises that use commands not supported by your version of MySQL, write the command to accomplish the task.

1. Define a view named LARGE_SLIP. It consists of the marina number, slip number, rental fee, boat name, and owner number for every slip whose length is 40 feet.

   a. Write and execute the CREATE VIEW command to create the LARGE_SLIP view.

   b. Write and execute the command to retrieve the marina number, slip number, rental fee, and boat name for every slip with a rental fee of $3,800 or more.

   c. Write and execute the query that the DBMS actually executes.

   d. Does updating the database through this view create any problems? If so, what are they? If not, why not?

2. Define a view named RAY_4025. It consists of the marina number, slip number, length, rental fee, boat name, and owner's last name for every slip in which the boat type is Ray 4025.

   a. Write and execute the CREATE VIEW command to create the RAY_4025 view.

   b. Write and execute the command to retrieve the marina number, slip number, rental fee, boat name, and owner's last name for every slip in the RAY_4025 view with a rental fee of less than $4,000.

   c. Write and execute the query that the DBMS actually executes.

   d. Does updating the database through this view create any problems? If so, what are they? If not, why not?

3. Define a view named SLIP_FEES. It consists of two columns: the first is the slip length, and the second is the average fee for all slips in the MARINA_SLIP table that have that length. Use AVERAGE_FEE as the name for the average fee. Group and order the rows by slip length.

   a. Write and execute the CREATE VIEW command to create the SLIP_FEES view.

   b. Write and execute the command to retrieve the slip length and average fee for each length for which the average fee is less than $3,500.

   c. Write and execute the query that the DBMS actually executes.

   d. Does updating the database through this view create any problems? If so, what are they? If not, why not?

4. Write, but do not execute, the commands to grant the following privileges:

   a. User Oliver must be able to retrieve data from the MARINA_SLIP table.

   b. Users Crandall and Perez must be able to add new owners and slips to the database.

   c. Users Johnson and Klein must be able to change the rental fee of any slip.

   d. All users must be able to retrieve the length, boat name, and owner number for every slip.

   e. User Klein must be able to add and delete service categories.

    f.   User Adams must be able to create an index on the SERVICE_REQUEST table.

    g.   Users Adams and Klein must be able to change the structure of the MARINA_SLIP table.

    h.   User Klein must have all privileges on the MARINA table.

5.   Write, but do not execute, the command to revoke all privileges from user Adams.

6.   Create the following indexes:

    a.   Create an index named BOAT_INDEX1 on the OWNER_NUM column in the MARINA_SLIP table.

    b.   Create an index named BOAT_INDEX2 on the BOAT_NAME column in the MARINA_SLIP table.

    c.   Create an index named BOAT_INDEX3 on the LENGTH and BOAT_NAME columns in the MARINA_SLIP table. List the lengths in descending order.

7.   Delete the index named BOAT_INDEX3; it is no longer necessary.

8.   Write the commands to obtain the following information from the system catalog. Do not execute these commands unless your instructor specifically asks you to do so.

    a.   List every table that you own.

    b.   List every column in the MARINA_SLIP table and its associated data type.

    c.   List the indexes associated with the MARINA_SLIP table.

    d.   List the privileges assigned to user Klein.

9.   Add OWNER_NUM as a foreign key in the MARINA_SLIP table.

CHAPTER 8

MYSQL SPECIAL TOPICS

LEARNING OBJECTIVES

Objectives

- Import data into a MySQL table
- Export data from a MySQL table
- Understand issues that affect database performance
- Analyze tables
- Optimize queries
- Understand and use the MySQL Query Browser
- Understand and use the MySQL Administrator

INTRODUCTION

In Chapter 7, you learned about database administration issues. In this chapter, you will expand your knowledge of database management and administration by learning how to use MySQL to import and export data. You also will learn how to fine-tune a database so it processes data quickly and efficiently. Finally, you will learn how to use two of the graphical user interface (GUI) tools that MySQL provides: MySQL Query Browser and MySQL Administrator.

IMPORTING AND EXPORTING DATA

Most database management systems provide some mechanism to import and export data. **Importing** is the process of converting data to a MySQL database. **Exporting** is the process of converting the data in a MySQL database to a file format for use in another program.

Importing Data into a Database

It is not uncommon for data stored in a database to originate from other sources. These other sources can come from within the organization, such as a file of potential customers maintained by the Marketing Department or from demographic files that are freely available on the Internet. Regardless of the reason for importing data, it is important to know how to import data from other sources into a MySQL database. In most cases, the easiest way to import data into a MySQL database is to use a text file. A **text file** contains unformatted data. A text file might contain line breaks, commas, or tabs to distinguish one piece of data from another. Many programs, such as Microsoft Excel, have features that let you save data as a text file and choose how to distinguish data in different fields. This distinguishing of data is called delimiting, and that is where the terms "tab-delimited" and "comma-delimited" get their names. A **comma-delimited file** uses a comma to separate data into fields; a **tab-delimited file** uses a tab character to separate data into fields.

To import a text file into MySQL, the text file must be tab-delimited and the data should not be enclosed in quotation marks. To help you understand the process of importing, suppose that Valerie has five new orders that she must add to the ORDERS table. Because these orders were input using another system, she has the data in a tab-delimited text file. Valerie examines the data before importing it by opening the file in Notepad, a text editor that is installed with Windows.

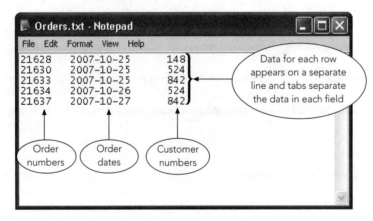

FIGURE 8-1 Tab-delimited text file in Notepad

EXAMPLE 1

Import the Orders.txt text file into the ORDERS table.

To import a file, use the **LOAD DATA INFILE** command, which includes the words LOAD DATA INFILE, followed by the name of the file to import in single quotation marks, the words INTO TABLE, and then the table name.

If you use Windows to create a text file, Windows uses two codes to indicate the end of each line (or paragraph) in the text file. To import data correctly, you might need to use two additional statements in the LOAD DATA INTO command. The FIELDS TERMINATED BY '\t' statement indicates that the fields in the rows are separated by tab characters (which in Windows are coded as \t). The LINES TERMINATED BY '\r\n' statement indicates that the rows end with hard return characters (which result from pressing the Enter key at the end of the line when creating the text file). The LOAD DATA INFILE command shown in Figure 8-2 adds five records to the ORDERS table.

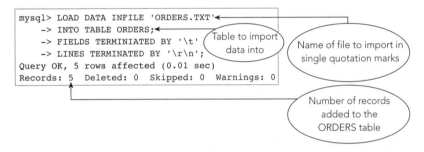

```
mysql> LOAD DATA INFILE 'ORDERS.TXT'
    -> INTO TABLE ORDERS;
    -> FIELDS TERMINIATED BY '\t'
    -> LINES TERMINATED BY '\r\n';
Query OK, 5 rows affected (0.01 sec)
Records: 5  Deleted: 0  Skipped: 0  Warnings: 0
```

Table to import data into

Name of file to import in single quotation marks

Number of records added to the ORDERS table

FIGURE 8-2   Importing a text file into the ORDERS table

NOTE

If the text file you are importing is located in a folder other than the default folder for your database, you must include the full path to the file as part of the filename. For example, if the file Orders.txt is located in a folder named Data on drive C, the command is:

```
LOAD DATA INFILE 'C:/Data/Orders.txt'
INTO TABLE ORDERS;
```

The filename in a LOAD DATA INFILE command is not case sensitive; the files ORDERS.TXT and Orders.txt are the same.

NOTE

The text file that you import should not contain any blank lines (empty paragraphs) that are created when you press Enter at the end of the last line of text. When you import a text file that contains blank lines, MySQL inserts a blank row at the end of your table. MySQL considers this blank row as containing null data. To check for blank lines, open the text file in Microsoft Word, enable the Show Formatting feature, delete any extra paragraph returns at the end of the file, and then save the file as a text file.

The ORDERS table now contains the data shown in Figure 8-3.


```
mysql> SELECT *
    -> FROM ORDERS;
+-----------+------------+--------------+
| ORDER_NUM | ORDER_DATE | CUSTOMER_NUM |
+-----------+------------+--------------+
| 21608     | 2007-10-20 | 148          |
| 21610     | 2007-10-20 | 356          |
| 21613     | 2007-10-21 | 408          |
| 21614     | 2007-10-21 | 282          |
| 21617     | 2007-10-23 | 608          |
| 21619     | 2007-10-23 | 148          |
| 21623     | 2007-10-23 | 608          |
| 21628     | 2007-10-25 | 148          |
| 21630     | 2007-10-25 | 524          |
| 21633     | 2007-10-25 | 842          |
| 21634     | 2007-10-26 | 524          |
| 21637     | 2007-10-27 | 842          |
+-----------+------------+--------------+
12 rows in set (0.00 sec)
```

Five rows appended to end of table

FIGURE 8-3 ORDERS table contains five imported rows

In Example 1, the imported data was appended (added to) the data in an existing table. To import data into a new table, you first must create the table using the CREATE TABLE command and then import the data into the new table using the LOAD DATA INFILE command, as illustrated in Example 2.

EXAMPLE 2

Create a new table named WAREHOUSE in the Premiere database. Import the data in the Ware.txt file into this new table.

To create the new WAREHOUSE table, use the following CREATE TABLE command:

```
CREATE TABLE WAREHOUSE
(WAREHOUSE CHAR(1) PRIMARY KEY,
LOCATION CHAR(15) );
```

Then use the LOAD DATA INFILE command shown in Figure 8-4 to load the WAREHOUSE table with the data saved in the Ware.txt file. The query in the figure shows the data in the WAREHOUSE table after importing the data into it.

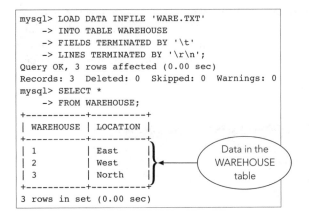

```
mysql> LOAD DATA INFILE 'WARE.TXT'
    -> INTO TABLE WAREHOUSE
    -> FIELDS TERMINATED BY '\t'
    -> LINES TERMINATED BY '\r\n';
Query OK, 3 rows affected (0.00 sec)
Records: 3  Deleted: 0  Skipped: 0  Warnings: 0
mysql> SELECT *
    -> FROM WAREHOUSE;
+-----------+----------+
| WAREHOUSE | LOCATION |
+-----------+----------+
| 1         | East     |
| 2         | West     |
| 3         | North    |
+-----------+----------+
3 rows in set (0.00 sec)
```

Data in the WAREHOUSE table

FIGURE 8-4   Importing text data into the WAREHOUSE table

Exporting Data from a Table

Sometimes it is necessary to export data stored in a MySQL database to a file so it can be used in other programs. In MySQL, you can export table data to a text file. Each row in the table becomes a row in the text file. By default, the columns in a row are separated by tabs.

For example, suppose that Richard needs to copy the part number, description, and price for each part in the warehouse so he can use this data in a report that he is preparing in Microsoft Word. Example 3 shows how to export data from the PART table.

EXAMPLE 3

Export the part number, description, and price for each part in the PART table to a text file named PartData.txt.

To export a table, use the **SELECT INTO OUTFILE** command, which includes the word SELECT, followed by the name of the column to export (or an asterisk to export all columns), the words INTO OUTFILE, the name of the text file in single quotation marks, the word FROM, and the table name. The SELECT INTO OUTFILE command shown in Figure 8-5 exports the data that Richard needs from the PART table into the PartData.txt file.

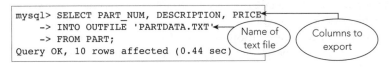

```
mysql> SELECT PART_NUM, DESCRIPTION, PRICE
    -> INTO OUTFILE 'PARTDATA.TXT'
    -> FROM PART;
Query OK, 10 rows affected (0.44 sec)
```

Name of text file   Columns to export

FIGURE 8-5   Exporting table data to a text file

You can open the PartData.txt file using any word-processing program or text editor. Figure 8-6 shows the contents of the PartData.txt file in Microsoft Word. The columns are separated by tabs (indicated as forward arrows when the Show Formatting feature is enabled). Using Word's features, Richard easily can convert the file to an appropriate format for his report. For example, he might convert the data to a table and add descriptive notes.

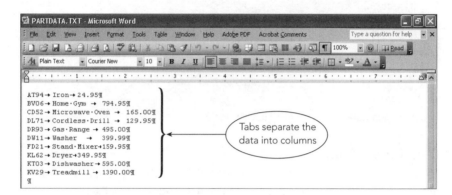

FIGURE 8-6 PartData.txt file in Word

NOTE

If you need to save the text file to a folder other than the default one for your database, you must include the full path to the file as part of the filename. For example, to save the PartData.txt file to a folder named Data on drive C, the command is:

```
SELECT *
INTO OUTFILE 'C:/Data/PartData.txt'
FROM PART;
```

DATABASE PERFORMANCE ISSUES

As a database becomes larger and more complex, database performance might suffer. **Database performance** is defined as the speed or rate with which the DBMS supplies information to the user. The addition of indexes to a database can speed up retrieval yet at the same time slow down the rate at which data is updated. Hardware constraints also impose physical constraints on database performance. The three most important factors that can affect database performance include the speed of the hardware, the design of the tables, and the performance of certain queries. To improve database performance, most DBMSs use optimizers. An **optimizer** is a built-in program or routine that the DBMS uses to monitor and improve database performance. Although a detailed discussion of database performance and optimization is beyond the scope of this text, there are techniques that you can use to fine-tune a database. You can find additional information about database performance and optimization at *http://dev.mysql.com/doc/*.

Optimizing the Tables in a Database

Three easy ways to ensure that your table designs are as efficient as possible are choosing the smallest possible size for columns, eliminating unnecessary columns from tables, and removing unnecessary tables from a database. You can also use MySQL to assess table performance by running the ANALYZE TABLE command after loading a table with data and creating any necessary indexes. The **ANALYZE TABLE** command analyzes the data in the table and creates statistics that the MySQL optimizer uses, as illustrated in Example 4.

EXAMPLE 4

Analyze the tables in the Premiere database.

The ANALYZE TABLE command starts with the words ANALYZE TABLE, followed by the name of the table to analyze. When more than one table is analyzed, separate the table names with commas. Figure 8-7 shows the command to analyze the tables in the Premiere database. The value in the Op column for each table is "analyze," indicating that the analyzer was used to examine the table. The Msg_type column displays one of the following values: status, error, info, or warning. If the Msg_type is "status" and the value in the Msg_text column is "OK," then there are no optimization issues present in the table. If the analyzer lists a Msg_type value of "error," "info," or "warning," these values indicate that resources in the database are low or there are problems with the table's indexes. These messages vary and depend on the particular result of analyzing the table.

```
mysql> ANALYZE TABLE REP, CUSTOMER, ORDERS,
    -> ORDER_LINE, PART, WAREHOUSE;
+---------------------+---------+----------+----------+
| Table               | Op      | Msg_type | Msg_text |
+---------------------+---------+----------+----------+
| premiere.rep        | analyze | status   | OK       |
| premiere.customer   | analyze | status   | OK       |
| premiere.orders     | analyze | status   | OK       |
| premiere.order_line | analyze | status   | OK       |
| premiere.part       | analyze | status   | OK       |
| premiere.warehouse  | analyze | status   | OK       |
+---------------------+---------+----------+----------+
6 rows in set (0.44 sec)
```

FIGURE 8-7 Analyzing the tables in the Premiere database

Another useful command for optimizing the tables in a database is the CHECK TABLE command. The **CHECK TABLE** command checks a table for errors, such as identifying corrupt tables resulting from not being closed properly.

EXAMPLE 5

Check the tables in the Premiere database.

The CHECK TABLE command starts with the words CHECK TABLE, followed by the names of the tables to check, separated by commas. Figure 8-8 shows the command to check the tables in the Premiere database. The value in the Op column for each table is "check," indicating that MySQL checked the tables. The values in the Msg_type and Msg_text columns are the same as those generated by the ANALYZE TABLE command.

```
mysql> CHECK TABLE REP, CUSTOMER, ORDERS,
    -> ORDER_LINE, PART, WAREHOUSE;
+---------------------+-------+----------+----------+
| Table               | Op    | Msg_type | Msg_text |
+---------------------+-------+----------+----------+
| premiere.rep        | check | status   | OK       |
| premiere.customer   | check | status   | OK       |
| premiere.orders     | check | status   | OK       |
| premiere.order_line | check | status   | OK       |
| premiere.part       | check | status   | OK       |
| premiere.warehouse  | check | status   | OK       |
+---------------------+-------+----------+----------+
6 rows in set (0.00 sec)
```

FIGURE 8-8   Checking the tables in the Premiere database

If the CHECK TABLE command determines that there is a problem with a table, you should issue a REPAIR TABLE command. The **REPAIR TABLE** command fixes damaged or corrupted tables. For example, if the CHECK TABLE command indicates that the ORDER_LINE table is corrupted, the command to fix the table would be:

```
REPAIR TABLE ORDER_LINE;
```

When you delete rows or columns from a table or make changes to a table with variable-length rows (tables with VARCHAR columns), running the OPTIMIZE TABLE command can be useful, as illustrated in Example 6.

EXAMPLE 6

Optimize the tables in the Premiere database.

The **OPTIMIZE TABLE** command recovers unused space caused by fragmented files. The OPTIMIZE TABLE command starts with the words OPTIMIZE TABLE, followed by the names of the tables to optimize, separated by commas. Figure 8-9 shows the command to optimize the tables in the Premiere database. The value in the Op column for each table is "optimize," indicating that MySQL optimized the tables. The values in the Msg_type and Msg_text columns are the same as those generated by the ANALYZE TABLE command.

```
mysql> OPTIMIZE TABLE REP, CUSTOMER, ORDERS,
    -> ORDER_LINE, PART, WAREHOUSE;
+----------------------+----------+----------+----------+
| Table                | Op       | Msg_type | Msg_text |
+----------------------+----------+----------+----------+
| premiere.rep         | optimize | status   | OK       |
| premiere.customer    | optimize | status   | OK       |
| premiere.orders      | optimize | status   | OK       |
| premiere.order_line  | optimize | status   | OK       |
| premiere.part        | optimize | status   | OK       |
| premiere.warehouse   | optimize | status   | OK       |
+----------------------+----------+----------+----------+
6 rows in set (1.52 sec)
```

FIGURE 8-9 Optimizing the tables in the Premiere database

Optimizing the Queries in a Database

Query optimization is an ongoing concern of database administrators because users become frustrated when it takes more than a few seconds to retrieve data from a database. Database administrators perform many of the tasks related to query optimization. For example, they use indexes (see Chapter 7) to ensure the queries in a database execute as efficiently as possible. There are also some commands that you can use to evaluate query performance.

You can obtain information about how MySQL executes a query by using the **EXPLAIN** command. When you precede a statement with the EXPLAIN command, MySQL identifies how it processes the statement, which might include information about how and in which order tables are joined. You also can use the EXPLAIN command to determine when you must add indexes to tables to improve query performance, as illustrated in Example 7.

E X A M P L E   7

Evaluate the performance of a query that selects the last name and first name from the REP table and the customer name and balance from the CUSTOMER table.

Figure 8-10 shows the EXPLAIN command used to evaluate the performance of the query. To make the results easier to read, the query includes the \G command to display the output vertically.

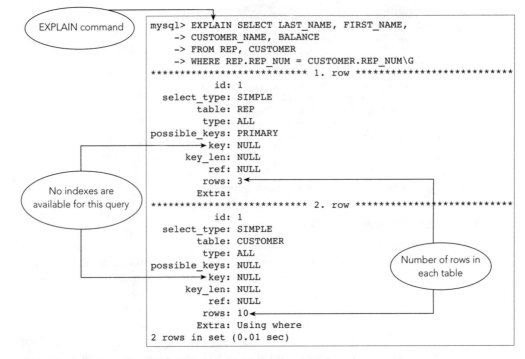

FIGURE 8-10 Using the EXPLAIN command to evaluate query performance

The EXPLAIN command starts with the word EXPLAIN and it precedes a normal SELECT command that selects the data for the query. Notice that MySQL does not execute the query; it is evaluated for performance only. The EXPLAIN command generates one row of output for each table involved in the query (in this case, the REP and CUSTOMER tables). You can use the output of the EXPLAIN command to determine if there is an index for a table involved in the query that might increase the speed at which the query is executed. The possible_keys column indicates which indexes are available to find the rows in these tables. If the column for the table is NULL, there are no relevant indexes. Because REP_NUM is the primary key of the REP table, the entry is PRIMARY. There is no index for the REP_NUM column in the CUSTOMER table. The key column indicates which key MySQL actually would use. If no index can be used, the key is NULL. Because the number of records to be searched for this query is small, indexes would not be used. The rows column indicates the number of rows present in each table. This is a join query and when you execute the query, MySQL must examine 30 total rows to find the data specified in the query (three rows in the REP table multiplied by 10 rows in the CUSTOMER table).

Another technique for evaluating query performance is to perform a procedure analysis. Whereas the EXPLAIN command examines the query statement before it is executed, the **PROCEDURE ANALYSE( )** function examines and analyzes the query results, as illustrated in Example 8.

EXAMPLE 8

Analyze the results of a query that selects descriptions from the PART table.

The PROCEDURE ANALYSE( ) function is added at the end of the SELECT command, as shown in Figure 8-11. Similar to the EXPLAIN command, including the PROCEDURE ANALYSE( ) function in a command analyzes the query results, but does not actually execute the query.

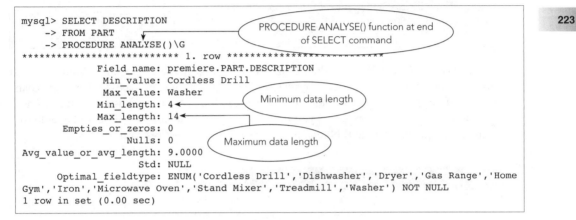

```
mysql> SELECT DESCRIPTION
    -> FROM PART
    -> PROCEDURE ANALYSE()\G
*************************** 1. row ***************************
             Field_name: premiere.PART.DESCRIPTION
              Min_value: Cordless Drill
              Max_value: Washer
             Min_length: 4
             Max_length: 14
       Empties_or_zeros: 0
                  Nulls: 0
Avg_value_or_avg_length: 9.0000
                    Std: NULL
       Optimal_fieldtype: ENUM('Cordless Drill','Dishwasher','Dryer','Gas Range','Home
Gym','Iron','Microwave Oven','Stand Mixer','Treadmill','Washer') NOT NULL
1 row in set (0.00 sec)
```

FIGURE 8-11   Using the PROCEDURE ANALYSE() function to analyze query results

The output from the PROCEDURE ANALYSE( ) function provides information about the table's columns, such as the minimum and maximum values, and suggests an optimal field type. In Figure 8-11, the optimal field (data) type suggested by the function is ENUM. The **ENUM** data type is an object type with a value chosen from a list of allowed values that are enumerated explicitly in the column specification at the time the table is created. Because PART data is dynamic, using ENUM is not a good suggestion. You also can use the output to determine if you can decrease a column size in the table. For example, the Max_length value for the DESCRIPTION column is 14 characters. This column is appropriately sized at 15 characters. However, if the DESCRIPTION column was defined as 50 characters, you might consider reducing the column size to more appropriately store the part description data, thereby saving storage space and improving query performance.

USING THE MYSQL QUERY BROWSER

The **MySQL Query Browser** is a separate MySQL program that you can use to create and execute queries using a graphical user interface. You also can use the Query Browser to create databases and tables, edit tables, create and run scripts, reformat query output, and export query results to various file formats. You can download the Query Browser from the MySQL Downloads page at *http://dev.mysql.com/downloads/*.

Starting and Using the Query Browser

The exact way you start the Query Browser depends on the operating environment in which you are working. In a Windows XP installation of MySQL 4.1, for example, you do the following:

STARTING THE QUERY BROWSER

- Click the Start button.
- Point to All Programs.
- Point to MySQL on the All Programs menu.
- Click MySQL Query Browser on the MySQL submenu.

The MySQL Query Browser dialog box shown in Figure 8-12 opens, in which you must enter the information for your server host, and your username and password. You also can enter a default database in the Default Schema text box. (A database is referenced as a **schema** in the Query Browser.) If you do not change the default database and decide to do so later, you can change the default database in the Query Browser.

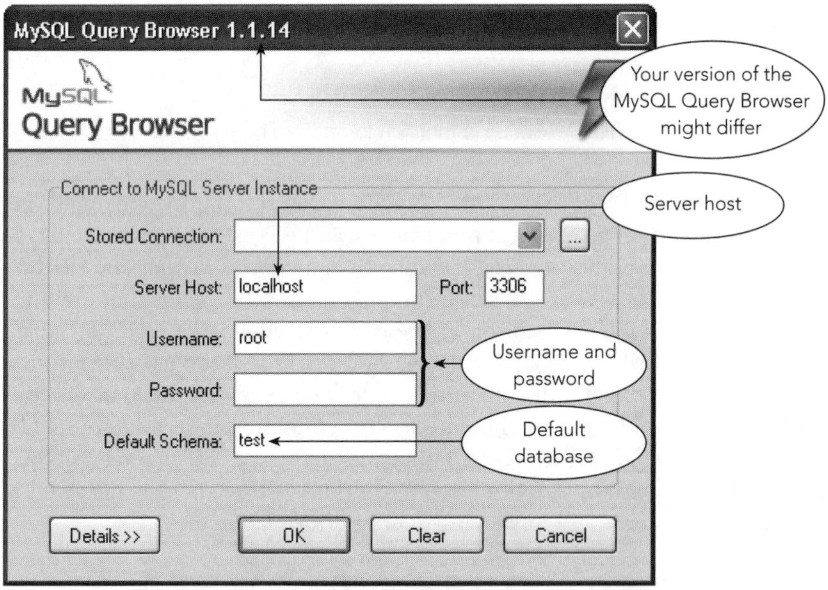

FIGURE 8-12 MySQL Query Browser dialog box

After connecting to MySQL Server, the Query Browser starts, as shown in Figure 8-13, and displays the Main Query window. The Main Query window has four sections: the Query toolbar, the Result Area, the Object Browser, and the Information Browser.

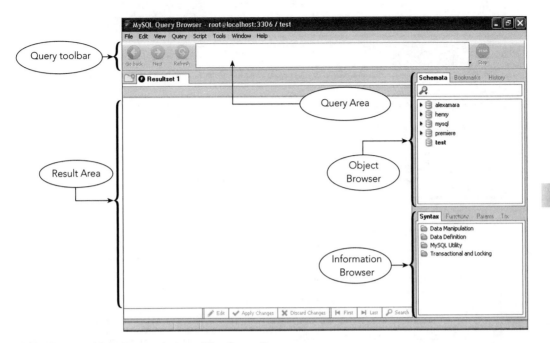

FIGURE 8-13   Main Query window of the Query Browser

You create queries in the **Query Area** on the Query toolbar. When visible, the Execute button executes the query and the Stop button stops execution. The Go back and Next navigation buttons allow you to review and execute previous queries. The Refresh button executes the most recently executed query.

Query results appear in the **Result Area** on tabbed pages. You can have multiple tabbed pages open and can split tabbed pages vertically or horizontally to compare query results.

The **Object Browser** has three tabbed pages entitled Schemata, Bookmarks, and History. The **Schemata Browser** (also called the **Database Browser**) displays all databases on the MySQL Server to which you are connected. The **Bookmarks Browser** allows you to save queries that you use frequently as bookmarks for quick retrieval. The **History Browser** lets you browse all the previously created queries during your session.

The **Information Browser** provides access to all information not directly related to actual data in the database. The **Syntax Browser** provides a quick reference to MySQL query syntax. The **Functions Browser** is a quick reference to the built-in functions available in MySQL. The **Params Browser** (pronounced "parameters browser") provides parameters that can help you build queries. The **Trx Browser** (pronounced "transaction browser") lists all queries that make up a single transaction.

Getting Help in the Query Browser

The simplest way to get help when using the Query Browser is to use the Help command on the Help menu. The MySQL Query Browser window is shown in Figure 8-14. You can click the topics on the left to learn more about using the Query Browser.

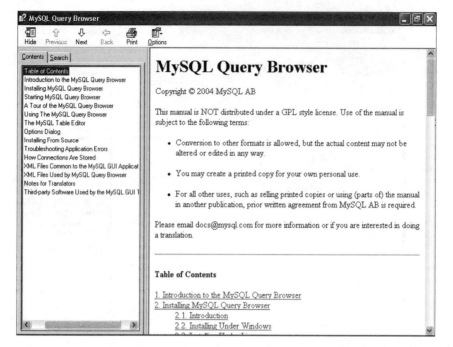

FIGURE 8-14 MySQL Query Browser (Help) window

Using the Database Browser

The Database Browser allows you to set the default database and to select the tables and columns to include in a query. You also can create databases, create and edit tables, and drop tables and databases. The database currently in use (the default database) appears in bold text in the list of databases on the server. To change the default database, right-click the database you want to use, and then click Make Default Schema on the shortcut menu, as shown in Figure 8-15. To display all the tables in the default database, double-click the database. To edit a table, right-click the table, and then click Edit Table on the shortcut menu.

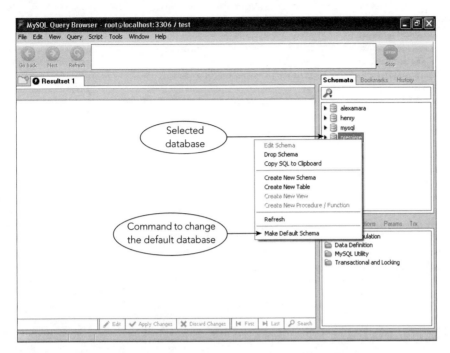

FIGURE 8-15   Using the Database Browser to change the default database

Using the Syntax Browser

The Syntax Browser provides an easy way to learn more about proper syntax for MySQL commands. The commands are organized into four categories: Data Manipulation, Data Definition, MySQL Utility, and Transactional and Locking. Double-clicking a category in the Syntax Browser displays the commands for that category. For example, Figure 8-16 shows the commands in the Data Manipulation category. Double-clicking a command opens the Inline Help tab and displays the syntax for the command. Figure 8-16 displays the syntax for the DELETE command.

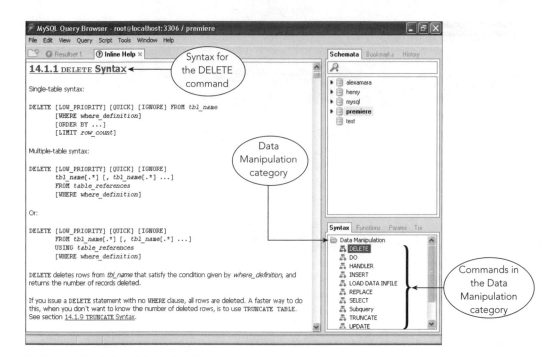

FIGURE 8-16 Inline Help for the DELETE command

Creating and Executing Queries

To create a query, type the query in the Query Area. You do not need to type a semicolon at the end of the command. As you type the query, the color of reserved words, such as SELECT, change to blue. You execute a query by using the Execute command on the Query menu, by pressing Ctrl+Enter, or by clicking the Execute button on the Query toolbar when it is visible.

NOTE

If your screen resolution is set to 800 x 600, you might not see the Execute button on the Query toolbar. You still can use the keyboard shortcut or the Query menu to execute your queries.

EXAMPLE 9

List the complete CUSTOMER table.

The SQL commands that you enter in the Query Area are identical to those that you used in the MySQL Command Line Client window. The only difference is that you execute the commands using one of the three previously discussed methods instead of typing a semicolon at the end of the command. The results appear in the Resultset 1 tab, as shown in Figure 8-17.

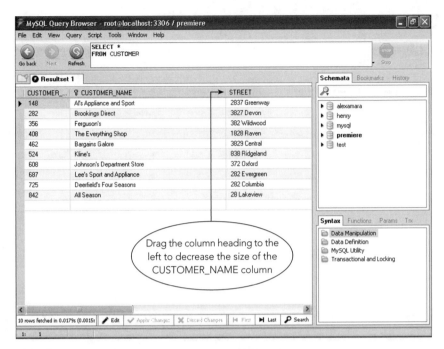

FIGURE 8-17 Query and query results in the Query Browser

Figure 8-17 shows the CUSTOMER_NUM, CUSTOMER_NAME, and STREET columns. You can view the rest of the columns in the query results by resizing the columns to eliminate blank space, by using the scroll bar at the bottom of the Result Area, or by closing the browsers (also called sidebars) on the right side of the screen. To resize a column, place the mouse pointer on the right side of the column heading, and then click and drag the column border to the left to decrease the column width. To increase a column's size, drag the right side of the column heading to the right. To close the browsers, click View on the menu bar, and then click Sidebar.

In the Query Browser, you can resize columns to produce more readable output as shown in Figure 8-18. You then can print the query results using the Print option on the File menu.

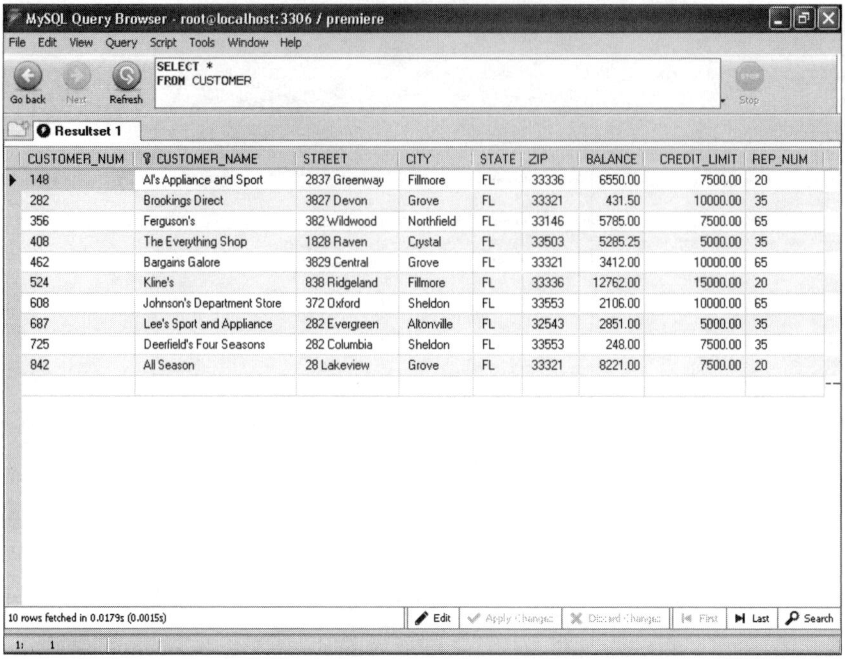

FIGURE 8-18 Query results with resized columns and hidden sidebars

Exporting a Resultset

After executing a query, you can view the query results (called the **resultset**) in the Result Area. You can also export the results to the following file formats: comma-delimited text files (also called comma-separated values), HTML (Hypertext Markup Language) files, XML (Extensible Markup Language) files, and Microsoft Excel files.

A **CSV** (comma-separated values) file is a text file with a .csv filename extension in which values are enclosed in quotation marks and separated by commas. You can open CSV files in many different programs, including word processors, spreadsheets, and databases. **HTML** files are text files with .htm or .html filename extensions that are used for creating and formatting Web pages. XML files are used for describing and delivering data on the Web. **XML** is a data interchange format that allows you to exchange data between dissimilar systems or applications. With XML, you can describe both the data and the structure of the data in one document.

EXAMPLE 10

Export the PART table as an XML file.

To export the table, create and run a SELECT query that displays all rows and all columns for the PART table. Then click File on the menu bar, point to Export Resultset, and click Export As XML File. In the Save Resultset to File dialog box, specify the folder in which to save the XML file and a filename, and then click the Save button. Figure 8-19 shows a portion of the Part.xml file in the XML editor for Windows, Microsoft Internet Explorer.

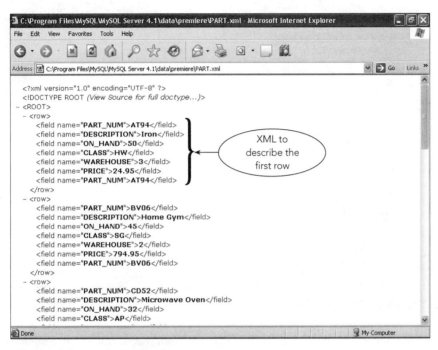

FIGURE 8-19   XML file in Microsoft Internet Explorer

Using the Script Editor

In Chapter 3, you learned how to create script files by using an editor such as Notepad or a word processor. The **Script Editor** provides another way to create and edit scripts, as illustrated in Example 11.

EXAMPLE 11

Open the script file that creates the tables in the Premiere database and loads them with data.

To open a script file, click File on the menu bar, and then click Open Script. Use the Open Script File dialog box to open the folder in which the script is saved and then double-click the script filename. The script opens on the Script 1 tab in the Result Area. When a Script tab is active, the buttons on the Query toolbar are replaced with script debugging and script execution buttons. The script file for the Premiere database is shown in Figure 8-20.

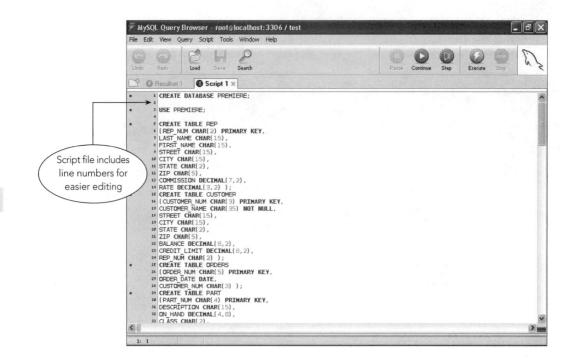

FIGURE 8-20 Script file in the Script Editor

If you need to change any of the data in the script, you can use the mouse and the keyboard arrow keys to move the insertion point, and then select and replace or type new data. Click the Close button on the Script tab to close the script file.

To create a new script, click File on the menu bar, and then click New Script Tab to open a new Script tab into which you can begin typing commands. You save changes to a script file by clicking the Save button on the toolbar.

NOTE

When a Script tab is active, you can click the Load button on the toolbar to open another script, or click the Execute button on the toolbar to run the script.

Using the MySQL Table Editor

In addition to editing script files, you can also use the Query Browser to change the structure of the tables in a database. The **MySQL Table Editor** lets you view and change the columns in a table and their data types. Other information is also available, including information about null columns, default values, indexes, and foreign keys. To start the Table Editor, click the arrow to the left of the default database in the Database Browser, right-click the table that you want to change, and then click Edit Table on the shortcut menu. Figure 8-21 shows the Table Editor for the PART table.

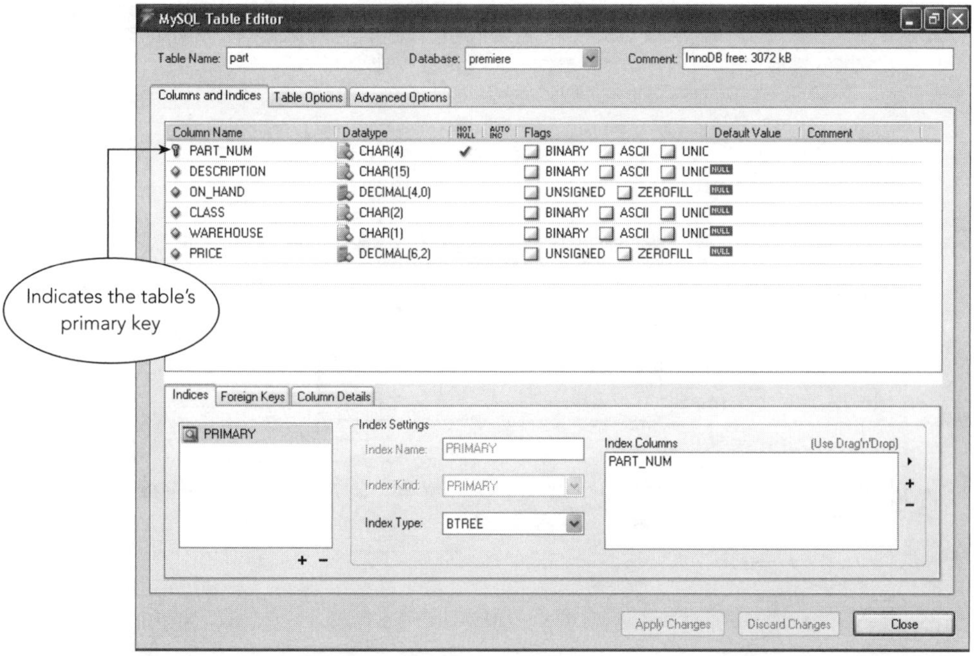

FIGURE 8-21 Table Editor for the PART table

To change the name, data type, default value, or comment for a column, double-click the value you want to change to select it and then type the new value. To change a column's status from null to not null, click the NOT NULL column to add or remove the check mark. To add or remove a column from the primary key, click the key or diamond icon to the left of the column name. A key indicates that the column is or is part of the primary key; a diamond indicates that the column is not part of the primary key. You can use the Indices tab to set and remove indexes and the Foreign Keys tab to set and remove foreign keys, as illustrated in Example 12. The Column Details tab provides more information about the selected column.

EXAMPLE 12

Specify the REP_NUM column in the CUSTOMER table as a foreign key that must match the REP_NUM column in the REP table.

To edit the CUSTOMER table, right-click the table in the Database Browser, and then click Edit Table on the shortcut menu. In the Table Editor window for the CUSTOMER table, click the Foreign Keys tab, and then click the plus sign (+) to open the Add Foreign Key dialog box shown in Figure 8-22.

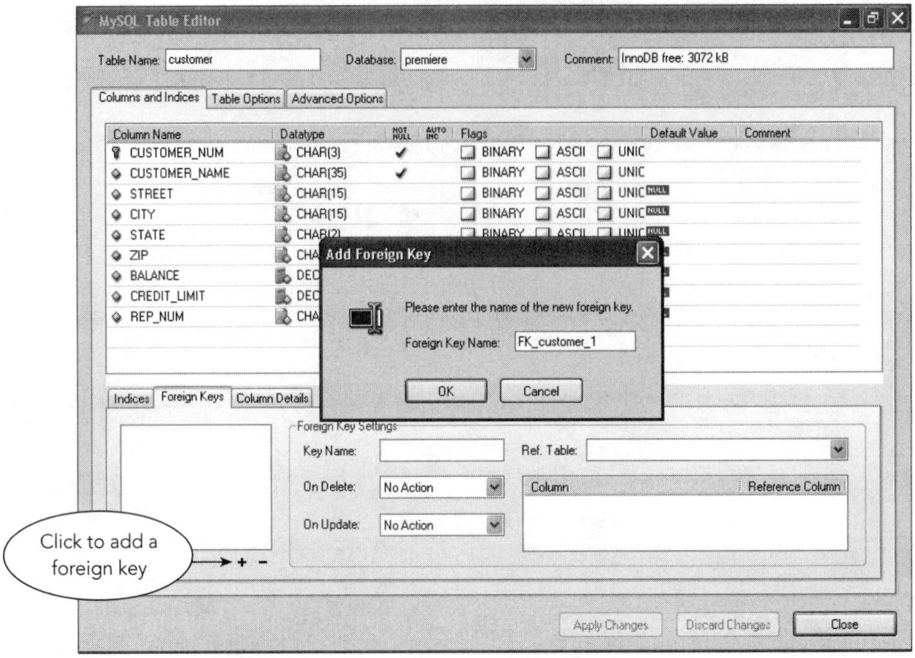

Click to add a foreign key

FIGURE 8-22 Add Foreign Key dialog box

You can accept the default name in the Foreign Key Name text box or assign one yourself. After clicking the OK button, click the Ref. Table list arrow, and then select the table whose primary key is required to match the foreign key, in this case, the REP table. Figure 8-23 shows the Foreign Keys tab specifying that REP_NUM in the CUSTOMER table is a foreign key that matches the REP_NUM column in the REP table. After finishing making changes in the Table Editor, click the Apply Changes button at the bottom of the window to save them. The Table Editor asks you to confirm your changes, and then it executes the command to make them.

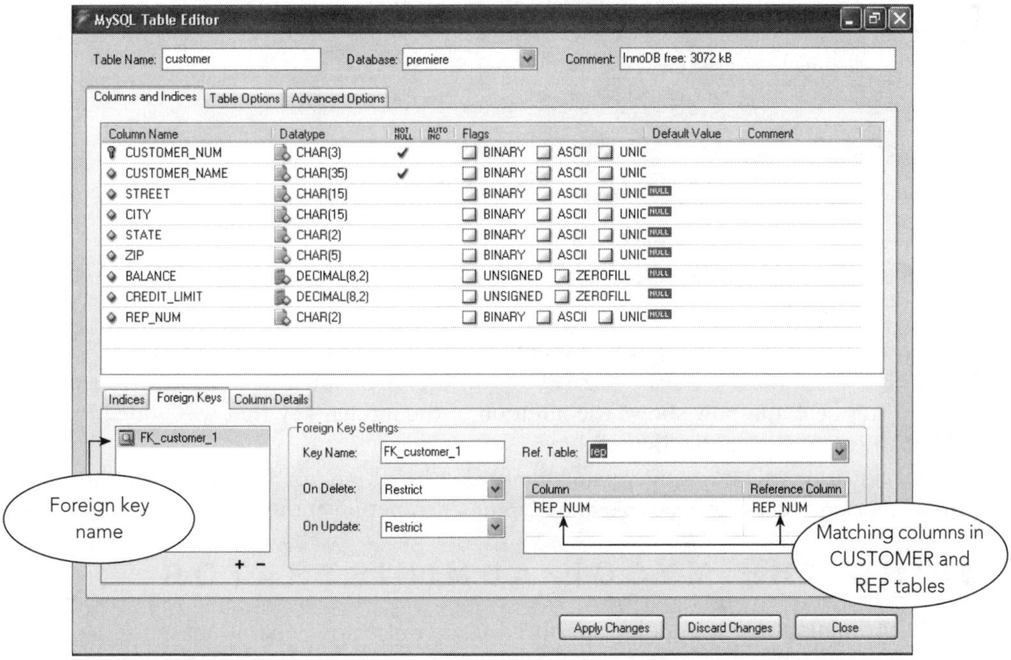

FIGURE 8-23   Foreign key added to the CUSTOMER table

Analyzing Query Performance

You already learned how to use the EXPLAIN command and the PROCEDURE ANALYSE( ) function at the MySQL command line to analyze query performance. You can also analyze queries using the Query Browser, as illustrated in Example 13.

EXAMPLE 13

Evaluate the performance of a query that selects the last name and first name from the REP table and the customer name and balance from the CUSTOMER table.

To use the EXPLAIN command in the Query Browser, type the EXPLAIN command and then type the query in the Query Area. Alternatively, you can type the query in the Query Area, click Query on the menu bar, and then click Explain. Figure 8-24 shows the result of using the EXPLAIN command to evaluate the query.

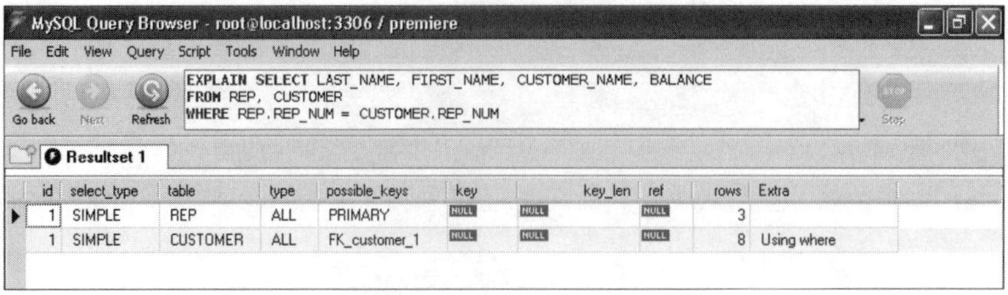

FIGURE 8-24 Using the EXPLAIN command to analyze query performance

You evaluated the same query in Example 7 and its results appear in Figure 8-10. Notice that the output is easier to read and interpret in the Query Browser. Also, the possible_keys column now shows the addition of the foreign key that was added to the CUSTOMER table using the Table Editor.

You can also evaluate a query using the PROCEDURE ANALYSE( ) function in the Query Browser, just as you did in Example 8, by typing the function at the end of a SELECT query.

USING THE MYSQL ADMINISTRATOR

MySQL Administrator is a tool for performing administrative operations, such as monitoring the status and performance of MySQL, performing and restoring backups, and managing users and connections to the database. You can download the Administrator from the MySQL Downloads page at *http://dev.mysql.com/downloads/*.

Starting the Administrator

Starting the Administrator is similar to the way you start the Query Browser: click the Start button on the Windows taskbar, point to All Programs, point to MySQL, and then click MySQL Administrator. The MySQL Administrator dialog box opens, into which you must enter your server host, username, and password to connect to the MySQL Server.

NOTE

If the Query Browser is open, you can click Tools on the menu bar, and then click MySQL Administrator to start the Administrator.

Viewing the Administrator Window

After clicking the OK button in the MySQL Administrator dialog box, the Administrator window shown in Figure 8-25 opens and displays a sidebar, a working area, and a menu bar.

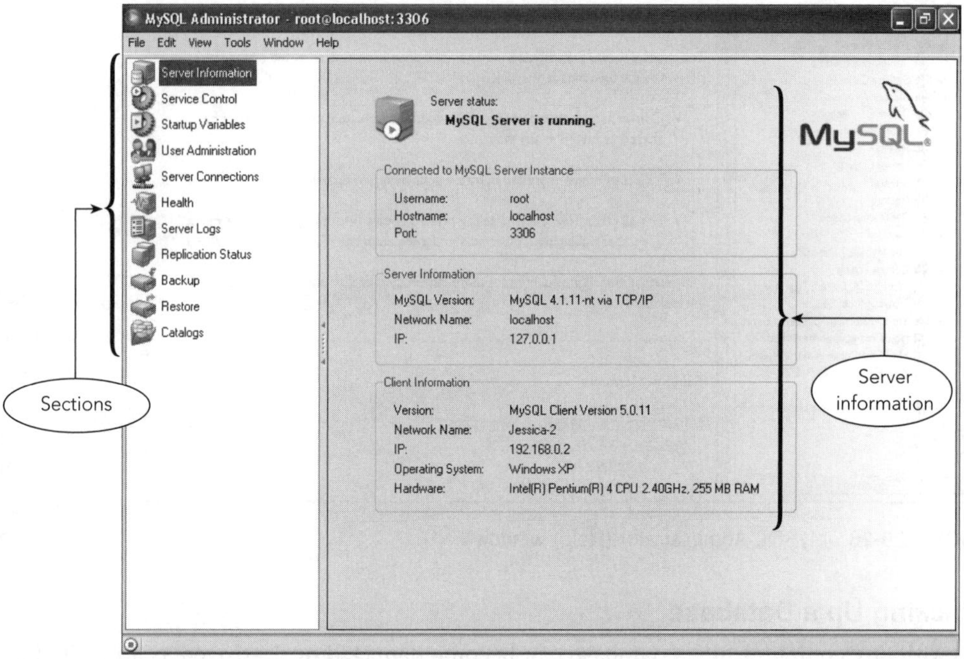

FIGURE 8-25 MySQL Administrator window

The sidebar has 11 sections. The Server Information, Service Control, Server Connections, and Server Logs sections are used to configure and manage the MySQL Server. The User Administration section is used to manage user privileges. The Startup Variables section is used to change the startup options for MySQL Server. The Health section is used to monitor database performance and the Replication Status section provides a visual overview of replicated databases. **Replication** is the process of making multiple copies of the database. The Backup section allows you to perform backups, and the Restore section allows you to restore backup files created in the Backup section. The Catalogs section allows you to view catalogs, databases, and tables. You also can perform table maintenance using the Catalogs section.

Getting Help in the Administrator

The simplest way to get help when using the Administrator is to click the Help command on the Help menu. The MySQL Administrator window is shown in Figure 8-26.

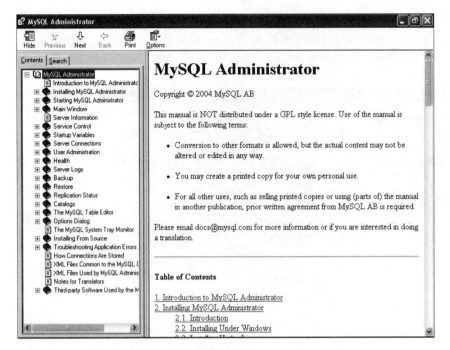

MySQL Administrator

Copyright © 2004 MySQL AB

This manual is NOT distributed under a GPL style license. Use of the manual is subject to the following terms:

- Conversion to other formats is allowed, but the actual content may not be altered or edited in any way.

- You may create a printed copy for your own personal use.

- For all other uses, such as selling printed copies or using (parts of) the manual in another publication, prior written agreement from MySQL AB is required.

Please email docs@mysql.com for more information or if you are interested in doing a translation.

Table of Contents

FIGURE 8-26   MySQL Administrator (Help) window

Backing Up a Database

As with any computer file, a database can become damaged or destroyed as a result of a variety of problems: users can enter incorrect data, programs that update the database can end abnormally during an update, a hardware problem can occur, and so on. After any such event has occurred, the database might contain invalid data, or worse, it might even be totally destroyed.

When data has been damaged or destroyed, you must have a process to return the database to its correct state. This process is called **recovery**; when you perform this process, you say that you "recover" the database.

The simplest approach to recovery involves periodically making a copy of the database (called a **backup copy**). This process is referred to as "backing up" the database. If a problem occurs, you correct the problem by copying the backup copy over the damaged database or installing the backup copy on a new system.

You can use the Backup section of the Administrator to back up a database, as illustrated in Example 14.

EXAMPLE 14

Back up the Premiere database.

To back up the database, click the Backup section on the sidebar, and then if necessary, click the Backup Project tab. Click the New Project button, assign a name to the backup, select the database to back up, and then click the forward arrow to move the database to the Backup Content pane. Finally, click the Execute Backup Now button and choose a location in which to store the backup file. Figure 8-27 shows the completed entries to back up the Premiere database.

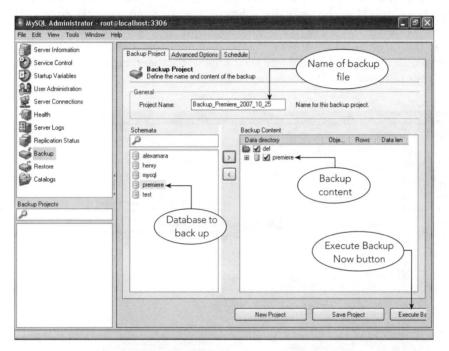

FIGURE 8-27 Using the Administrator to back up a database

NOTE

You should always include the date of the backup in the backup filename. By doing so, it is easy to distinguish between all the backup copies you have made to determine which one is the most recent. It is a good idea to store backup copies of databases on removable media, and to store the media in a safe place. Most organizations store backup copies off site so that a disaster at the location of the main database does not also result in the loss of the backup copies.

Restoring a Database

If you are ever in a situation that requires you to restore a database to its correct and current state, you can use the Restore section of the MySQL Administrator.

EXAMPLE 15

The Premiere database is corrupt. Restore the database to its correct state using the most recent backup.

To restore the database, click the Restore section on the sidebar, and then click the Open Backup File button. Use the Open dialog box to browse to and select the backup file to restore; that is, the name of the most current backup file. After selecting the backup file to restore, use the Target Schema list arrow to specify a target database. If you choose Original Schema, all tables are restored into their original database. Figure 8-28 shows the completed entries to restore the Premiere database.

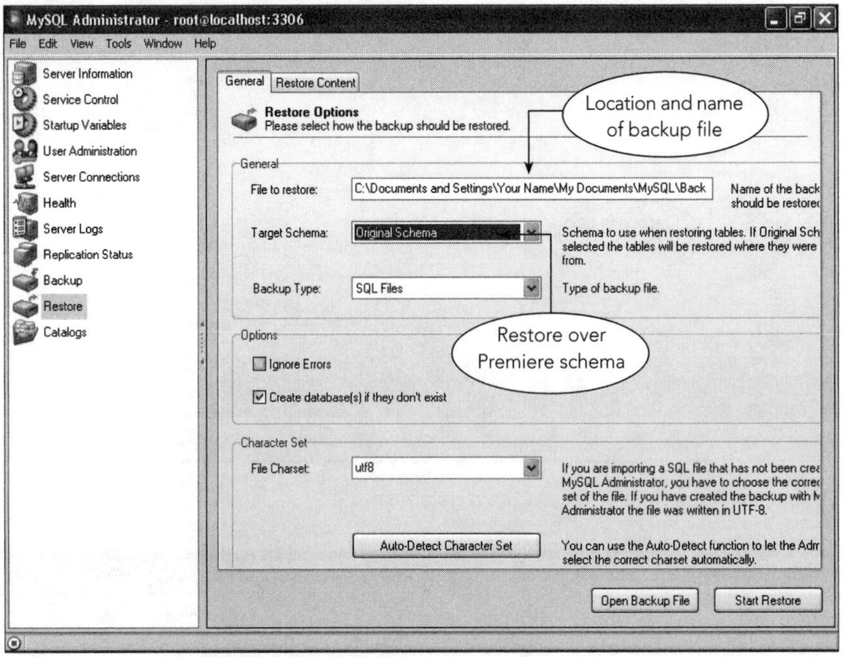

FIGURE 8-28 Using the Administrator to restore a database

Maintaining a Database

You can use the Catalogs section to create, edit, and maintain tables and indexes. The Catalogs section also provides a Maintenance dialog box that allows you to optimize tables, check tables, and repair tables.

EXAMPLE 16

Check the CUSTOMER table for errors.

To check the CUSTOMER table for errors, click the Catalogs section on the sidebar, click the database that you want to check, click the CUSTOMER table in the Table Name column on the Schema Tables tab, and then click the Maintenance button. When the dialog box shown in Figure 8-29 opens, make sure the Check Tables option button is selected, and then click the Next button. The Administrator checks the CUSTOMER table for errors.

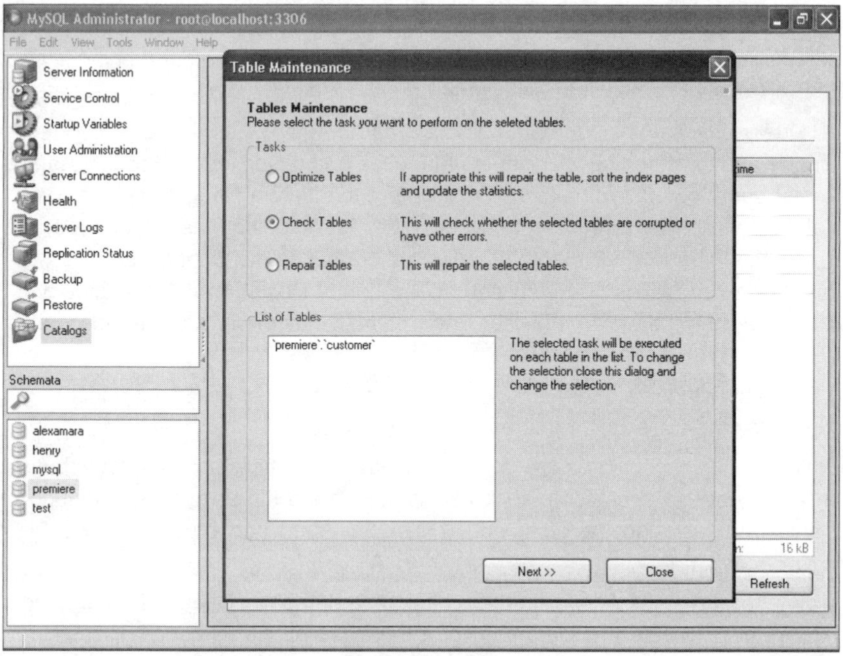

FIGURE 8-29 Table Maintenance dialog box

You also can use the Table Maintenance dialog box to optimize and repair tables by selecting the appropriate option button.

Chapter Summary

Importing is the process of converting data to a MySQL database. To import a file, use the LOAD DATA INFILE command.

Exporting is the process of converting the data in a MySQL database to a file format for use in another program. To export a table, use the SELECT INTO OUTFILE command.

Database performance is the speed or rate with which the DBMS supplies information to the user. An optimizer is a built-in program or routine that the DBMS uses to monitor and improve database performance.

Use the ANALYZE TABLE, CHECK TABLE, and OPTIMIZE TABLE commands to evaluate the performance of tables in the database. Use the REPAIR TABLE command to repair a damaged or corrupted table.

Use the EXPLAIN command to evaluate the performance of a query before running it. Use the PROCEDURE ANALYSE() function to analyze the query results.

The MySQL Query Browser is a separate MySQL program with a graphical user interface that is used to create and execute queries, create databases and tables, edit tables, create and run scripts, reformat query output, and export query output to different file formats. The Main Query Window of the Query Browser has four sections: the Query toolbar, the Result Area, the Object Browser, and the Information Browser. Queries are created in the Query Area on the Query toolbar and the query results (the resultset) appear in the Result Area. Databases and tables are manipulated using the Object Browser. The Information Browser provides information on SQL syntax.

The Query Browser includes a Script Editor and a Table Editor. Use the Script Editor to create and edit scripts. Use the Table Editor to create and edit tables.

MySQL Administrator is a separate MySQL program with a graphical user interface that is used to perform administrative operations, such as monitoring the status and performance of MySQL, performing and restoring backups, and managing users and connections to the database.

Use the Backup section of the Administrator to back up a database. Use the Restore section of the Administrator to restore a backup copy of a database over a damaged or destroyed database. Use the Catalogs section of the Administrator to create, edit, and maintain tables and indexes.

Key Terms

ANALYZE TABLE	ENUM
backup copy	EXPLAIN
Bookmarks Browser	exporting
CHECK TABLE	Functions Browser
comma-delimited file	History Browser
CSV	HTML
Database Browser	importing
database performance	Information Browser

LOAD DATA INFILE

MySQL Administrator

MySQL Query Browser

MySQL Table Editor

Object Browser

OPTIMIZE TABLE

optimizer

Params Browser

PROCEDURE ANALYSE()

Query Area

recovery

REPAIR TABLE

replication

Result Area

resultset

schema

Schemata Browser

Script Editor

SELECT INTO OUTFILE

Syntax Browser

tab-delimited file

text file

Trx Browser

XML

Review Questions

1. How do you import data into a MySQL database? Are there any formatting requirements on the data that you are importing?

2. How do you export data stored in a MySQL table into a file?

3. What is database performance?

4. What is an optimizer?

5. What is the purpose of the ANALYZE TABLE command?

6. What is the purpose of the CHECK TABLE command?

7. When do you use the OPTIMIZE TABLE command?

8. What is the purpose of the EXPLAIN command?

9. What is the purpose of PROCEDURE ANALYSE() function?

10. How do you start the Query Browser?

11. What information is provided by the Database Browser?

12. How do you use the Syntax Browser?

13. Name four file types that you can use to store data that you export from MySQL, and describe the function of each.

14. Name and describe two tasks that you can complete using the Script Editor.

15. Name and describe two tasks that you can complete using the MySQL Table Editor.

16. What is replication?

17. How do you back up and restore a MySQL database?

Exercises

Premiere Products

Use MySQL, the MySQL Query Browser, and the MySQL Administrator to make the following changes to the Premiere Products database (see Figure 1-2 in Chapter 1). Use the notes at the end of Chapter 3 or the Print command on the File menu to print your output if directed to do so by your instructor. Check with your instructor before doing exercises that require the Query Browser and the Administrator.

1. Premiere Products recently acquired some additional parts from a distributor that is going out of business. Data about the new parts is stored in the Parts.txt file on your Data Disk. Use the MySQL Command Line Client to import these parts into the PART table in the Premiere database. Display the complete PART table to verify that the parts were added.

2. Premiere database wants to add a new table to the database to store class descriptions for parts. Complete the following tasks at the command line:

    a. Create a new table named ITEM_CLASS for the Premiere database. The ITEM_CLASS table has two character columns: CLASS has a length of 2 characters and is the table's primary key, and DESCRIPTION has a length of 20 characters.

    b. Import the data in the Class.txt file on your Data Disk into the ITEM_CLASS table. Display the complete ITEM_CLASS table. (*Hint*: Replace the semicolon at the end of the command with \G to display the output correctly if necessary.)

3. The Premiere Products Marketing department wants to create a mailing list of customers. Export the customer name, street, city, state, and zip from the CUSTOMER table to a file named Address.txt on your data disk.

4. What is the command to check the tables in the Premiere Products database for errors? Run this command and then print the results.

5. Evaluate the following query, and then answer the questions that follow it.

```
SELECT ORDERS.ORDER_NUM, ORDER_DATE
FROM ORDERS, ORDER_LINE, PART
WHERE ORDERS.ORDER_NUM = ORDER_LINE.ORDER_NUM
AND ORDER_LINE.PART_NUM = PART.PART_NUM
AND DESCRIPTION = 'Iron'
```

    a. In what order will the tables be joined?

    b. What are the possible keys listed for each table?

6. Analyze the query used in Exercise 5, and then answer the following questions:

    a. What are the minimum values for each field in the result?

    b. What are the optimal field types for each field in the result?

7. Use the Query Browser to create a query that joins the ORDER_LINE and PART tables. Display the order number, part number, description, warehouse, number ordered, quoted price, and total price. (Total price is a computed column that is the result of multiplying the number ordered by the quoted price.)

    a. Run the query and resize the columns to display all the data on the screen. Print the query using the Print command on the File menu.

    b. Export the resultset to a CSV file named Orders.csv on your Data Disk.

8. Use the Script Editor to add a command to the MySQL-DropPremiere script file to drop the ITEM_CLASS table. Save and close the script file.

9. Use the MySQL Table Editor to make the part number a foreign key in the ORDER_LINE table.

10. Use the Query Browser to evaluate the query shown in Exercise 5 using the EXPLAIN command and PROCEDURE ANALYSE( ) function. Resize the columns in each resultset, and then print the resultsets.

11. Use the MySQL Administrator to back up the Premiere database on your Data Disk. Include today's date in the backup filename.

12. Use the MySQL Administrator to optimize the tables in the Premiere database. How did you perform this task, and what did the output tell you?

Henry Books

Use MySQL, the MySQL Query Browser, and the MySQL Administrator to make the following changes to the Henry Books database (Figures 1-4 through 1-7 in Chapter 1). Use the notes at the end of Chapter 3 or the Print command on the File menu to print your output if directed to do so by your instructor. Check with your instructor before doing exercises that require the Query Browser and the Administrator.

1. Henry Books acquired some new inventory. The data about the new books is in the Books.txt file on your Data Disk. Use the MySQL Command Line Client to import the new books into the BOOK table in the Henry database. Display the complete BOOK table to verify that the books were added.

2. Ray Henry wants to add a table to the Henry database to store a description of book types. Complete the following tasks at the command line:

    a. Create a new table named BOOK_TYPE in the Henry database. The BOOK_TYPE table has two character columns: TYPE has a length of 3 characters and is the table's primary key, and DESCRIPTION has a length of 20 characters.

    b. Import the data in the Types.txt file on your Data Disk into the BOOK_TYPE table. Display the complete BOOK_TYPE table. (*Hint*: Replace the semicolon at the end of the command with \G to display the output correctly if necessary.)

3. The Accounting department at Henry Books wants to create a list of book codes, titles, and prices. Export the necessary columns from the BOOK table to a file named Prices.txt on your Data Disk.

4. What is the command to check the tables in the Henry database for errors? Run this command and then print the results.

5. Evaluate the following query, and then answer the questions that follow it.

```
SELECT BOOK.BOOK_CODE, TITLE
FROM BOOK, INVENTORY, WROTE
WHERE BOOK.BOOK_CODE = INVENTORY.BOOK_CODE
AND BOOK.BOOK_CODE = WROTE.BOOK_CODE
AND BRANCH_NUM = 2
AND AUTHOR_NUM = 20
```

    a. In what order will the tables be joined?

    b. What are the possible keys listed for each table?

6. Analyze the query used in Exercise 5, and then answer the following questions:

    a. What are the minimum values for each field in the result?

    b. What are the optimal field types for each field in the result?

7. Use the Query Browser to create a query that joins the PUBLISHER and BOOK tables and displays the publisher name, book code, title, type, and price. Sort the results by title within publisher name.

    a. Run the query and resize the columns to display all the columns. Print the query using the Print command on the File menu.

    b. Export the resultset to a CSV file named Pub_Book.csv on your Data Disk.

8. Use the Script Editor to add a command to the MySQL-DropHenry script file to drop the BOOK_TYPE table. Save and close the script.

9. Use the Table Editor to make the branch number and book code foreign keys in the INVENTORY table.

10. Use the Query Browser to evaluate the query shown in Exercise 5 using the EXPLAIN command and PROCEDURE ANALYSE() function. Resize the columns in each resultset and then print the resultsets.

11. Use the MySQL Administrator to back up the Henry database on your Data Disk. Include today's date in the backup filename.

12. Use the MySQL Administrator to optimize the tables in the Henry database. How did you perform this task, and what did the output tell you?

Alexamara Marina Group

Use MySQL, the MySQL Query Browser, and the MySQL Administrator to make the following changes to the Alexamara Marina Group database (Figures 1-8 through 1-12 in Chapter 1). Use the notes at the end of Chapter 3 or the Print command on the File menu to print your output if directed to do so by your instructor. Check with your instructor before doing exercises that require the Query Browser and the Administrator.

1. Alexamara Marina Group recently acquired two new marinas. The data about these marinas is stored in the Marinas.txt file on your Data Disk. Use the MySQL Command Line Client to import the data in the Marinas.txt file into the MARINA table. Display the complete MARINA table to verify that the marinas were added.

2. The database administrator for the Alexamara database wants to add a table to the database to store descriptions of the boat types. Complete the following tasks at the command line:

    a. Create a new table named TYPE in the Alexamara database. The TYPE table has two character columns: BOAT_TYPE has a length of 50 characters and is the table's primary key, and DESCRIPTION has a length of 50 characters.

    b. Import the data in the BoatDesc.txt file into the TYPE table. Display the complete TYPE table. (*Hint*: Replace the semicolon at the end of the command with \G to display the output correctly if necessary.)

3. Alexamara needs to create a mailing list of owners. Export all the data except the owner number from the OWNER table into a file named Owners.txt on your Data Disk.

4. What is the command to check the tables in the Alexamara database for errors? Run this command and then print the results.

5. Evaluate the following query and then answer the questions that follow it:

```
SELECT MARINA_SLIP.SLIP_ID, BOAT_NAME,
    OWNER_NUM, SERVICE_ID, EST_HOURS, SPENT_HOURS
FROM MARINA_SLIP, SERVICE_REQUEST
WHERE MARINA_SLIP.SLIP_ID = SERVICE_REQUEST.SLIP_ID
AND CATEGORY_NUM = 2
```

    a.   In what order will the tables be joined?

    b.   What are the possible keys listed for each table?

6. Analyze the query used in Exercise 5, and then answer the following questions:

    a.   What are the minimum values for each field in the result?

    b.   What are the optimal field types for each field in the result?

7. Use the Query Browser to create a query that joins the MARINA_SLIP and OWNER tables and displays the marina number, slip number, owner first name, owner last name, address, city, state, and zip code.

    a.   Run the query and resize the columns to display all the columns. Print the query using the Print command on the File menu.

    b.   Export the resultset to an HTML file named Owners.html on your Data Disk.

8. Use the Script Editor to add a command to the MySQL-DropAlexamara script file to drop the TYPE table. Save and close the script file.

9. Use the MySQL Table Editor to make the marina number and owner number foreign keys in the MARINA_SLIP table.

10. Use the Query Browser to evaluate the query shown in Exercise 5 using the EXPLAIN command and PROCEDURE ANALYSE() function. Resize the columns in each resultset, and then print the resultsets.

11. Use the MySQL Administrator to back up the Alexamara database on your Data Disk. Include today's date in the backup filename.

12. Use the MySQL Administrator to optimize the tables in the Alexamara database. How did you perform this task, and what did the output tell you?

SQL REFERENCE

INTRODUCTION

You can use this appendix to obtain details concerning important components and syntax of the SQL

language. Items are arranged alphabetically. Each item contains a description, a reference to where the

item is covered in the text, and, where appropriate, both an example and a description of the query results.

Some SQL commands also include a description of the clauses associated with them. For each clause,

there is a brief description and an indication of whether the clause is required or optional.

ALIASES (PAGES 139–143)

You can specify an alias (alternative name) for each table in a query. You can use the alias in the rest of the command by following the name of the table with a space and the alias name.

The following command creates an alias named R for the REP table and an alias named C for the CUSTOMER table:

```
SELECT R.REP_NUM, R.LAST_NAME, R.FIRST_NAME, C.CUSTOMER_NUM, C.CUSTOMER_NAME
FROM REP R, CUSTOMER C
WHERE R.REP_NUM = C.REP_NUM;
```

ALTER TABLE (PAGES 168–170, 200–202)

Use the ALTER TABLE command to change a table's structure. As shown in Figure A-1, you type the ALTER TABLE command, followed by the table name, and then the alteration to perform.

Clause	Description	Required?
ALTER TABLE *table name*	Indicates name of table to be altered.	Yes
alteration	Indicates type of alteration to be performed.	Yes

FIGURE A-1   ALTER TABLE command

The following command alters the CUSTOMER table by adding a new CUSTOMER_TYPE column:

```
ALTER TABLE CUSTOMER
ADD CUSTOMER_TYPE CHAR(1);
```

The following command changes the CITY column in the CUSTOMER table so that it cannot accept nulls:

```
ALTER TABLE CUSTOMER
MODIFY CITY NOT NULL;
```

ANALYZE TABLE (PAGES 218–219)

Use the ANALYZE TABLE command to analyze the data in a table and create statistics that the MySQL optimizer uses. Figure A-2 describes the ANALYZE TABLE command.

Clause	Description	Required?
ANALYZE TABLE *table name*	Indicates name of table to be analyzed.	Yes

FIGURE A-2   ANALYZE TABLE command

The following command analyzes the CUSTOMER table:

```
ANALYZE TABLE CUSTOMER;
```

CHECK TABLE (PAGES 219–220)

Use the CHECK TABLE command to check a table for errors, such as identifying corrupt tables that result from not being closed properly. Figure A-3 describes the CHECK TABLE command.

Clause	Description	Required?
CHECK TABLE *table name*	Indicates name of table to be checked.	Yes

FIGURE A-3 CHECK TABLE command

The following command checks the CUSTOMER table for errors:

```
CHECK TABLE CUSTOMER;
```

COLUMN OR EXPRESSION LIST (SELECT CLAUSE) (PAGES 94-96)

To select columns, use the SELECT clause followed by the list of columns, separated by commas.

The following SELECT clause selects the CUSTOMER_NUM, CUSTOMER_NAME, and BALANCE columns:

```
SELECT CUSTOMER_NUM, CUSTOMER_NAME, BALANCE
```

Use an asterisk in a SELECT clause to select all columns in a table. The following SELECT clause selects all columns:

```
SELECT *
```

Computed Columns (Pages 102-104)

You can use a computation in place of a column by typing the computation. For readability, you can type the computation in parentheses, although it is not necessary to do so.

The following SELECT clause selects the CUSTOMER_NUM and CUSTOMER_NAME columns as well as the results of subtracting the BALANCE column from the CREDIT_LIMIT column:

```
SELECT CUSTOMER_NUM, CUSTOMER_NAME, (CREDIT_LIMIT - BALANCE)
```

The DISTINCT Operator (Pages 111-112)

To avoid selecting duplicate values in a command, use the DISTINCT operator. If you omit the DISTINCT operator from the command and the same value appears on multiple rows in the table, that value will appear on multiple rows in the query results.

The following query selects all customer numbers from the ORDERS table, but it lists each customer number only once in the results:

```
SELECT DISTINCT(CUSTOMER_NUM)
FROM ORDERS;
```

Functions (Pages 108–113)

You can use functions in a SELECT clause. The most commonly used functions are AVG (to calculate an average), COUNT (to count the number of rows), MAX (to determine the maximum value), MIN (to determine the minimum value), and SUM (to calculate a total).

The following SELECT clause calculates the average balance:

```
SELECT AVG(BALANCE)
```

COMMIT (PAGES 172–174)

Use the COMMIT command to make permanent any updates made since the last command. If no previous COMMIT command has been executed, the COMMIT command will make all the updates during the current work session permanent immediately. All updates become permanent automatically when you exit SQL. Figure A-4 describes the COMMIT command.

Clause	Description	Required?
COMMIT	Indicates that a COMMIT is to be performed.	Yes

FIGURE A-4 COMMIT command

The following command makes all updates since the most recent COMMIT command permanent:

```
COMMIT;
```

CONDITIONS (PAGES 96–102)

A condition is an expression that can be evaluated as either true or false. When you use a condition in a WHERE clause, the results of the query contains those rows for which the condition is true. You can create simple conditions and compound conditions using the BETWEEN, LIKE, IN, EXISTS, ALL, and ANY operators, as described in the following sections.

Simple Conditions (Pages 96–98)

A simple condition has the form: column name, comparison operator, and then either another column name or a value. The available comparison operators are = (equal to), < (less than), > (greater than), <= (less than or equal to), >= (greater than or equal to), and < > or != (not equal to).

The following WHERE clause uses a condition to select rows on which the balance is greater than the credit limit:

```
WHERE BALANCE > CREDIT_LIMIT
```

Compound Conditions (Pages 98–100)

Compound conditions are formed by connecting two or more simple conditions using the AND, OR, and NOT operators. When the AND operator connects simple conditions, all the simple conditions must be true in order for the compound condition to be true. When the OR operator connects the simple conditions, the compound condition will be true whenever any one of the simple conditions is true. Preceding a condition by the NOT operator reverses the truth of the original condition.

The following WHERE clause is true if the warehouse number is equal to 3 *or* the units on hand is greater than 100, *or* both:

```
WHERE (WAREHOUSE = '3') OR (ON_HAND > 100)
```

The following WHERE clause is true if the warehouse number is equal to 3 *and* the units on hand is greater than 100:

```
WHERE (WAREHOUSE = '3') AND (ON_HAND > 100)
```

The following WHERE clause is true if the warehouse number is *not* equal to 3:

```
WHERE NOT (WAREHOUSE = '3')
```

BETWEEN Conditions (Pages 101–102)

You can use the BETWEEN operator to determine if a value is within a range of values.

The following WHERE clause is true if the balance is between 2,000 and 5,000:

```
WHERE BALANCE BETWEEN 2000 AND 5000
```

LIKE Conditions (Pages 104–105)

LIKE conditions use wildcards to select rows. Use the percent (%) wildcard to represent any collection of characters. The condition LIKE '%Central%' will be true for data consisting of any character or characters, followed by the letters "Central," followed potentially by some additional characters. Another wildcard symbol is the underscore (_), which represents any individual character.

The following WHERE clause is true if the value in the STREET column is Central, Centralia, or any other value that contains the letters "Central":

```
WHERE STREET LIKE '%Central%'
```

IN Conditions (Pages 105–106, 114–116, 134)

You can use the IN operator to determine whether a value is in some specific collection of values.

The following WHERE clause is true if the credit limit is $5,000, $10,000, or $15,000:

```
WHERE CREDIT_LIMIT IN (5000, 10000, 15000)
```

The following WHERE clause is true if the part number is in the collection of part numbers associated with order number 21610:

```
WHERE PART_NUM IN
(SELECT PART_NUM
FROM ORDER_LINE
WHERE ORDER_NUM = '21610')
```

EXISTS Conditions (Pages 134–136)

You can use the EXISTS operator to determine whether the results of a subquery contain at least one row.

The following WHERE clause is true if the results of the subquery contain at least one row, that is, there is at least one order line with the desired order number and on which the part number is DR93:

```
WHERE EXISTS
(SELECT *
FROM ORDER_LINE
WHERE ORDERS.ORDER_NUM = ORDER_LINE.ORDER_NUM
AND PART_NUM = 'DR93')
```

ALL and ANY (Pages 150–152)

You can use the ALL or ANY operators with subqueries. If you precede the subquery by ALL, the condition is true only if it satisfies *all* values produced by the subquery. If you precede the subquery by ANY, the condition is true if it satisfies *any* value (one or more) produced by the subquery.

The following WHERE clause is true if the balance is greater than every balance contained in the results of the subquery:

```
WHERE BALANCE > ALL
(SELECT BALANCE
FROM CUSTOMER
WHERE REP_NUM = '65')
```

The following WHERE clause is true if the balance is greater than at least one balance contained in the results of the subquery:

```
WHERE BALANCE > ANY
(SELECT BALANCE
FROM CUSTOMER
WHERE REP_NUM = '65')
```

CREATE DATABASE (PAGE 66)

Use the CREATE DATABASE command to create a new database. Figure A-5 describes the CREATE DATABASE command.

Clause	Description	Required?
CREATE DATABASE *database name*	Indicates the name of the database to create.	Yes

FIGURE A-5   CREATE DATABASE command

The following CREATE DATABASE command creates a database named PREMIERE:

```
CREATE DATABASE PREMIERE;
```

CREATE INDEX (PAGES 193–197)

Use the CREATE INDEX command to create an index for a table. Figure A-6 describes the CREATE INDEX command.

Clause	Description	Required?
CREATE INDEX *index name*	Indicates the name of the index.	Yes
ON *table name*	Indicates the table for which the index is to be created.	Yes
(column list)	Indicates the column or columns on which the index is to be based.	Yes

FIGURE A-6   CREATE INDEX command

The following CREATE INDEX command creates an index named REPNAME for the REP table on the combination of the LAST_NAME and FIRST_NAME columns:

```
CREATE INDEX REPNAME ON REP(LAST_NAME, FIRST_NAME);
```

When you need to create an index on a nonprimary key column so that it stores unique values, use the CREATE UNIQUE INDEX command. The following CREATE UNIQUE INDEX command creates an index named SSN on the SOC_SEC_NUM field in the REP table:

```
CREATE UNIQUE INDEX SSN ON REP(SOC_SEC_NUM);
```

CREATE TABLE (PAGES 67–68)

Use the CREATE TABLE command to define the structure of a new table. Figure A-7 describes the CREATE TABLE command.

Clause	Description	Required?
CREATE TABLE *table name*	Indicates the name of the table to be created.	Yes
(column and data type list)	Indicates the columns that comprise the table along with their corresponding data types (see Data Types section).	Yes

FIGURE A-7   CREATE TABLE command

The following CREATE TABLE command creates the REP table and its associated columns and data types. REP_NUM is the table's primary key.

```
CREATE TABLE REP
(REP_NUM CHAR(2) PRIMARY KEY,
LAST_NAME CHAR(15),
FIRST_NAME CHAR(15),
STREET CHAR(15),
CITY CHAR(15),
STATE CHAR(2),
ZIP CHAR(5),
COMMISSION DECIMAL(7,2),
RATE DECIMAL(3,2) );
```

CREATE VIEW (PAGES 180–190)

Use the CREATE VIEW command to create a view. Figure A-8 describes the CREATE VIEW command.

Clause	Description	Required?
CREATE VIEW *view name* AS	Indicates the name of the view to be created.	Yes
query	Indicates the defining query for the view.	Yes

FIGURE A-8   CREATE VIEW command

The following CREATE VIEW command creates a view named HOUSEWARES, which consists of the part number, part description, units on hand, and unit price for all rows in the PART table on which the item class is HW:

```
CREATE VIEW HOUSEWARES AS
SELECT PART_NUM, DESCRIPTION, ON_HAND, PRICE
FROM PART
WHERE CLASS = 'HW';
```

Figure A-9 describes some common data types that you can use in a CREATE TABLE command.

Data type	Description
CHAR(n)	Stores a character string n characters long. You use the CHAR data type for columns that contain letters and special characters and for columns containing numbers that will not be used in any calculations. Because neither sales rep numbers nor customer numbers will be used in any calculations, for example, the REP_NUM and CUSTOMER_NUM columns are both assigned the CHAR data type.
VARCHAR(n)	An alternative to CHAR that stores a character string up to n characters long. Unlike CHAR, all that is stored is the actual character string. If a character string 20 characters long is stored in a CHAR(30) column, for example, it will occupy 30 characters (20 characters plus 10 blank spaces). If it is stored in a VARCHAR(30) column, it will only occupy 20 characters. In general, tables that use VARCHAR instead of CHAR occupy less space, but will not process as rapidly during queries and updates. Both are legitimate choices. This text uses CHAR, but VARCHAR would work equally well.
DATE	Stores date data. In MySQL, dates are enclosed in single quotation marks and have the form YYYY-MM-DD (for example, '2007-10-15' is October 15, 2007).
DECIMAL(p,q)	Stores a decimal number p digits long with q of these digits being decimal places to the right of the decimal point. For example, the data type DECIMAL(5,2) represents a number with three places to the left and two places to the right of the decimal (for example, 100.00). You can use the contents of DECIMAL columns in calculations.
INT	Stores integers, which are numbers without a decimal part. The valid range is –2147483648 to 2147483647. You can use the contents of INT columns in calculations. If you follow the word INT with AUTO_INCREMENT, you create a column for which MySQL will automatically generate a new sequence number each time you add a new row. This would be the appropriate choice, for example, if you want to let the DBMS generate a value for a primary key.
SMALLINT	Stores integers, but uses less space than the INT data type. The valid range is –32768 to 32767. SMALLINT is a better choice than INT when you are certain that the column will store numbers within the indicated range. You can use the contents of SMALLINT columns in calculations.

FIGURE A-9 Commonly used data types

DELETE (ROWS) (PAGES 79–80, 166)

Use the DELETE command to delete one or more rows from a table. Figure A-10 describes the DELETE command.

Clause	Description	Required?
DELETE FROM *table name*	Indicates the table from which the row or rows are to be deleted.	Yes
WHERE *condition*	Indicates a condition. Those rows for which the condition is true will be retrieved and deleted.	No (If you omit the WHERE clause, all rows will be deleted.)

FIGURE A-10   DELETE command

The following DELETE command deletes any row from the LEVEL1_CUSTOMER table on which the customer number is 895:

```
DELETE FROM LEVEL1_CUSTOMER
WHERE CUSTOMER_NUM = '895';
```

DROP INDEX (PAGE 197)

Use the DROP INDEX command to delete an index, as shown in Figure A-11.

Clause	Description	Required?
DROP INDEX *index name*	Indicates the name of the index to be dropped.	Yes
ON *table name*	Indicates the name of the table on which the index was built.	Yes

FIGURE A-11   DROP INDEX command

The following DROP INDEX command deletes the index named CREDNAME on the CUSTOMER table:

```
DROP INDEX CREDNAME ON CUSTOMER;
```

DROP TABLE (PAGES 71, 174)

Use the DROP TABLE command to delete a table, as shown in Figure A-12.

Clause	Description	Required?
DROP TABLE *table name*	Indicates name of table to be dropped.	Yes

FIGURE A-12 DROP TABLE command

The following DROP TABLE command deletes the table named LEVEL1_CUSTOMER:

```
DROP TABLE LEVEL1_CUSTOMER;
```

DROP VIEW (PAGE 190)

Use the DROP VIEW command to delete a view, as shown in Figure A-13.

Clause	Description	Required?
DROP VIEW *view name*	Indicates the name of the view to be dropped.	Yes

FIGURE A-13 DROP VIEW command

The following DROP VIEW command deletes the view named HSEWRES:

```
DROP VIEW HSEWRES;
```

EXPLAIN (PAGES 221–222, 235–236)

Use the EXPLAIN command to obtain information about how MySQL executes a query. When you precede a statement with the EXPLAIN command, MySQL identifies how it processes the query, which might include information about how tables are joined and in which order. Figure A-14 describes the EXPLAIN command.

Clause	Description	Required?
EXPLAIN		Yes
query	Indicates the query to be evaluated.	Yes

FIGURE A-14 EXPLAIN command (query)

The following EXPLAIN command evaluates the performance of a query that selects the last name and first name from the REP table and the customer name and balance from the CUSTOMER table:

```
EXPLAIN SELECT LAST_NAME, FIRST_NAME, CUSTOMER_NAME, BALANCE
FROM REP, CUSTOMER
WHERE REP.REP_NUM = CUSTOMER.REP_NUM;
```

GRANT (PAGES 190–193)

Use the GRANT command to grant privileges to a user. Figure A-15 describes the GRANT command.

Clause	Description	Required?
GRANT *privilege*	Indicates the type of privilege(s) to be granted.	Yes
(column list)	Indicates the collection of columns on which the privilege is to be granted.	No
ON *database object*	Indicates the database object(s) to which the privilege(s) pertain.	Yes
TO *user name*	Indicates the user(s) to whom the privilege(s) are to be granted. To grant the privilege(s) to all users, use the TO PUBLIC clause.	Yes

FIGURE A-15   GRANT command

The following GRANT command grants the user named Johnson the privilege of selecting part numbers, descriptions, and classes from the PART table:

```
GRANT SELECT (PART_NUM, DESCRIPTION, CLASS) ON PART TO JOHNSON;
```

INSERT INTO (QUERY) (PAGES 162–163)

Use the INSERT INTO command with a query to insert the rows retrieved by a query into a table. As shown in Figure A-16, you must indicate the name of the table into which the row(s) will be inserted and the query whose results will be inserted into the named table.

Clause	Description	Required?
INSERT INTO *table name*	Indicates the name of the table into which the row(s) will be inserted.	Yes
query	Indicates the query whose results will be inserted into the table.	Yes

FIGURE A-16 INSERT INTO (query) command

The following INSERT INTO command inserts rows selected by a query into the LEVEL1_CUSTOMER table:

```
INSERT INTO LEVEL1_CUSTOMER
SELECT CUSTOMER_NUM, CUSTOMER_NAME, BALANCE, CREDIT_LIMIT, REP_NUM
FROM CUSTOMER
WHERE CREDIT_LIMIT = 7500;
```

INSERT INTO (VALUES) (PAGES 75–77, 165–166)

Use the INSERT INTO command and the VALUES clause to insert a row into a table by specifying the values for each of the columns. As shown in Figure A-17, you must indicate the table into which to insert the values, and then list the values to insert in parentheses.

Clause	Description	Required?
INSERT INTO *table name*	Indicates the name of the table into which the row will be inserted.	Yes
VALUES *(values list)*	Indicates the values for each of the columns on the new row.	Yes

FIGURE A-17 INSERT INTO (values) command

The following INSERT INTO command inserts the values shown in parentheses as a new row in the REP table:

```
INSERT INTO REP
VALUES
('20','Kaiser','Valerie','624 Randall','Grove','FL','33321',20542.50,0.05);
```

INTEGRITY (PAGES 200–202)

You can use the ALTER TABLE command with an appropriate ADD PRIMARY KEY or ADD FOREIGN KEY clause to specify integrity. Figure A-18 describes the ALTER TABLE command for specifying integrity.

Clause	Description	Required?
ALTER TABLE *table name*	Indicates the table for which integrity is being specified.	Yes
ADD PRIMARY KEY *(column name)* Or ADD FOREIGN KEY *(column name)* REFERENCES *table name (column name)*	Creates a primary key using the specified column or creates a foreign key that references the specified column in the indicated table.	Yes

FIGURE A-18   Integrity options

The following ALTER TABLE command changes the REP table so that the REP_NUM column is the table's primary key:

```
ALTER TABLE REP
ADD PRIMARY KEY (REP_NUM);
```

The following ALTER TABLE command changes the CUSTOMER table so that the REP_NUM column in the CUSTOMER table is a foreign key referencing the primary key of the REP table:

```
ALTER TABLE CUSTOMER
ADD FOREIGN KEY (REP_NUM) REFERENCES REP(REP_NUM);
```

LOAD DATA INFILE (PAGES 215–217)

Use the LOAD DATA INFILE command to import a tab-delimited text file into MySQL. As shown in Figure A-19, you must indicate the name of the text file containing the data to import and the name of the table into which the data will be inserted. The filename must be enclosed in single quotation marks.

Clause	Description	Required?
LOAD DATA INFILE *'filename'*	Indicates the name of the text file containing the data.	Yes
INTO *table name*	Indicates the name of the table into which the data will be inserted.	Yes
FIELDS TERMINATED BY *'delimiter'*	Indicates the way that field data is separated (for example, '\t' indicates a tab character).	No
LINES TERMINATED BY *'delimiter'*	Indicates the way that row data is separated (for example, '\r\n' indicates a paragraph).	No

FIGURE A-19 LOAD DATA INFILE

The following LOAD DATA INFILE command imports the data in the file named ORDERS.TXT into the ORDERS table:

```
LOAD DATA INFILE 'ORDERS.TXT'
INTO TABLE ORDERS;
```

OPTIMIZE TABLE (PAGES 220–221)

Use the OPTIMIZE TABLE command to recover unused space caused by fragmented files as shown in Figure A-20.

Clause	Description	Required?
OPTIMIZE TABLE *table name*	Indicates name of table to be analyzed.	Yes

FIGURE A-20 OPTIMIZE TABLE command

The following command optimizes the tables in the Premiere Products database:

```
OPTIMIZE TABLE REP, CUSTOMER, ORDERS, ORDER_LINE, PART;
```

PROCEDURE ANALYSE() (PAGES 222–223)

Use the PROCEDURE ANALYSE() function to examine and analyze a query's results. Figure A-21 describes the PROCEDURE ANALYSE() function.

Clause	Description	Required?
query	Indicates the query on which the analysis will be performed.	Yes
PROCEDURE ANALYSE()		Yes

FIGURE A-21 PROCEDURE ANALYSE() function

The following command analyzes the results of a query that selects descriptions from the PART table:

```
SELECT DESCRIPTION
FROM PART
PROCEDURE ANALYSE();
```

REPAIR TABLE (PAGE 220)

Use the REPAIR TABLE command to fix damaged or corrupted tables, as shown in Figure A-22.

Clause	Description	Required?
REPAIR TABLE *table name*	Indicates name of table to be repaired.	Yes

FIGURE A-22 REPAIR TABLE command

The following command repairs the ORDER_LINE table:

```
REPAIR TABLE ORDER_LINE;
```

REVOKE (PAGE 193)

Use the REVOKE command to revoke privileges from a user. Figure A-23 describes the REVOKE command.

Clause	Description	Required?
REVOKE *privilege*	Indicates the type of privilege(s) to be revoked.	Yes
ON *database object*	Indicates the database object(s) to which the privilege pertains.	Yes
FROM *user name*	Indicates the user name(s) from whom the privilege(s) are to be revoked.	Yes

FIGURE A-23 REVOKE command

The following REVOKE command revokes the SELECT privilege for the REP table from the user named Johnson:

```
REVOKE SELECT
ON REP
FROM JOHNSON;
```

ROLLBACK (PAGES 172–174)

Use the ROLLBACK command to reverse (undo) all updates since the execution of the previous COMMIT command. If no COMMIT command has been executed, the command will undo all changes made during the current work session. Figure A-24 describes the ROLLBACK command.

Clause	Description	Required?
ROLLBACK	Indicates that a rollback is to be performed.	Yes

FIGURE A-24 ROLLBACK command

The following command reverses all updates made since the time of the last COMMIT command:

```
ROLLBACK;
```

SELECT (PAGES 77–78, 94–122, 130–133)

Use the SELECT command to retrieve data from a table or from multiple tables. Figure A-25 describes the SELECT command.

Clause	Description	Required?
SELECT *column or expression list*	Indicates the column(s) and/or expression(s) to be retrieved.	Yes
FROM *table list*	Indicates the table(s) required for the query.	Yes
WHERE *condition*	Indicates one or more conditions. Only the rows for which the condition(s) are true will be retrieved.	No (If you omit the WHERE clause, all rows will be retrieved.)
GROUP BY *column list*	Indicates column(s) on which rows are to be grouped.	No (If you omit the GROUP BY clause, no grouping will occur.)
HAVING *condition involving groups*	Indicates a condition for groups. Only groups for which the condition is true will be included in query results. Use the HAVING clause only if the query output is grouped.	No (If you omit the HAVING clause, all groups will be included.)
ORDER BY *column or expression list*	Indicates column(s) on which the query output is to be sorted.	No (If you omit the ORDER BY clause, no sorting will occur.)

FIGURE A-25 SELECT command

The following SELECT command joins the ORDERS and ORDER_LINE tables. The command selects the customer number, order number, order date, and the sum of the product of the number ordered and unit price, renamed as ORDER_TOTAL. Records are grouped by order number, customer number, and date. Only groups on which the order total is greater than 1,000 are included. Groups are ordered by order number.

```
SELECT CUSTOMER_NUM, ORDERS.ORDER_NUM, ORDER_DATE,
     SUM(NUM_ORDERED * QUOTED_PRICE) AS ORDER_TOTAL
FROM ORDERS, ORDER_LINE
WHERE ORDERS.ORDER_NUM = ORDER_LINE.ORDER_NUM
GROUP BY ORDERS.ORDER_NUM, CUSTOMER_NUM, ORDER_DATE
HAVING SUM(NUM_ORDERED * QUOTED_PRICE) > 1000
ORDER BY ORDERS.ORDER_NUM;
```

SELECT INTO OUTFILE (PAGES 217–218)

Use the SELECT INTO OUTFILE command to export a table from MySQL to a text file. As shown in Figure A-26, you must indicate the name of the table to be exported and the name of the file to contain the text data. The filename must be enclosed in single quotation marks.

Clause	Description	Required?
SELECT *columns*	Indicates the columns to be exported.	Yes
INTO OUTFILE *'filename'*	Indicates the name of the text file to be created.	Yes
FROM *table name*	Indicates the name of table containing columns to be exported.	Yes

FIGURE A-26　SELECT INTO OUTFILE

The following SELECT INTO OUTFILE command exports the part number, description, and price columns from the PART table to a text file named PARTDATA.TXT.

```
SELECT PART_NUM, DESCRIPTION, PRICE
INTO OUTFILE 'PARTDATA.TXT'
FROM PART;
```

SHOW COLUMNS (PAGES 85, 198–199)

Use the SHOW COLUMNS command to list all the columns in a table and their characteristics. Figure A-27 describes the SHOW COLUMNS command.

Clause	Description	Required?
SHOW COLUMNS FROM *table*	Indicates the table from which to list and describe columns.	Yes

FIGURE A-27　SHOW COLUMNS command

SHOW GRANTS (PAGE 200)

Use the SHOW GRANTS command to list all the privileges assigned to a given user. Figure A-28 describes the SHOW GRANTS command.

Clause	Description	Required?
SHOW GRANTS FOR *user name*	Indicates the user for which to list the granted privileges.	Yes

FIGURE A-28　SHOW GRANTS command

SHOW INDEX (PAGES 199–200)

Use the SHOW INDEX command to list all the indexes associated with a given table. Figure A-29 describes the SHOW INDEX command.

Clause	Description	Required?
SHOW INDEX FROM *table*	Indicates the table from which to list indexes.	Yes

FIGURE A-29 SHOW INDEX command

SHOW TABLES (PAGE 198)

Use the SHOW TABLES command to list all the tables in the system catalog for the default database, as follows:

```
SHOW TABLES;
```

SUBQUERIES (PAGES 113–116, 134–137)

You can use one query within another. The inner query is called a subquery and it is evaluated first. The outer query is evaluated next, producing the part description for each part whose part number is in the list.

The following command contains a subquery that produces a list of part numbers included in order number 21610:

```
SELECT PART_DESCRIPTION
FROM PART
WHERE PART_NUM IN
(SELECT PART_NUM
FROM ORDER_LINE
WHERE ORDER_NUM = '21610');
```

UNION, INTERSECT, AND MINUS (PAGES 145–149)

Connecting two SELECT commands with the UNION operator produces all the rows that would be in the results of the first query, the second query, or both queries. Connecting two SELECT commands with the INTERSECT operator produces all the rows that would be in the results of both queries. Connecting two SELECT commands with the MINUS operator produces all the rows that would be in the results of the first query, but *not* in the results of the second query. Figure A-30 describes the UNION, INTERSECT, and MINUS operators.

Operator	Description	Required?
UNION	Produces all the rows that would be in the results of the first query, the second query, or both queries.	Yes
INTERSECT	Produces all the rows that would be in the results of both queries.	Yes
MINUS	Produces all the rows that would be in the results of the first query but not in the results of the second query.	Yes

FIGURE A-30   UNION, INTERSECT, and MINUS operators

The following query displays the customer number and customer name of all customers that are represented by sales rep 65, *or* that have orders, *or* both:

```
SELECT CUSTOMER_NUM, CUSTOMER_NAME
FROM CUSTOMER
WHERE REP_NUM = '65'
UNION
SELECT CUSTOMER.CUSTOMER_NUM, CUSTOMER_NAME
FROM CUSTOMER, ORDERS
WHERE CUSTOMER.CUSTOMER_NUM = ORDERS.CUSTOMER_NUM;
```

The following query displays the customer number and customer name of all customers that are represented by sales rep 65 *and* that have orders:

```
SELECT CUSTOMER_NUM, CUSTOMER_NAME
FROM CUSTOMER
WHERE REP_NUM = '65'
INTERSECT
SELECT CUSTOMER.CUSTOMER_NUM, CUSTOMER_NAME
FROM CUSTOMER, ORDERS
WHERE CUSTOMER.CUSTOMER_NUM = ORDERS.CUSTOMER_NUM;
```

MySQL does not support the INTERSECT operator; the following MySQL command produces the same results:

```
SELECT CUSTOMER_NUM, CUSTOMER_NAME
FROM CUSTOMER
WHERE REP_NUM = '65'
AND CUSTOMER_NUM IN
(SELECT CUSTOMER_NUM
FROM ORDERS);
```

The following query displays the customer number and customer name of all customers that are represented by sales rep 65 but that do *not* have orders:

```
SELECT CUSTOMER_NUM, CUSTOMER_NAME
FROM CUSTOMER
WHERE REP_NUM = '65'
MINUS
SELECT CUSTOMER.CUSTOMER_NUM, CUSTOMER_NAME
FROM CUSTOMER, ORDERS
WHERE CUSTOMER.CUSTOMER_NUM = ORDERS.CUSTOMER_NUM;
```

MySQL does not support the MINUS operator; the following MySQL command produces the same results:

```
SELECT CUSTOMER_NUM, CUSTOMER_NAME
FROM CUSTOMER
WHERE REP_NUM = '65'
AND CUSTOMER_NUM NOT IN
(SELECT CUSTOMER_NUM
FROM ORDERS);
```

UPDATE (PAGES 79–80, 163–165)

Use the UPDATE command to change the contents of one or more rows in a table. Figure A-31 describes the UPDATE command.

Clause	Description	Required?
UPDATE *table name*	Indicates the table whose contents will be changed.	Yes
SET *column = expression*	Indicates the column to be changed, along with an expression that provides the new value.	Yes
WHERE *condition*	Indicates a condition. The change will occur only on those rows for which the condition is true.	No (If you omit the WHERE clause, all rows will be updated.)

FIGURE A-31   UPDATE command

The following UPDATE command changes the customer name on the row in the LEVEL1_CUSTOMER table on which the customer number is 842 to All Season Sport:

```
UPDATE LEVEL1_CUSTOMER
SET CUSTOMER_NAME = 'All Season Sport'
WHERE CUSTOMER_NUM = '842';
```

Use the USE command to change the default database to the one that you want to use. Figure A-32 describes the USE command.

Clause	Description	Required?
USE *database name*	Changes the default database to the named database.	Yes

FIGURE A-32   USE command

The following USE command changes the default database to the one named PREMIERE:

```
USE PREMIERE;
```

APPENDIX **B**

HOW DO I REFERENCE

This appendix answers frequently asked questions about how to accomplish a variety of tasks using

MySQL. Use the second column to locate the correct section in Appendix A that answers your question.

How do I	Review the named section(s) in Appendix A
Add columns to an existing table?	ALTER TABLE
Add rows?	INSERT INTO (Values)
Analyze a table?	ANALYZE TABLE
Calculate a statistic (sum, average, maximum, minimum, or count)?	1. SELECT 2. Column or Expression List (SELECT Clause) (Use the appropriate function in the query.)
Change rows?	UPDATE
Change the default database?	USE
Check a table for errors?	CHECK TABLE
Create a data type for a column?	1. Data Types 2. CREATE TABLE
Create a database?	CREATE DATABASE
Create a table?	CREATE TABLE
Create a view?	CREATE VIEW
Create an index?	CREATE INDEX
Delete a table?	DROP TABLE
Delete a view?	DROP VIEW
Delete an index?	DROP INDEX
Delete rows?	DELETE Rows
Drop a table?	DROP TABLE
Drop a view?	DROP VIEW
Drop an index?	DROP INDEX
Export a resultset to a file?	SELECT INTO OUTFILE
Grant a privilege?	GRANT
Group data in a query?	SELECT (Use a GROUP BY clause.)
Import data in a text file into a table?	LOAD DATA INFILE
Insert rows?	INSERT INTO (Values)
Insert rows using a query?	INSERT INTO (Query)

FIGURE B-1 How do I reference

How do I	Review the named section(s) in Appendix A
Join tables?	Conditions (Include a WHERE clause to relate the tables.)
List the columns in a table and their characteristics?	SHOW COLUMNS
List the indexes associated with a given table?	SHOW INDEX
List the privileges assigned to a given user?	SHOW GRANTS
List the tables in the default database?	SHOW TABLES
Make updates permanent?	COMMIT
Optimize query performance?	1. EXPLAIN 2. PROCEDURE ANALYSE()
Optimize table performance?	OPTIMIZE TABLE
Prohibit nulls?	1. CREATE TABLE 2. ALTER TABLE (Include the NOT NULL clause in a CREATE TABLE or ALTER TABLE command.)
Remove a privilege?	REVOKE
Repair a table?	REPAIR TABLE
Retrieve all columns?	1. SELECT 2. Column or Expression List (SELECT Clause) (Type * in the SELECT clause.)
Retrieve all rows?	SELECT (Omit the WHERE clause.)
Retrieve only certain columns?	1. SELECT 2. Column or Expression List (SELECT Clause) (Type the list of columns in the SELECT clause.)
Revoke a privilege?	REVOKE
Select all columns?	1. SELECT 2. Column or Expression List (SELECT Clause) (Type * in the SELECT clause.)

FIGURE B-1   How do I reference (continued)

How do I	Review the named section(s) in Appendix A
Select all rows?	SELECT (Omit the WHERE clause.)
Select only certain columns?	1. SELECT 2. Column or Expression List (SELECT Clause) (Type the list of columns in the SELECT clause.)
Select only certain rows?	1. SELECT 2. Conditions (Use a WHERE clause.)
Sort query results?	SELECT (Use an ORDER BY clause.)
Specify a foreign key?	Integrity (Use the ADD FOREIGN KEY clause in an ALTER TABLE command.)
Specify a primary key?	Integrity (Use the ADD PRIMARY KEY clause in an ALTER TABLE command.)
Specify a privilege?	GRANT
Undo updates?	ROLLBACK
Update rows?	UPDATE
Use a calculated field?	1. SELECT 2. Column or Expression List (SELECT Clause) (Enter a calculation in the query.)
Use a compound condition?	1. SELECT 2. Conditions (Use simple conditions connected by AND, OR, or NOT in a WHERE clause.)
Use a compound condition in a query?	Conditions
Use a condition in a query?	1. SELECT 2. Conditions (Use a WHERE clause.)
Use a subquery?	Subqueries
Use a wildcard?	1. SELECT 2. Conditions (Use LIKE and a wildcard in a WHERE clause.)
Use an alias?	Aliases (Enter an alias after the name of each table in the FROM clause.)
Use set operations (union, inter-section, difference)?	UNION, INTERSECT, and MINUS (Connect two SELECT commands with UNION, INTERSECT, or MINUS.)

FIGURE B-1 How do I reference (continued)

ANSWERS TO ODD-NUMBERED REVIEW QUESTIONS

CHAPTER 1—INTRODUCTION TO PREMIERE PRODUCTS, HENRY BOOKS, AND ALEXAMARA MARINA GROUP

Due to the nature of the material in Chapter 1, there are no Review Questions.

CHAPTER 2—DATABASE DESIGN FUNDAMENTALS

1. An entity is a person, place, thing, or event.
3. A relationship is an association between tables (entities). A one-to-many relationship between two tables is a relationship in which each row in the first table can be associated with many rows in the second table, but each row in the second table is associated with only one row in the first table.
5. A relation is a two-dimensional table in which the entries in the table are single-valued (each location in the table contains a single entry), each column has a distinct name, all values in the column match this name, the order of the rows and columns is immaterial, and each row contains unique values.
7. For each table, you write the name of the table and then within parentheses list all of the columns in the table. Underline the primary keys. The Henry Books database is represented as follows:

```
BRANCH (BRANCH_NUM, BRANCH_NAME, BRANCH_LOCATION, NUM_EMPLOYEES)
PUBLISHER (PUBLISHER_CODE, PUBLISHER_NAME, CITY)
AUTHOR (AUTHOR_NUM, AUTHOR_LAST, AUTHOR_FIRST)
BOOK (BOOK_CODE, TITLE, PUBLISHER_CODE, TYPE, PRICE, PAPERBACK)
WROTE (BOOK_CODE, AUTHOR_NUM, SEQUENCE)
INVENTORY (BOOK_CODE, BRANCH_NUM, ON_HAND)
```

9. Column B is functionally dependent on another column (or a collection of columns), A, if at any point in time a value for A determines a single value for B.
11. Functional dependencies:

```
DEPARTMENT_NUM → DEPARTMENT_NAME
ADVISOR_NUM → ADVISOR_LAST_NAME, ADVISOR_FIRST_NAME,
    DEPARTMENT_NUM
COURSE_CODE → DESCRIPTION
STUDENT_NUM → STUDENT_LAST_NAME, STUDENT_FIRST_NAME, ADVISOR_NUM
STUDENT_NUM, COURSE_CODE → GRADE
```

Tables and columns:

```
DEPARTMENT (DEPARTMENT_NUM, DEPARTMENT_NAME)
ADVISOR (ADVISOR_NUM, ADVISOR_LAST_NAME, ADVISOR_FIRST_NAME,
     DEPARTMENT_NUM)
COURSE (COURSE_CODE, DESCRIPTION)
STUDENT (STUDENT_NUM, STUDENT_LAST_NAME, STUDENT_FIRST_NAME,
     ADVISOR_NUM)
STUDENT_COURSE (STUDENT_NUM, COURSE_CODE, GRADE)
```

E-R diagram: (*Note:* Your rectangles can be in different positions as long as they are connected by the same arrows.)

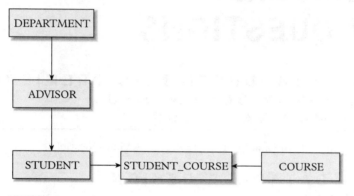

FIGURE C-1

13. A table (relation) is in second normal form if it is in first normal form and no nonkey column is dependent on only a portion of the primary key. If a table is not in second normal form, the table contains redundancy, which leads to a variety of update anomalies. A change in a value can require not just one change, but several. There is the possibility of inconsistent data. Adding additional data to the database may not be possible without creating artificial values for part of the key. Finally, deletions of certain items can result in inadvertently deleting crucial information from the database.

15.

```
STUDENT (STUDENT_NUM, STUDENT_LAST_NAME, STUDENT_FIRST_NAME,
     ADVISOR_NUM)
ADVISOR (ADVISOR_NUM, ADVISOR_LAST_NAME, ADVISOR_FIRST_NAME)
COURSE (COURSE_CODE, DESCRIPTION)
STUDENT_COURSE (STUDENT_NUM, COURSE_CODE, GRADE)
```

CHAPTER 3—AN INTRODUCTION TO SQL

1. The manner in which you start MySQL depends on the operating environment in which you are working. In a Windows installation, click the Start button, point to All Programs, point to MySQL, point to MySQL Server 4.1, and then click MySQL Command Line Client. You would then need to enter your password.

3. To create a database, use the CREATE DATABASE command followed by the database name.
5. Use the CREATE TABLE command to create a table by typing the table name and then listing within a single set of parentheses the columns in the table and their data types.

7. The common data types in MySQL are INT, SMALLINT, DECIMAL, CHAR, VARCHAR, and DATE.
9. The INSERT command.
11. The UPDATE command.
13. Use the SHOW COLUMNS command.

CHAPTER 4—SINGLE-TABLE QUERIES

1. The basic form of the SELECT command is SELECT-FROM. Specify the columns to be listed after the word SELECT (or type * to select all columns), and then specify the table name that contains these columns after the word FROM. Optionally, you can include conditions after the word WHERE.
3. You can form compound conditions by combining simple conditions connected by the operators AND, OR, or NOT.
5. Use arithmetic operators and write the computation in place of a column name. You can assign a name to the computation by following the computation with the word AS and then the desired name.
7. The percent (%) wildcard represents any collection of characters. The underscore (_) wildcard represents any single character.
9. Use the ORDER BY clause to sort data.
11. To sort in descending order, follow the sort key with the DESC operator.
13. To avoid duplicates, precede the column name with the DISTINCT operator.
15. Use the GROUP BY clause.
17. Use the IS NULL operator in the WHERE clause.

CHAPTER 5—MULTIPLE-TABLE QUERIES

1. Indicate in the SELECT clause all columns to display, list in the FROM clause all tables to join, and then include in the WHERE clause any conditions requiring values in matching columns to be equal.
3. IN and EXISTS
5. An alias is an alternate name for a table. To specify an alias in a command, follow the name of the table with the name of the alias. You use the alias just like a table name throughout the command.
7. The UNION command creates a union of two tables. The INTERSECT command creates the intersection of two tables. To create an intersection of two tables in MySQL, use the IN operator with a subquery. To create a difference of two tables in MySQL, use the NOT IN operator with a subquery. To perform any of these operations, the tables must be union-compatible.

9. If a subquery is preceded by the ALL operator, the condition is true only if it is satisfied by all values produced by the subquery.

11. In an inner join, only matching rows from both tables are included. You can use the INNER JOIN clause to perform an inner join.

13. In a right outer join, all rows from the right table (that is, the second table listed) are included whether or not they match. Only matching rows from the left table are included. You can use the RIGHT JOIN clause to perform a right outer join.

CHAPTER 6—UPDATING DATA

1. CREATE TABLE
3. Use the INSERT command with a SELECT clause.
5. COMMIT
7. DELETE
9. The ALTER TABLE command with the ADD clause.
11. Before beginning the updates for a transaction, commit any previous updates by executing the COMMIT command. Complete the updates for the transaction. If any update cannot be completed, execute the ROLLBACK command and discontinue the updates for the current transaction. If you can complete all updates successfully, execute the COMMIT command after completing the final update.

CHAPTER 7—DATABASE ADMINISTRATION

1. A view contains data that is derived from existing base tables when users attempt to access the view.
3. The portion of the CREATE VIEW command that describes the data to include in the view.
5. Views provide data independence, allow database access control, and simplify the database structure for users.
7. DROP VIEW
9. REVOKE
11. Use the CREATE INDEX command to create an index. Use the CREATE UNIQUE INDEX command to create a unique index. A unique index enforces a rule that only unique values are allowed in the column (or columns) on which the index is created.
13. The DBMS
15. Use the SHOW INDEX command and the table name.
17. Integrity constraints are rules that the data in the database must follow to ensure that only legal values are accepted in specified columns, or that primary and foreign key values match between tables.
19. Use the ADD FOREIGN KEY clause of the ALTER TABLE command.

1. Use the LOAD DATA INFILE command. The data must be in a tab-delimited text file.

3. Database performance is defined as the speed or rate with which the DBMS supplies information to the user.

5. The ANALYZE TABLE command analyzes the data in a table and creates statistics that the MySQL optimizer uses. You should run the ANALYZE TABLE command after loading a table with data and creating any necessary indexes.

7. Use the OPTIMIZE TABLE command to recover unused space caused by fragmented files.

9. The PROCEDURE ANALYSE( ) function is added to the end of a SELECT statement. It examines and analyzes the query results, but does not actually execute the query. The output from the PROCEDURE ANALYSE( ) function provides information about the table's columns, such as the minimum and maximum values, and suggests an optimal field type.

11. The Database Browser (also called the Schemata Browser) displays all databases on the MySQL Server to which you are connected.

13. You can export to the following file formats: comma-delimited text files (also called comma separated values), HTML (Hypertext Markup Language) files, XML (Extensible Markup Language) files, and Microsoft Excel files. You can open CSV files in many different programs, including word processors, spreadsheets, and databases. HTML files are text files with .htm or .html filename extensions that are used for creating and formatting Web pages. XML files are used for describing and delivering data on the Web. Microsoft Excel is a spreadsheet application.

15. The MySQL Table Editor lets you view and change the columns in a table and their data types. You can use the Indices tab to set and remove indexes and the Foreign Keys tab to set and remove foreign keys.

17. Use the MySQL Administrator; use the Backup section to perform backups and the Restore section to restore backup files created using the Backup section.

INDEX